AN INSPECTOR RECALLS

The entrance hall

AN INSPECTOR RECALLS

Saving our Heritage

Derek Sherborn

The Book Guild Ltd
Sussex, England

First published in Great Britain in 2003 by
The Book Guild Ltd,
25 High Street,
Lewes, East Sussex
BN7 2LU

Typesetting in Times by
IML Typographers, Birkenhead, Merseyside

Printed in Great Britain by
Bookcraft (Bath) Ltd, Avon

A catalogue record for this book is available from
The British Library

ISBN 1 85776 653 6

Dedicated to my great friends
Brian Leach and Jack Anderson
without whose constant support
and encouragement I would
never have completed this book nor had
their companionship in visiting so many
historic buildings, never found my new house
in Brighton and never enjoyed the best years
of my life.
June, 2002.

CONTENTS

ACKNOWLEDGEMENTS

This book would never had been possible without the constant help and encouragement of my cousin and godson, John Wilsdon, who has been a most wonderful inspiration for me all the way through. I am also enormously grateful to my very great friend, Tim Knox, who most generously volunteered to read the text for me and made many helpful suggestions. I am also hugely indebted to my distant cousin, Commander General Selous DSO, for allowing me to quote from the unpublished private memoirs of his great grandmother, the former Ann Holgate Sherborn, the wife of Frederick Lokes Selous, and mother of Frederick Courtney Selous DSO, the distinguished naturalist and big game hunter. Also of very great help to me has been Peter Reid who has most generously shared with me his incredibly vast knowledge of the Country Houses and Stately Homes of the United Kingdom.

I also wish to thank John and Eileen Harris for their kindness and help down the years but I must warn readers of John Harris's latest book that I failed to reconcile his account of me, my mother and my house; the facts as I now remember them, nor our visit to Stanwell Place!

Among the numerous people who have helped in other ways with the preparation of the book I would particularly like to thank Stephen Bennett, Clive Goodwin, Philip Duggan, Brenda and Sid Bailey, Melanie Samuel, Janet Wrench and Carol Biss of The Book Guild, and my esteemed former colleagues Carole Ryan and Dolly Potter of English Heritage.

Photographs in the book where not taken by myself were largely supplied from the collections of the National Monuments Record Division of English Heritage in Swindon, for which I am truly grateful. The photograph of the water colour by George Engleheart of Bedfont Lodge was kindly supplied by the Engleheart family and is reproduced here for the first time. Others were kindly supplied by Mukesh Pattni, Walter Scott, Brian Leach, The Paul Mellon Centre, the Antique Collector, Mrs M StClair, *The Architectural Review*, Mrs Clarissa Lewis (the daughter of Sir John Piper) *The Car Illustrated*, The Sheffield Theatres Trust and *Country Life*.

INTRODUCTION

In a book dealing largely with historic houses and their families, their contents and collections, it is inevitable that one has to have a system provided. And the great fault with the book is that it is all true and difficult to digest! One would love to have the space to champion the old house, to extol the virtues of moss grown paths, the scent of walled gardens, the crackle of log fires, the smell of methane gas from kennels and stables and the murky images of long gone ancestors hanging all over the walls.

Such combinations of events and happenings inherited down the ages are natural accidents and cannot be manufactured with any amount of money. And, whether one approves or disapproves of the people involved, their combination illustrates an irreplaceable part of English History. Once broken up it is gone forever.

I became fascinated by historic family homes in my early teens and research into them has been one of my greatest interests.

The War in progress, I became fascinated by domestic bygones, in particular the contents of kitchens. The kitchen in my house in Bedfont when I finally sold it is a testament to my continued fascination in this area. I was interested in how things worked. Why did a kitchen need such implements? When were they used, and by whom? It was this type of curiosity that I later transferred to my interest in country houses and other historic buildings. Who built them? When and for whom? How did they function? Are the features original or added later on? And if the latter, why, who for and by whom? And so on.

As you will see in the following pages, my 'magpie' instinct and my inherent love of old buildings led [perhaps inevitably] to a long career with the Ministry of Town and Country Planning. I became a listing inspector, and spent several decades touring the country and visiting places of potential interest. Some I saved by persuading the powers that be they deserved to be listed, and hence preserved. Many, however, were pulled down.

Like so many other things, we are far more enlightened over such matters these days than we were in the post-war years.

This book is divided into three parts. The first provides a history of my family. The second covers my own formative years, and the third is a distillation of my own diaries and notes, describing my time with the Ministry, and what we tried to achieve for England's national heritage. This section concludes with the early years of my retirement in Brighton, when I found myself able to travel for pleasure instead of work, and visit places that I had played a part in saving from destruction years before.

PART ONE

A HISTORY OF THE
SHERBORN FAMILY

1

Suburban Squires: The Oldest Family

'So what, say I? So what?' said the very grand lady from the Victoria and Albert Museum. Not that she was speaking on behalf of the museum, she was just a very great friend who always spoke her mind, except when she was trying to chat up rich Americans or great aristocrats. Intellectually she was entitled to be a great snob for she had an enormous knowledge of works of art, languages and a smart Swiss background. She was also a great hostess in the sense that she was always entertaining, modestly but well, people of intelligence from all countries and backgrounds. She had invented the summer schools at Attingham Park in Shropshire, and had enormous energy, making a great point of drawing mutually interesting and acceptable people together. Her name was Helen Lowenthal. The remark I made that had upset her was that I thought my family was probably the oldest in Greater London and I was actually quite interested in that fact. She was not, and thought it silly.

There are few things less interesting to others than one's own ancestors, and mine are the same. Our own family tree reads like that of a dog from the Kennel Club, or that of a horse from Tattersall's, Inherited Blood rather than anything else at all.

The greater part of the western half of Middlesex was a flat and featureless tract of unpopulated and dangerous wasteland known as Hounslow Heath. Embracing parts of fifteen parishes including Bedfont, Cranford, Staines, Stanwell and Heston, it was almost featureless. There were random outbreaks of gorse and scrub and little else save for the odd corpse-hung gibbet. There were also scattered survivals of ancient burials and the site of a substantial ancient British temple. Throughout the seventeenth century Hounslow Heath embraced well over 4,000 acres, but by the end of the eighteenth century most of it had been parcelled up in enclosures and given to neighbouring landowners. Before then it included the whole of what is now Heathrow Airport and extended right down to the churchyard in Bedfont. Right in the middle was once a place called Hatton Grange, belonging to King Edward III who used it as a hunting lodge.

Bedfont had two manor houses of medieval date. One of these, called Pates, has survived to the present day in a remarkably well preserved state. The other, Fawns, is much less well preserved, but also very well documented. This house was to become my home (and the home of the last of the Sherborns of Bedfont), and was the principal feature of a compound of manorial buildings to the south of Bedfont Green and its church. It was described in 1438 as 'an halhous with cross chambers with a prevee therto, a kechyne with a treasaunce between the hall and the kechyne, a loft in the keychen, a lede in the kechyne, a netehous, a newe tofalle for eight kyne, a newe house of five rownes ay house with stables and other offices, two pairs gatehouses, a new colverhouse, all the houses above said tyled, a barne of foure rownes and an hoggesty thacched and two ponds for fyshe in the Culverhouse'. The property had 150 acres of land which remained with the house until William Sherborn's death in 1912. No Sherborn was living in the house then, one supposes, but Richard Sherborn is mentioned as having land adjoining on the east side. Perhaps the family arrived in the 1330s in Edward III's baggage train en route to Hatton Grange.

During the 1330s the Black Death swept across Europe. Oxford lost two thirds of her academic population and it was estimated that three quarters of the population of Europe died. However, the Sherborns survived this catastrophe and actually remained in Bedfont until I left in 1983.

There is not a great deal to be said about the various generations; it is better to relegate these faceless people to a family tree and try not to burden the bones with flesh. There is, however, more information about a certain Henry Sherborn who leased Fawns Manor from one Felix Wilson of Colnbrook in the mid-seventeenth century. Wilson was a landowner and he complained to the Manorial Court that, although in

6

1648 he owned Fawns with all its lands, Henry had refused to sign the new lease because the premises had been badly damaged by soldiers during the Civil War. By 1654 Henry was so hard up that the parish beadle was instructed to distrain on his goods for non-payment of rent!

One of Henry's descendants, Thomas Sherborn who died in 1731, left a will in which he lists his land and houses, as well as detailing furnishings like his second best bedstead with curtains, valance and all the furniture, three pairs of sheets and his second best chest of drawers with half a dozen cane chairs. These were destined for his son Thomas and his other son Charles was to have one bed and bedstead, mattress, valance and covering, another chest of drawers with half a dozen cane chairs and two pairs of sheets. What little furniture they had in their houses in those days!

In January 1732, the cousins Mary and Rachel Sherborn, returning to their home in Bedfont, witnessed an attack by two highwaymen on a coach belonging to General Honywood. 'Putting him in fear' they 'robbed him of a silver watch with a steel chain, a gold seal and a Bath metal seal, value £3 and 2 guineas in money'. Two men, Thomas Timms and John Bye, were arrested and charged with the offence and the case was tried at the Old Bailey. The general and the lady with him were travelling in a Berlin and four towards his house which appears to have been in or near Staines. In evidence, Mary Sherborn said: 'As I and my cousin Rachel came from Brentford Market the General's coach passed us a little on the other side of the Powder Mills, and being a little before us, about a mile or less from Bedfont, these two highwaymen came from London . . . they stopped the coach and robbed it. We were on horseback but went at foot pace and when we came to Bedfont the parish clock struck twelve. We passed by the coach when the men were robbing it and then they rode off to London.' Timms asked her, 'Are we the two persons who robbed the coach?' Mary was forced to say that she saw little of their faces and simply couldn't think that they were the 'right ones'. The men were acquitted because the Sherborns couldn't identify them.

Another member of the family, Charles Sherborn, baptised in Bedfont in 1716, was apprenticed to James Wigley in 1731 and was admitted a Freeman off the Clothworkers Company. He became an engraver of trade cards, book plates and brass monuments in churches, and also developed a great interest in heraldry and genealogy. One of his trade cards reads: "'Charles Sherborn of Gutter Lane, Cheapside, London, Engraver, begs leave to inform the public that having made Heraldry his peculiar study for many years". He had built up a great collection of books and manuscripts including those of, "the celebrated Sir Joseph Barrett of Cheapside consisting of many scarce books with grants by Sir Edward Walker, Knight, Garter Principal King at Arms, Henry St George and Peter LeNeve Esq., Clarencieux and Richard St George Norroy, together with many others, containing the pedigrees of noble families, their marriages, alliances etc. Also Visitations of Counties, many of which are in the handwriting of the said Kings at Arms ... The nobility, gentry and others who may have occasion of searching for arms, pedigrees etc. are hereby informed that an office is open for that purpose at the Kings Arms, 41 Gutter Lane Cheapside". N.B. no office fee required, where the arms or pedigrees are not found. "Arms painted on vellum and seals engraved".' He is sure to have found the arms and pedigrees, whether genuine or not, because it was his living! 'Heraldry had for more than a half a century been his peculiar study and being so fortunate in his pursuits as to acquire a valuable collection of many experts in the field, in the opinions of the late Sir Charles Townley and Rafe Bigland Esq., the Principal Kings of Arms, they were by far the most extensive and curious manuscripts in that science of any private person in the kingdom.' I have not found his collections nor is there any trace of those of Joseph Barrett which he mentions having bought. Among Charles Sherborn's engraved works were many book plates, including those of John Clerke, Esq. of Aston, Oxfordshire, and among the trade cards were those of George Yardley, carver and gilder of Noble Street, Aldersgate; Thomas Silk, cabinet maker of St Paul's churchyard. (I have recently added to my collection in Brighton a very fine mahogany toilet mirror by Thomas Silk.) Gray's Coffee House in Norwich, and Dare & Hitchcock, Mercers of Cheapside. He also engraved the brass wall monument to the Escott family at Carhampton, near Dunster in Somerset and I am fairly certain that he engraved the brass wall monument to the Sherborns in Bedfont Church. He was followed, much later on, as an engraver in the family by Charles William Sherborn, and in his interest in genealogy by Charles Davies Sherborn, his son.

Another Georgian Sherborn was William, who was born in 1751 and died in 1825. He became quite prosperous and was on friendly terms with George Engleheart, the eminent miniature painter who built himself a splendid house on the green called Bedfont Lodge. Engleheart painted William Sherborn's miniature as a gift, as well as one of Francis Sherborn and another of Peter Henderson, deputy lieutenant of the county, who lived in the village at a house called the White House. Uncle Charlie gave two of these miniatures to the British Museum. It was William Sherborn who championed the cause of the poor when there was a harmful proposal to enclose the common lands of the village. In gratitude he was presented with a tea tray painted with a scene of the village green with its houses and church. He himself is shown engaged in conversation with Beilby Porteous, then Bishop of London, who has alighted from his coach. A long inscription runs along the bottom: 'A witness for William Sherborn, of his abhorrence to robbing the poor by Enclosures, Bedfont, 10th March 1801 on which day the Duke of Northumberland, the Bishop of London, the Governors of Christ's Hospital etc., withdrew their signatures from the petition which they had signed for the Enclosure to their perpetual honour on being informed of the great evil the poor would sustain by it'. I love it and still have it. I am glad he felt for other people.

William Sherborn was a 'patient' of Saka Deen Mahomed, the celebrated Turkish bather of Brighton. William was often in Brighton being steamed and smacked for the good of his health. Mahomed was not Turkish, he was Indian, but he became a very prominent character and is well remembered in Brighton.

The next eldest of the brothers was Francis, who was born in 1786. When he married, his father took Heston Farm for him to lease. 'It was too late to get it ploughed and prepared for the coming season,' wrote Ann Sherborn, but 'my uncle Frank was extremely popular and as soon as this ill-luck was known it was remedied, a day was appointed. The whole county sent their ploughmen and teams; when my grandfather Sherborn knew what was coming he made a fête of it, tents were fixed, casks breached and indoors and out was feasting and revelry. In two or three days the land was quite prepared.' Francis had become tenant of Heston Farm with his brother Matthew on 27 September 1833, and their local friends voluntarily performed the extraordinary task of ploughing 320 acres of land, harrowing 20 acres and manuring 8 acres in seven hours. The number of horses employed was 1,062, along with twenty-four oxen. 'It had been my intention to celebrate the 150th anniversary of this event at Bedfont, but alas, it was not to be. I was to be gone.

Another of William Sherborn's nine children, John was born in April 1795 and became an artist's colourman. He had premises at 321 Oxford Street in partnership with his cousin, James Tillier. Their painted signboard for the shop is now in the Museum of London. He was one of the first occupants of Ladbroke Square in 1848 and he married Sarah Holgate of Staines. The Holgates came from the Yorkshire and Lancashire borders but had settled in Saffron Walden in Essex at the end of the sixteenth century. They believed they were of the same family as Robert Holgate, Archbishop of York, and later President of the North. After Thomas Holgate and Jane Bruce married at St John's Hackney on 24 February 1705, future generations claimed that they were descended from the Bruces of Clackmannanshire and thus perhaps from Robert the Bruce himself! John Sherborn died on 26 July 1859 and is buried at Warlingham. Their children included Ann Holgate Sherborn who married Frederick Lokes Selous and left some interesting memoirs, which I have drawn on here. She was the mother of Frederick Courtenay Selous DSO, the distinguished naturalist and big game hunter, after whom the Selous Scouts were named. Ann's sister Emily married her brother-in-law, Angelo Selous who was a dramatist and a singer, while a third brother, Henry Courteney Selous was an artist who painted, among other things, the celebrated picture of the opening of the Great Exhibition of 1851 by Queen Victoria. While Selous was painting this picture he was given a studio at Buckingham Palace which the Queen used to come to for sittings dressed just in a straw bonnet and plain shawl.

Of the eight children William Sherborn and Ann (Berryman) had only Matthew, born in 1793, was to achieve great wealth. He married Eleanor Catherine Wilkinson in 1823 and became a sleeping partner with John Sams: 'Oil and Italian Warehousemen to the Royal Family' at 173 Piccadilly. Their only child Ellen married William Crowther of Aston Somerville in Gloucestershire and, unusually for a Victorian marriage, it went wrong. She was sued for divorce and married the correspondent William Higford Griffiths. They set

10

themselves up in an aggrandised Georgian house encrusted with Gothic battlements calling itself Weddington Castle, near Nuneaton in Warwickshire. The building no longer survives.

Ellen and William later moved to Chipping Camden in Gloucestershire, buying the finest Georgian classical house in the main street rechristening it 'Bedfont House' where they had several children. Matthew left a huge fortune and had provided for them magnanimously. It is OK to be a rich grocer. After all everyone needs food. Ellen is believed to haunt Bedfont House to this day.

Ann's grandfather, William Henry Holgate, bought a very pretty place called Knowle Green, near Staines Moor. The moor stream ran through the grounds for some distance. He gave it to Ann's mother for as long as she chose to live in it and there, Ann Holgate Selous whose memoirs I am quoting from here was born. The Staines Church being closed for repairs she was christened 'in an ugly square brick building in the corner of the old orchard. My grandfather let the parish use it for a boys' schoolroom.'

Bedfont must have been a pleasant place in his time. In the lease particulars for Bedfont Lodge in the Engleheart archives at Stoke Priory the agents glowingly describe it: 'The situation is beautiful and remarkably healthy and commands extensive and rich views of the Surrey Hills and the surrounding scenery. It is in the immediate vicinity of His Majesty's Staghounds and embraces every advantage combined with field sports. The neighbourhood is distinguished for the respectability of its inhabitants and coaches are passing hourly!' Was it really?

The Sherborns were the lay rectors and had the right to control works to the chancel and the erection of monuments there. On 3 February 1834 Henry Engleheart wrote to Francis Sherborn sending him sincere thanks and a cheque for four guineas for permission to erect a tablet in Bedfont church chancel in memory of his brother. An earlier letter from the Engleheart family, this time from the famous miniaturist George, sends greetings to him and his children and requests him to avoid altering the level of the watercourse near his house, Bedfont Lodge, because of the injury it would do to his one and only drain!

One of Francis Sherborn's diaries survives for 1845, but

what can one say of a man who records on 10 January, 'Went to Bushy Park deer taking. Took 13'; on 13 January, 'Stable lanthorns all put in repair'; on 20 January, 'Killed above 100 rats in Dukes Barn'; on 21 January, 'Out with P. Alberts Harriers at Heathrow. Very good sport'; on 25 January, 'Went to Dorney with the Princes Harriers. Very good sport'; and on 5 February, 'Queens Hounds met at Bedfont Gate. Took at Hawick, very good run'. It was all blood and guts save for the odd dance at Heathrow Hall. How terribly dull country life was then. And bloodthirsty! How I would have hated it all.

Francis, with his brother and sisters, was largely responsible for the restoration and partial rebuilding of Bedfont Church in 1865.

In 1867 the owners of Pates Manor and its estate, Christ's Hospital in London, carried out one of its periodic reviews of the property. The report is detailed and, discussing the house itself, says that it has 'From time immemorial been in the occupation of the Sherborn family and for about seven years past in that of Mr Francis Sherborn; the eldest son of the lessee who relinquished it to him about five years before his own death which took place in December 1864 at an advanced age. The three daughters of the late tenant also reside with their brother and the aspect of the house and garden betokens a good deal of the care and interest taken therein by them. The family own a considerable quantity of land in Bedfont ... On the general question of the farm we may say that it is in high condition as to cultivation and management and receives every justice at the hands of Mr Sherborn ... The house is very commodious and in nice order generally, a very large sum (about £700) having been laid out in substantially repairing and improving it (including the erection of new out offices thereto) at the commencement of the present lease. It bears now indeed rather the aspect of a genteel villa residence than that of an old farmhouse.'

In 1874 Francis won a silver cup for root crops from the Middlesex Agricultural Society and, in 1879, another silver cup for the best cultivated farm, so things were still being maintained to a high standard. However, financial disaster was not far off. In 1882, with the lease at an end he wrote to his landlords: 'I have the comforting reflection that I have performed my part of the bargain to the letter. But, gentlemen, there is another side to the question. I have suffered most serious losses and considering the liberal remissions that have been made by landlords generally throughout the country I cannot help saying that I should not be unmindful of the compliment, were you, gentlemen, to show your kind sympathy with my case, by offering me that as a gift which my conscience would not allow me to claim as a right or ask as a boon. 1882 unfortunately promises to be the worst year of all, being the worst crop all round I ever remember.' He lost £4,500 in twelve years. His bankruptcy in June 1888 was not his fault at all, the whole of his debt being caused by the failure of Lord Huntingtower (son of the eighth Earl of Dysart) to pay moneys owing to him. It transpired that the late Lord Dysart had actually owned Francis' father £21,000 from years before, and in addition to that had lost £10,000 over a period of twelve years.

The appalling depression in agriculture at the time meant that land had become a positive burden to owners. Bigger crops in foreign countries and the colonies, along with appalling weather in the years 1878 to 1881 had aggravated matters even more. There had been severe outbreaks of liver fluke in sheep (the Sherborns actually farmed sheep at Bedfont) and consequently a tremendous loss of animal stock.

Boys no longer worked for cheap rates for their place was now in school. The price of wheat fell by half in fifty years. The repeal of the Corn Laws in 1846, which enabled cheap wheat to be imported and thus benefited the poor, had done considerable harm to England's farmers. They were in a woebegone state, not able to face the next crisis and wondering from day to day what the future could possibly have in store or them. Farmers lost money and went bankrupt all over England and it became even worse! During the next decade over 2 million acres reverted to rough grass without any increase in livestock. As Oscar Wilde made Lady Bracknell say, 'Land had ceased to be either a profit or a pleasure. It gives one position and prevents one from keeping it up.' Francis Sherborn's bankruptcy was a frightful disaster which rocked the whole family. Lands and stock had to be sold by public auction.

A rather tragic note from Francis in the archives of Christ's Hospital records his regret at his money problems: 'Having been born at Pates Manor Farm in the year 1822 it has always been my desire – and especially since I have become tenant of the same – to end my days there.' Notwithstanding his troubles he did stay on in the house because his sisters took on the lease in his place.

Ann Holgate Selous recorded 'Poor Frank, I went to see him soon after the sale; he looked horribly ill and could scarcely walk; I hurried to him, he threw his arms round me and fairly wept on my shoulder. I had never thought about those acres before, but seeing what their loss was to Frank, I too felt it to be intolerable and we grieved and cried desperately. But silly as this proceeding was, it really seemed to do him good. Of my six cousins, Frank alone inherits his father's tastes; he visited everywhere and after his death, Emma showed me the packets and packets of sympathising letters she had to answer. At the funeral the little church was packed from far and near. If among my descendants any child is fearfully passionate let not his or her parents be too anxious. My delightful Uncle Frank – widely known for probity and justice, was fearful at times and would in such moments break up furniture etc.; right and left, and cousin Frank once in a passion at its disobedience shot his favourite dog dead.' Can one excuse that in any way at all?

Ann's memoirs also record her meeting with the 'Duke of Clarence, poor fellow – there was a Colonel McDonald (I think) equerry or aide-de-camp to the Prince of Wales, and the little fellow was constantly with him. One day when he called Emma, who felt an interest in the boy who was to be King, asked some questions about him. The Colonel said, "Would you like to see him Miss Sherborn? Your brother has a hunting breakfast soon, shall I bring him?" Emma was delighted and took care to order a grand supply of tarts and such things. When the guests came into the drawing room Emma was amused by them making the little fellow the centre figure of the semicircle. My cousins were all good looking, she the beauty of the neighbourhood, but they could not be persuaded to marry, nor their brothers either.'

Prince Albert Victor Christian Edward, Duke of Clarence, was born in 1864 and died in 1892. I suppose the visit was in about 1870. The eldest son of Edward VII, he was engaged to be married to Princess May of Teck in 1891, but dying at the age of 28 the following year, he never married nor succeeded to the throne. He was said always to have had bad health. Very soon after Princess May became engaged to his younger brother George. They married in 1893 and succeeded to the throne on the death of King Edward. Clarence was a doubtful character and just before his death was involved in the scandal of the male brothel in Cleveland Street. His nickname was 'cuffs and collars'. The second engagement to Princess May raised many eyebrows. She was evidently determined to be Queen of England.

We know exactly what Pates Manor was like at the time of the young Prince Eddie's visit as there is an inventory for 1865 and a sale catalogue for when the contents of the house were dispersed in 1907. It sounds as though nothing had changed. His Royal Highness probably only saw the entrance hall, dining and drawing rooms. Above the chimneypiece in the latter was a large gilt framed mirror measuring 50″ × 40″ and on the chimneypiece were a pair of cut glass lustres. The carpet was fitted to the room and of Brussels manufacture, and a bordered hearthrug lay in front of a brass fender and fire irons. The curtains were of crimson merino damask hung from maplewood poles and there were Venetian blinds. The furniture consisted of eight, rosewood grained, drawing-room chairs with green Utrecht velvet seats, and there was a mahogany couch with needleworked cloth and bolster. There were easy chairs, various tables, oil paintings and engravings, and later an upright piano by Hopkinson was added, with a music stool and canterbury, and an ormolu and marble clock. We know nothing of the chimneypiece itself, but it concealed a very good Tudor stone fireplace surround, rediscovered a century later in 1970. The dining room contained a set of 4′ 6″ mahogany dining tables, certainly Georgian from the description; a set of ten mahogany dining chairs covered in leather; a fine old bookcase nearly eight feet long, a Turkey carpet and hearthrug; more crimson merino damask window curtains, but this time with a mahogany pole and roller blinds; various easy chairs and tables; and 200 books. The pictures included a painting of one of the windows of King's College Chapel, Cambridge; a lithograph of Dr Frogley; and four miniatures by George Engleheart. The other rooms included best bedrooms with four-poster beds with dimity hangings and matching window curtains; lesser rooms with 'Japanned' bedsteads and others with 'French' bedsteads; and chintz and muslin curtains. The two maids' rooms sound appalling, with poor bedsteads, odd lengths of carpet and 'four old chairs covered in leather'. The kitchen and mangle room are described in much detail, the only surprise being a shower bath in the latter – an unusual luxury at this date (possibly acquired by William Sherborn for use while working in

Portugal on the construction of the railways in 1856). There was an immense amount of silver and the small wine cellar was stocked to bursting. At the sale in 1907 there were four dozen bottles of 1873 sherry, surely then of no use at all. The outside effects in 1907 included a phaeton and a dog cart, a farm cart and a trap, an Alderney cow, a shorthorn cow in calf and thirty-four fowls. The garden had a box-edged parterre to the south of the house, a vinery with black grapes, a well, barns, outbuildings, and on the west front of the house a cedar tree planted by Uncle Frank in 1808.

The family pews were in the chancel of the church of Bedfont, and when it became the fashion for a choir 'of nice little boys' to sing the psalms, the vicar wished the chancel to be given up to them; but Frank absolutely refused to give up the pews where his family had sat for generations and never missed services. He wrote at last to the bishop, who immediately decided it as Frank wished.

Certainly the Royal Family knew how to please country gentlemen. Frank was at an agricultural dinner where the Prince of Wales presided, and a servant made his way to him and announced that HRH wished to take wine with him. One day, returning quietly from a hunt, a lady with a strikingly fine figure passed Frank, who a minute or two after heard his name called; knowing the voice, he turned and it was the Prince of Wales. 'Who is she, Sherborn? Who is she? Do you know her? Have you seen her before?' panted the prince, hurrying after the fine figure. There were so many.

Ann detested school, although she was fond of her governess and liked the teachers, but being in Brighton so long away from home was too dreadful: 'One Easter, Emily and I were not to go home as usual and our melancholy was interrupted by a summons to the dining room and there, by the fire, sat mama, looking, I thought, most beautiful with large leghorn flaps tied down over her ears and angel plumes [They were really white ostrich.] Mama, being as disconsolate as Emily and I but being free had suddenly taken off and come to us. We always went to Brighton, papa and a four horse coach – a heavenly journey if school had not been at the end. We were staying at Brighton after I left school. One day on the old Chain Pier and under where the work was all open, we were looking at the waves when up came a monster. Daniel Chapman caught up a little child who was standing by to his shoulder and Sarah and I climbed onto the fence. He was over six feet and big and strong. Unfortunately the solid green water was above our waists and the foam half smothered the child on Daniel's shoulders, and our new shot green and ruby silk dresses were ruined. Daniel Chapman, who my sister married, descended straight from the old dramatist George Chapman (or so it was said). He (George) was chiefly known for his translation of Homer and wrote a number of tragedies and comedies. For two years I went to school in Brighton and I remember seeing in 1842 the Queen in dark blue velvet and white feathered hat, walking with Prince Albert on Kemp Town Parade, then just made. My memory next journeys to the Isle of Wight when we were staying at Ryde, Emily still at school and some cousins with us on a calm day. We went round the Island on a steamer called *Lord Yarborough* and off the Needles "crash", we had run on a rock. I found myself at full length on the deck, everyone else was the same, and by the time we had picked ourselves up the vessel was slowly vibrating, descending on one side so the top of the bulwarks was nearly level with the water, when we all ran up to the higher side which then commenced to descend to the same level and then we rushed to the ascending side. I heard a cry of "Back her" which roused into life a quiet, brown, wrinkled old gentleman with a face like a walnut who suddenly shouted through a speaking trumpet that he was Captain Milner of the Royal Navy and that he took command of the vessel. Apparently they were on the submerged rocks Pepper and Mustard which had previously sunk a boat called *Penelope*. She had eventually been beached and her crew, all that were found, were buried on the cliffs above, and so should we. There were fishing boats not too far to hear and we would shout till they heard and tiny fishing boats came and took us off. But what a scene the deck was. Some fainting, some praying. Some men comforting the prostrate, some awaiting the proper moment to swim off. Before our little boat was reached by the fishing vessels, the *Ruby*, a steam boat, came up and carried us all into Cowes. I had not felt at all afraid, but for days and nights after when I closed my eyes or looked towards darkness, I saw the sea with one vessel which immediately went down and then reappeared and did the same again.'

The *Lord Yarborough* was a 37-ton steamer, its figurehead being that of its namesake, the first commodore of the Royal Yacht Squadron and the owner of the Appuldurcombe estate on the island. The ship was the property of the Portsmouth and Ryde Steam Packet Company and was launched in June 1826. She had a wooden hull, two engines, and was single-masted and schooner rigged. Apart from sailing around the island, she also went to Cowes, Ryde, Portsmouth, Worthing, Brighton, Yarmouth, Lymington and Poole.

At another house on the Isle of Wight Ann met the famous Guilia Grisi, whose farewell performance in London was given on 7 August 1854. She sat out and talked to her. She had such a sweet smile and winning dimpled face and she told her that she had to give up the stage because no one believed that her voice at her age could get through an opera, but she herself thought she could as well as ever. Afterwards, for a charity, she sang at the lecture hall and 'really I thought the roof must rise for the volume of sweet sound'. Ann was quite fond of travel and succeeded in visiting France, Morocco, Algiers and elsewhere, but her favourite places apart from home were her visits to Burnham-on-Sea and Brighton. The family later bought a pretty place in the Isle of Wight called Melville Lodge, with the sea on three sides of them, and the Boniface Downs on the fourth. Their most amusing guest there was Baron Bramwell, the lawyer, and they used to go on long walks together. One day they went to bathe near Appuldurcombe, swimming out a great way, the Baron wearing an enormous straw hat as the heat was so great. As they returned to the shore an angry man told them they were trespassing on Lord Yarborough's estate and that he was his bailiff. The judge at once laid down the law as if he were on the bench, as the seashore between high and low water belongs to no one, the bailiff found himself defeated.

They had several friends and acquaintances on the island, notably the Pulskis, Hungarian patriot refugees, and met at another house Lady Elizabeth Pringle, daughter of Lord Breadalbane (died 1878). 'Also there was a Mr Cope from Niton who always spoke of his house as his mansion. He begged us to come and see him at his "mansion". We called him Mansion Cope and how Lady Elizabeth, refrained from laughing at him I don't know.'

They also met Princess Louise of Hesse, not long married. Born in 1817 she was the daughter of William Landgrave of Hesse and Princess Charlotte of Denmark, her marriage taking place in 1842. They became the King and Queen of Denmark in 1863 and were the parents of our Queen Alexandra. Ann records that 'Princess Louise went picnicking just outside the grounds and the Freres knew where they were for they had begged to have their kettle boiled for their picnic. As a tremendous shower came on, Mr Frere [a local landowner] immediately offered them the shelter of his house which they accepted. The Princess had a very strong foreign accent.' Most remarkable of their acquaintances was Miss Dick of Bonchurch, who 'being refused permission to marry the man she loved, went to bed and stayed there for years'.

After the Isle of Wight they moved to Barrymore at Wargrave, the home of the celebrated Earl of Barrymore in the eighteenth century, whose private theatre attached to his house had considerable contemporary fame. The theatre had gone by the time the Selous family arrived but the associations intrigued them. 'My sister Emily was very beautiful. As school she was called Faerie Queen and I've heard girls say "Look at Emily Sherborn, how beautiful she looks".' She had a wonderful complexion, dark brown hair with a good deal of burnt skin and open highlights. Angelo Selous fell in love with her when she was a schoolgirl and waited for years before he gained her father's consent. Emily Sherborn was twenty when she married, and though her father greatly esteemed her proposed husband, Angelo Selous, he was twenty-five years her senior. She was her father's favourite child and they had greatly enjoyed their visits to the Royal Academy, going over the pictures conscientiously from first to last. On the day of her marriage, 13 June 1848, her father locked himself in his room until her uncle, Frank, actually swore at the top of his voice, to break the door in. 'After the marriage they eventually moved in to 25 Ladbroke Square, the Square still unfinished, its unrailed opposite side apparently stretching out to the horizon, and from our drawing room balcony I used to watch haymaking and sunsets and I set free the lark father bought me. The house was built by my husband and when I returned from Switzerland I was so appalled by its large rooms and the probable difficulty of managing an adequate household that I sat down on the sofa and burst into tears. We took a house in Boulogne and found it a most amusing place, the Keeleys [a famous theatrical couple] were there ... and made the whist rooms of the casino delightful. We used to go there to watch them play for they looked and spoke and acted everything exactly as if they were on stage. That year a French camp was close to Boulogne and the camp brought the Emperor Louis Napoleon and the Emperor Louis Napoleon brought Prince Albert and a crowd of other people. Cholera then came and infected the camp. Fortunately our house was at the healthiest part of town but there often came hurried requests for hot water, all about the streets were processions of priests on their way to the dying, holding branches of sweet herbs to their faces and the streets were melancholy, with black hangings on their houses where people lay dead and on these hangings were represented large tears ... We were terrified for our three babies and would have left but the English doctor there strongly advised us to stay. Cholera, he said, was everywhere and more likely to be taken in a new air so we stayed, keeping sheets hung over the staircase, always wet with chloride of lime, and Angelo, whenever indoors, always smoked up and down the house. At last, one night Frederick was ill and through the darkness I stumbled – there were no lamps anywhere – down to the town below for a doctor and medicine.' A Scottish doctor supplied medicines through a window, and probably saved their lives.

Emily's son, Frederick Courteney Selous, had shown a great interest in wild animals as a child and he eventually became one of the foremost big game hunters of all time. It was through him that Ann Holgate Sherborn, Mrs Selous, entertained at a little dinner Princess Murat. She was Princess Caroline Letizia Murat, born on the 31st December 1832, who was married first, in Paris, 6th June 1850, to Charles Baron de Chassira, was widowed in 1870 and married secondly in 1871, John Garden of Little Redisham Hall in Suffolk. She was living at 12 Mandeville Place in 1891, and was the grand-daughter of the King of Naples, the celebrated General Joachim Murat, created King in 1808 by Napoleon, whose sister he had married. John Garden assisted in the escape of Napoleon III and the Empress Eugenie from France in 1871. At the same time she entertained a nephew of Lord Carnarvon's 'the Honorable Mr Drummond, who was later killed in Africa. The Princess was later to find English life too dull and returned to the Continent.'

The Sherborns soldiered on at Pates Manor until the death of Miss Eliza in 1907, when the whole of the contents were sold by auction on the premises. All family letters, diaries, and personal papers were consigned to bonfires lit in the grounds, only the estate papers being saved. William remained alone at Fawns until he too died in 1912. It seemed that the Sherborns had died out now forever. But William had left part of his property to a distant cousin, descended from a mid-eighteenth century Sherborn and that is how Great Uncle Charlie got his nickname of Squire, my father inherited, and so did I.

When I was young I had always understood that one day there would be a fairy-tale inheritance. Mother was always saying that we would be able to afford everything we needed one day when 'our ship' came home. I was not clear what kind of 'ship' it was, what it might be or what it was called, Why was it that we had a ship? Grandma Allman had no ships and we had no connection whatsoever with the sea.

The truth was that Uncle Charlie, a remote, grumpy old man living in Peterborough Road, Parsons Green, in London, had inherited a house in Bedfont in Middlesex called Fawns Manor, with the Lordship of the Manor of Fawns and Cockbell, from an old boy called William Sherborn whom he had discovered while writing the history of the Sherborns which he published in 1901. William of Bedfont was the last Sherborn still living in Bedfont when he died in 1912. Uncle Charlie's inheritance was quite complicated it seemed. It was only because the solicitor, Sir George Barber, had agreed to swap Fawns for a few acres of land left to Uncle Charlie that the house had come to him at all. My father would be head of the family after Uncle Charlie died and I remember being taken to Bedfont as a small boy and peeping over the walls and through hedges at a grey and gloomy house at the end of a drive. It all looked rather neglected and Uncle Charlie himself had never lived there. He was to die in 1942.

The open hall at Fawns was divided into two storeys during the sixteenth century; its east wing rebuilt, the west wing lost and an entrance hall wing added in 1889. Very odd it was too. The works necessary to make the house into a gentleman's residence after years of use as three cottages were carried out with characteristic Victorian vigour, but without much care for the past. However, somehow the house did acquire some additional character, and the losses were archaeological more than architectural. William Sherborn who did the work was quite a character in his own right.

William became interested in concrete quite early on and there was a concrete wall surrounding the fruit garden, studded and wired for fruit.

It had the unique feature of a pipe running around inside, connecting the pump house at one end with a slate horse trough facing the stables, a cast iron circular copper at the south end, and a slate tank at the return, or western end, of the garden. He also built a range of buildings containing wine bins constructed of concrete, although in cold weather the bottles froze and burst. Concrete was spread everywhere, with huge concrete walls around many of the fields and a pair of concrete estate cottages. William started using Joseph Tall's patent for building walls, registered in 1865, as early as 1868. The object was 'to effect an economy in building cottages and dwelling houses, and other erections in concrete combined with brick rubble or hard durable substance in place of employing costly brickwork'.

William knew that he had an inexhaustible deposit of gravel, so he could make Tall's concrete very easily. On an ordinary foundation, vertical boards were set up to form boxes into which the concrete was poured. The boxes were filled, the outsides were removed and the structure carried up in stages. Windows and doorframes were built in. Moulds made from zinc were used for ornaments, arches and curves, and a removable trellis frame of metal or wood, covered in concrete, formed the roofs. William threw himself into this novel form of construction with enthusiasm. Although Fawns had ceased to be the chief home of the family (with the White House and Pates Manor being preferred) he proceeded to 'restore' the fabric by embedding it in Tall's patent concrete. An entrance hall was added along the south side of the house and the whole edifice, including its lofty barrel vaulted ceiling, was built of concrete. The staircase was wholly of the same material save for its splendid oak balustrade, given to him by a friend as a present. Concrete arches, niches and vaulted ceilings were created all over the house. All the walls of Fawns Manor were encased in the same way, and an extraordinary chimney with flying buttresses was added on the north side of the house. I had a strange dream only recently in which I imagined that William's inspiration for the design was from his days in Portugal building the railways, and that he might have intended decorating the interior with tiling and pottery in bright colours in the Portuguese manner. Indeed, the vaulted ceilings, arches, niches, and recesses would have looked marvellous covered with Portuguese *azulejos*!

William also farmed his lands with enthusiasm and flair, using oxen teams until well into the 1890s. For his household arrangements, he had Mr and Mrs Washbourn with their two daughters to look after him. One of the daughters, Mrs Searle, came to see me in 1967 and told me that half of my bedroom, with its oak and glass-fronted cupboard doors, had been the estate muniment room and that the other half, then divided off by a cross wall, had been Mr and Mrs Washbourn's room. The rest of the house was scarcely furnished or finished at all. The housekeeper's room became in my day the family sitting room.

I would have liked to have met William Sherborn, but obviously never did, for he died in 1912. He was a highly eccentric bachelor, remembered for riding round his fields at midnight wearing nothing but his nightshirt, riding a tricycle around the drawing room at Fawns, having his horse brought up the stairs to his bedroom to see him in bed and staying there for six months of the year. In the summer he had his cat tethered to a stake near to his strawberry bed to keep birds away from the fruit!!

2

The Sherborns' Civil War and the Return of the Prodigal Sons

Of course there was no civil war in the family, but certainly there was one almighty row. Way back, following the death of Henry Sherborn of Bedfont in 1729, there was an upset over land and his son, another Henry, found himself sent packing with a horse and a shilling. He arrived at Windsor, just a few miles away, and stayed there until his death in 1784. It took more than a century and a half for the two sides of the family to be reconciled and speak again.

Of his eleven children, a son, William, moved on to Newbury in Berkshire and had five children, of whom Charles, born in 1796, was my own great-great grandfather. After Bedfont and Windsor the family moved to Newbury and indigence. Indeed, the eldest William Sherborn (1753–1809) actually became a humble wheelwright. He married Maria Carter of Newbury on 14 February 1785 and had five children, the eldest son (also William) being born on 1 January 1786. According to family tradition he was involved in making the Throckmorton Coat in Newbury (he was about twenty-five at the time), a kind of *Guinness Book of Records* effort in which a sheep was shorn, the wool carded, treated, spun, woven, dyed and made into a smart cutaway coat for Sir Robert Throckmorton, all in one day, 25 June, 1811. The sheep was then killed, roasted and eaten. The coat is still preserved at the Throckmortons' home, Coughton Court in Warwickshire. William eventually became a tailor and habit-maker at 60 Princes Court in London in 1829, and a leather brace and belt maker at 65 Princes Street, Leicester Square from 1835 to 1850. There he was helped in his shop by a daughter of his old friend the barefist boxer, Tom Cribb, the Champion of all England. Cribb, in his retirement from the ring, set himself up as landlord of a pub then called the Union Arms, on the corner of Oxenden Street and Panton Street, and he was there from 1828 to 1839. In recent years the pub has been renamed the 'Tom Cribb' after him and contains a collection of prints of the celebrated man. Cribb died in 1848, evidently ruined financially.

Henry, another brother, married a Mary Woollwright from Berkeley in Gloucestershire and they took a house called 24 Mornington Place. It was here that they had Alfred Lord Tennyson stay for a number of years and when the manuscript of his great *In Memoriam*, written about his friend and lover, Arthur Hallam, went missing, it was found in Mary Sherborn's kitchen cupboard. The thing almost lost for ever.

Henry's brother, Charles Sherborn, was born in 1796, was apprenticed to William Davis, an upholsterer in Newbury in 1810, and in about 1830 set up shop in London as a cabinet-maker, upholsterer and upholder at 9 Princes Street, just off Leicester Square, and then moved into the Square to 43 (1830–1839) and then 52 (1840–1846). He married Mary Bance of Newbury, a member of an armigerous French Huguenot family of cloth weavers, on 5 May 1829. He lived over the shop and his family were all born there. Leicester Square was by now given over entirely to trade and the days when Frederick, Prince of Wales, Sir Philip Parker Long, Reynolds and Hogarth lived there were long gone. Charles was already in Soho when he married Mary Bance and they had two children, Mary Hannah (who married John Hill of Cow Hill & Co., India rubber and gutta percha merchants) and Charles William, the most noteworthy of the Sherborn clan.

Charles had a ticket to view George IV's coronation banquet in Westminster Hall in 1820, and left a diary in which he records his curiosity in events by going to Horace Walpole's sale at Strawberry Hill in April 1842, to see the picture gallery at Dulwich in May 1849, skating on the Serpentine in January 1850, seeing the hippopotamus in Regents Park and later in June 1850, the House of Lords and Commons and was chilling in his description, 'superfluity beyond use or necessity in my opinion'. In September 1850 he saw the Exposition building (the Crystal Palace) in Hyde Park, heard Mrs Kemble read at the St James's Theatre, and in 1853 went to Paris with his son and others. He witnessed the launch of the *Prince Albert* at Woolwich in May 1854 and on 7 March 1856 was present when Covent Garden Theatre was burnt down. He had moved from Leicester Square to No. 10 King Street, St James in 1847 next door to Christies, the auctioneers. He died there in 1858. Mary supported herself in widowhood until her own death in 1890 by taking in rather grand lodgers: John Bramley Moore, the chairman of Liverpool Docks (and with other interests), and Colonel Sir Chandos Hoskyns Tenth Baronet. Hoskyns left his military chests and his campaign couch behind in the house and they remained in my family until recent years.

I suppose that I never took any great interest in the Huguenot Bances, Charles' wife's family, but to my grandfather and his generation they were all very real because Grandmother Sherborn had been a Bance and there were cousins and their offspring. Thomas Bance, Mary's brother, who was a tailor, packed his things, married Harriet Bailey, the daughter of a baker and pastry cook in Lewes in Sussex, settled there and by her had eleven children. He was a prominent citizen in his adopted town, becoming deputy high constable in the 1870s and high constable later (a title changed a few years later to mayor). His eldest son, Thomas, eventually followed him into business. By a unique stroke of good fortune, there is in Lewes in Messrs Reeve's, probably the oldest established firm of photographers in England. It is still run by the same family and still has its original premises with all the furnishings, records and negatives. Through visiting them I found something like seventy negatives of the Bances, their relatives, their shop and their monuments and wedding groups. The Bances established themselves quite well in Lewes, two daughters marrying into landed families, the Wetheralls of Pashley and the Botelers of Eastry, and another a member of the Falconer family.

There were however, two tragic deaths – Fanny at the age of 22 and later Frank Arnold, a palefaced lad who was lost at sea at the early age of 17. The *Sussex Express* for May 1872 regretted to state 'That there is every reason to fear that Franklin Arnold the youngest son of our respected fellow Townsman Mr T. Bance the High Constable of Lewes had been lost at sea. The young gentleman was a "midi" on board the *Golden Fleece*, Indiaman Captain Fife, and not long since returned from his first voyage round the world. He was warmly welcomed home again by a host of acquaintances, who found that a few months absence had changed the high spirited boisterous schoolboy into the young man of gentlemanly feelings and polished manners. How travel does improve one! After a few weeks holiday the ship was ready for sea, and once more young Frank left his friends and his brothers and his dear native land on the ocean to roame.'

The ship was bound from London for Calcutta, and on Saturday was off the Isle of Wight, beating down Channel against a heavy gale into the south west. On the morning following the gale, Francis' mess mates reported that his place was vacant, enquiries were made, the ship was searched, but nothing of him could be seen or heard. The captain sent a letter to Mr Bance and a letter written by Frank a day or two before. He had just celebrated his seventeenth birthday.

Did he fall, or was he pushed? Was that a veiled criticism in the article? Polished manners?!

Thomas had a house in Abinger Place near the Church of St John and lived in modest style. As a tailor in a county town he was quite well-to-do, and in 1871 had 14 men working for him as well as three boys and four women. His politics were liberal. He was eventually buried with his wife, who had died in 1860, in All Saints Church in Lewes. His son Thomas followed him in the business, but his grandson, Thomas Percival (born in 1870) had predeceased him.

Pashley at Ticehurst in East Sussex, no longer Wetherall property and for many of its later Wetherall years kept empty and unused, is a very grand house standing in extensive grounds. For years it was renowned for the importance of its fine old carved oak panelling. No doubt of medieval origin, its Tudor timbered walls and Georgian brick garden elevation stand as ample witness to the importance of the family years ago. Harriet Bance, who married William Squires Wetherall and went to live in South Africa with him, had three daughters, of whom one still lives in London.

The Botelers are a little more difficult to trace, but here was a family of very considerable importance in the Middle Ages, two obtaining peerages. In recent years there had been William Fuller Boteler KC, Recorder of Canterbury and Commissioner of Bankruptcy (1777–1846). He married Charlotte Joynes of Mount Pleasant, a substantial seat just south of Gravesend, had three sons and six daughters, and was father of Richard Boteler of Eastry. Others had been parliamentary clerks. Of the other Bance siblings, Frederick lived and died in South

Africa, Caroline married George James Wood of the Customs in Liverpool and Dover, Charles William (named after his godfather Charles William Sherborn) who married Edith Harrison, a doctor of medicine, John Edgar who had a wife, Suzanne and had four children, Emily Sherborn (Bance) who married Angus Falconer, and two spinsters, Eveline Mary and Annie Florence. Thomas Percival, the eldest son and heir, by his first wife Elizabeth had a son also named Thomas Percival and by his second (Anne Nye of Hamsey, perhaps a member of the family of Tunbridge ware makers in Tunbridge Wells, or the Nyes who ran the Theatre Royal in Brighton) had a daughter, Elizabeth. There are still several Bance descendants about.

It was with much regret that the *Sussex Express* of 14 August 1880 announced the death of Thomas Bance after 'a long and melancholy illness – Dr Braden had done all he could to prolong life and his family had exerted themselves to the utmost to render his efforts effective, but it was all in vain and he died last Wednesday evening surrounded by his relatives. He always did all the good he could, and never shirked the public duties which naturally devolved on one in whom general confidence was ever reposed. He supported every movement for the benefit of the town and neighbourhood, took great interest in agricultural matters, and was never wanting when well-directed activity and energy were required. He served the office of head-borough, junior high constable and senior high constable, being elected to the latter office in 1874.'

Thomas Bance senior by his will left his four unmarried daughters £50 each and the tenancy of the house free for six months. His estate was left to his nephew John Bance of Newbury, a woollen draper, and to a friend, James Broad of Lewes, tallow chandler. The remainder of his family were all disinherited.

I know little about Charles Sherborn's life as a collector, but no doubt he was in and out of Christies and also Robinson and Fishers who occupied as auction rooms the once fashionable Almack's Ballroom on the opposite side of King Street. He certainly acquired two of the original medieval carved wood roof bosses of the 1530s from Newbury parish church; a carved limewood overthrow from one of Wren's City churches and a pair of Wouverman's fancy bandit pictures. Charles' and Mary's eldest son was Charles William Sherborn. One of his mother's uncles was George Holmes, a partner in the firm Holmes and Griffin, sedan chair manufacturers to the royal family in Whitcomb Street. I have one of their chairs at home. George Holmes' brother had in Regency times been the proprietor of the London Oxford stagecoach.

Charles William was born on 14 June 1831 at 43 Leicester Square and educated at a local diocesan school and afterwards at Cave House, Uxbridge. A few copies survive of the school magazine, called the *Cave House Monthly Miscellany*, for dates from February 1845 to August 1846. They have charming engraved views of literary shrines like Milton's cottage at Chalfont, Sloperton Cottage near Devizes (the 'home of Thomas Moore'), Newstead Abbey, home of Lord Byron, Pope's Villa at Twickenham, Thomson's cottage at Kew Lane, Richmond Abbotsford; Sir Walter Scott's and Sir Richard Steele's cottage at Haverstock Hill. Cave House has long since gone, of course, but it was a substantial Georgian mansion and evidently had quite a decent reputation.

Charles William was sent on the 'Grand Tour', living in Paris, Geneva, Rome, Naples, Pisa and Florence for many years. In Rome he enjoyed the friendship of Pietro Girometti, the medallist and cameo worker, and also the very eminent Welsh sculptor John Gibson from whom he acquired a marble statuette of Venus, which I now have. Charles William studied art in all its aspects and was quite good in oils and watercolour and extremely proficient in metalwork, engraving and enamelling. He was admitted as a goldsmith. He is best known for his splendid series of book plates executed over a period of half a century and numbering over 400. There is scarcely a good library without his work. A sideline were his etched and engraved views, often of threatened historic buildings, and portraits produced as illustrations for books or for framing. He was an avaricious collector and apart from pictures by Wilson, Constable and contemporary artists, he amassed a great collection of old master etchings and engravings by Durer, Rembrandt, Rubens and others, all of which were later to be given to London University. His early working life was not easy, just engraving monograms and crests on silver, and he went bust in 1860, a temporary difficulty he swiftly overcame by seeking solace in the arms of a rich woman – a 25 year old widow. He was hardly the first or last person to marry for money! Hannah Wait, born Davies, was the young widow of a successful draper of social pretensions in Bold Street in Liverpool. She was able to solve Charles' money problems immediately and he achieved stability two years later, but financial tragedy again overtook him twelve years later, and from then on he lived entirely on art and his wife's good fortune.

A parcel of letters sent to him over the years has come down to me, quite a few of them dating from the 1850s and written by Pietro Girometti from Rome, referring to the International Art Exhibition in Manchester in 1854, talking about his work in cameo, pietra dura and steel, his rich American lady patrons, the absence of English ones, the excitement of a railway about to be built from Rome to Civitavecchia as part of one from Rome to Naples and the further project of a railway to Bologna: 'This is the first step towards civilisation that we make at last! ... Your Christmas spent in the English style, with delicious roast beef, and plum pudding, amused me very much, and if to this it may be added a sufficient quantity of good wine to make you gay and tipsy, the amusement must have reached the utmost degree of pleasure and *ne plus ultra* of satisfaction.' How grateful he was for the gift of buttons he had engraved for him and sent. He notes the taking of Sebastopol as a great victory, and talks of doing 'a very large cameo on a beautiful stone, this represents Achilles with the helmet and shield. The beauty of the stone is wonderful, the ground being sardonyx, the face of a fine pearly colour, the shield and helmet of a very fine violet colour quite equal to the steel, and the rest white. Both the helmet and shield will be covered with ornaments and basso relievos. I hope this will make a great noise among objects of this kind.' This last letter is dated November 1855 and he ends by saying how much he would like Charles to 'pay another visit to Rome – this would afford me the opportunity of passing some other weeks in your company and talking again about *spiders* and *snakes* ... You would find me always with the sentiments of esteem and friendship with which, I remain, your very affectionate friend, Pietro Girometti.'

Later there were to be quite a few letters from other artists such as Lord Leighton, Francis Seymour Haden, Stacey Marks and Sir Frank Short, but the really interesting ones are those from Frederick Sandys, few actually dated at all, but seemingly all of the 1890s and all begging for money – tragic letters, asking for five or six shillings, written on scraps of paper and sometimes just in pencil. One letter of 27 August 1897 asks for ten shillings or a sovereign because he was unable to finish a portrait because he had no brown or black chalk. He said that he ought to get fifty or sixty guineas for it, but was prepared to sell it for thirty and had to pawn it over the weekend. He already owed Charles money.

Another large series of letters is from Alfred Gilbert. They refer to cooperation between the two men on sculptural work in which my great grandfather helped by doing engraving and enamelling on metals. It is not clear to me what works they were collaborating over but the Earl of Derby's arms are mentioned, a motto, 'Sol Mea Testis', garters round the escutcheons of Henry I and Henry II to match those of other kings, and a plaque, but maybe the work for Gilbert was on the Duke of Clarence's great tomb for St George's Chapel, Windsor. He was often represented at the Academy exhibitions, and when the Royal Society of Painter Etchers was founded in 1884 he was one of its original members. One of his best works was the line-engraved portrait of the president of the Society, Sir Francis Seymour Haden. In 1892 the Grolier Club of New York exhibited many of his works, and in 1893 Frederick Keppel gave him another exhibition. In 1899 a special series of his works formed the feature of that year's exhibition at the Society of Painter Etchers in London. Small details of him are that he always wore a black velvet jacket and a smoking cap indoors and that there was always bloater paste for tea. He was very fond of it.

Hannah Simpson Sherborn's grandsons remembered her as a rather imperious old lady who insisted on her small change being washed, and her shoelaces and newspapers being ironed to make them flat. She carried the handbag and kept it shut. She had an interesting grandfather Thomas Davies of Bold Street, Liverpool (1770–1823), an eminent watch and chronometer maker who was in partnership with Peter Litherland of that city and ultimately took the name Litherland in consideration of a bequest, becoming Litherland Davies. One clock, a gold watch, his silver-topped cane and his death mask remain in my family, but a bracket clock, two watches and a silver mounted marble snuffbox have all been stolen at various times.

Hannah outlived Charles in the tall, large house at No. 1, Finborough

Road, with its rows of servant's bells in the kitchen and speaking tubes by each fireplace. The rooms retained her husband's collection of pictures which included works by Constable, Turner, Morland, Wilson and others, along with his old master drawings and rather unfashionable furniture. Right up to her death she wore the traditional widow's cap of fine lace. She was of strong stuff.

Charles William was a brilliant etcher and engraver. Rather oddly, since it was well outside his usual work, the Baroness Burdett-Coutts persuaded him to design a set of toiletware for her. Hannah was an autocratic Victorian wife, first living at 540 Kings Road, Chelsea and latterly in Finborough Road, round the corner. Both houses have now fallen from the rather higher estate they had in those days. She died two years before I was born, and had five children, of whom one, Charles Davies, was even more extraordinary than his father. Of him more later.

Every flock, it is said, has its black sheep. One cannot chose one's relations or ancestors hard as one may try. Charles William had a very strange brother of whom much is now unfortunately known. It is a pity that he ever lived; astonishing that any letters have survived at all! Edwin John was born on 23 July 1837. He served 'before the mast' as first Cuddy servant from June 1858 to April 1859 on the tea clipper *Copenhagen*, an 876-tonner built in 1855 and in service on the London Australia run. She was launched a little while before the famous *Cutty Sark* and was slightly smaller in gross tonnage. Edwin later settled in Dayton, Ohio, and I recently discovered a collection of letters written by his mother to him, and very odd they are too! On 14 February 1855, his mother wrote to him and his wife Emma: 'I am sure I need not say what pleasure I felt at the receipt of your nice long letter, for strange to say again the same post brought tidings of both my children, the one [Charlie] in Rome and he in America. If I dare only hope that you Emma and Charlie would ever meet in England in my lifetime what a happy time it would be for all, improbable as it now seems. I received the gold coin safely – but am sorry to say the *Journal of Physiological Medicine* will not go by post. Books are only allowed by post to our own Colonies. I am more than grieved that you are to leave Dayton . . . I am daily more convinced than ever that England was at the height of her prosperity the year of the Great Exhibition [in 1851]. She has seen her day and like other great nations she will fall. Never has she been so disgraced as lately, ten whole days without a Ministry, the disgraceful manner in which the War has been conducted [in the Crimea] and the heavy taxation which it must necessarily bring upon us. The great failures in the City, the discontent of the people, rich and poor, all convince me that we have seen the best of our times here. What will the pages of England's future history contain? Why our army [in the Crimea] of 54,000 men, where are they? Nearly annihilated by starvation, neglect, no shelter, no clothing! I send *The Times* more frequently lately so that you may read the accounts yourself. I will send you others when Gladstone finishes us with his Budget which I think will make all the Americans call us English fools...'

After her husband's death in April 1858 she had a letter of sympathy from her daughter-in-law to which she replied: 'My dear Emma, how good and kind of you in my hour of sorrow to write a few lines of sympathy to your friend whom you have never seen or known. Such attentions as these, dear, soften and soothe our sorrows tho' for a short moment it renews as it were a fresh grief. I have had much trouble, anxiety, and sorrow since your former letter dated June 28, 1857. Soon after that my poor husband's appetite began to decline...' and here follows the details of his eventual death, 'when it came it was like a dream at first but the sad reality soon became so evident when I saw the vacant place, the empty chair that was for so many years occupied. [Oh dear! Those Victorian widows!!] I am in my 53rd year, my dear husband was 11 years older, so that our ages were considered pretty equal! I cannot therefore expect to last many years and as I get older my troubles increase.' She was actually to live another 23 years, not dying until 1890!

Another part letter of 1859 refers to the birth of another child to them. She hopes 'that it may prove a treble source of happiness and comfort and delight to you all. Charlie has done pretty well, he has a very nice little office in Jermyn Street close by and still lives at home with me, and now the evenings are getting long we begin chess again. I can play much better but of course not equal to Charlie. I often think of you – I think it almost time he was married. Polly is really getting old ... "I have been into Kent to see Mrs Henry Sherborn, she has such a lovely house; situated at the top of a very high hill and a beautiful garden"...' It was called Berkeley Lodge and is at Dunkirk, near Canterbury.

Another part letter, probably dating about 1860 refers to much she has to be thankful for: 'Charlie is most happily settled, such a dear, affectionate wife, he has such a nice home, then again I have dear Polly at home which is a source of great comfort to me and her health is much improved since she has left off teaching. Ted is still at Mr Howitt's in Holborn but he is of very different disposition to the others. My house looks very nice, it is very clean and comfortable now. I think I told you it cost me nearly £700. I have a lease at a rental of £100 per annum instead of my old rent of £175 per annum. Do you still reside in the same house or shall you remove into Dr Casey's [or Carey's] when he leaves ... I long to know if this War will or does affect Dayton much; what a sad thing it is. Give my most affectionate love to dear Emma, tell her how I regret not sending my box of toys for dear Lottie and Charlie. Kiss them both for me ...'

A letter of 19 May 1862 reads: 'My dear John, Time flies so rapidly that I had no idea the length that has elapsed since I wrote to you ... I congratulate you first of all on your success in your profession [he was thought to be studying medicine] and I dare say now you have the whole it is not any too much for your expenses now that your dear little ones get older. I deeply sympathise with dear Emma on the loss of her dear babe. No one can enter into a mother's feelings unless they too lose one themselves. I am so happy to hear of the welfare of your dear girl and boy. Lottie must be a nice girl by this time. How I longed and wished your old servant you wrote about would call, it would have been a great treat to have heard all about you and the dear children from one who had known you all personally. She never called and I suppose she never will. What an unfortunate affair this Civil War [in America] is – who would have thought of it some years ago? It seems to me that it never would or could be settled.

'I have received an unusual amount of papers, accept my best thanks dear John for them, though I am almost ashamed to confess I did not see the account of your dear babe's death. I send you some ... the last an account of the opening of our Great Exhibition in 1862. I wish you could afford to come and bring dear Emma to see the Exhibition, how happy we should be. I think that there is a proposal (tho' distant at present) of Polly's marrying [she married John Hill and died aged just 40]. If it should come off I shall be equally satisfied as I am with

34

Charlie. I am sorry to say that she has been much out of health, I suppose that it may be termed a sluggish liver. She has frequently a bad pain in her right side and is frequently so dreadfully nervous that some nights she gets no sleep at all ... and then she is obliged to have a course of morphine which composes her and she gets better for a time. She is at present on a visit to her uncle my brother [Thomas Bance at Lewes]. She has been five weeks today and I do not know when she will return. Last March I was sent for into Kent to see the last of poor Henry Sherborn, he died the day after my arrival [9 October 1863], it was very sad because, poor man, he had long been anticipating the return of Rev Mr and Mrs Butt (son-in-law and daughter) from India whom if nothing happens will arrive in England on 7th June with the addition of two children, a boy and girl, both born in India. Mrs Butt received my letter announcing her poor father's death just as she would be sailing for England. Mr William Sherborn is a wonder, he's 77 years old but wonderfully well – he spends his Sundays always here and many evenings besides. I greatly fear he will live not to want because I must take care of that but he will no doubt live to be a burden to us as he is spending fast the few pounds he has, poor old man. He must feel very lonely, he is the only one of his family left. Fanny Buxton wishes to be kindly remembered to you.

'With sincere affection for you and Emma and your dear little ones and with every good wish and blessing from your affectionate Mother Mary Sherborn.'

Another part letter of 1864 to John: 'You will be pleased to hear Charlie is doing very well though his expenses are very great. His family increases, he has three, the sweetest tempered and two of the finest children you could see for their respective ages, the elder a boy $3\frac{1}{2}$ years, the youngest a boy 4 months – he has a smile for everybody, the little girl just two years is very fair ... When I wrote to congratulate you on the birth of your last babe I made mention of the fact that there was no prospect of Polly producing a family. It is grievous to think how much better a position you would be in if it were not for the very high rate of provisions caused by this unhappy war. I have just read with horror that another call is made for the frightful number of 300,000 – it seems incredible to me that they can be promised, then to read that about 1,000,000 men have perished since 1861. What an awful thought and what good has it achieved? I shall send you my paper by this post. I hope dear little Lottie received the pictures from the *Illustrated News* and you the other part. Charlie and Hannah, Polly, and Fanny Buxton desire to be most kindly remembered. My warmest and best love to your own dear Emma and your beloved children ... pray you may both be spared many many years to see your children grow up and become useful members of society. Tell Emma we shall never see each other but I often think of her. Believe me, my dear John, to remain your affectionate Mother Mary Sherborn.'

The letters sound all right, but are they? Did Edwin John have a wife Emma, three children, Lottie the eldest, Charlie, the second, a baby who died young? Why does Charles Davies Sherborn, his nephew, say that John died unmarried in Chicago in 1880, if in fact he had married and had children? Where are the photogaphs that might have been sent of Emma and the children? And what career did he follow? Was he escaping from a possessive mother and felt he had to invent a family to keep her quiet? There seem to be doubts in Mary's mind at times, for why does she say that she knows that she will never see Emma and the children? Why does she query the fact that she has been through the parcel of American papers she has been sent and cannot find any mention of the death of the baby? The letters are here now, returned after his death, back from America. It is very odd, writing this now, when the letters have been accessible for 130 years, that I had never read them, and no one in the family, just no one, had ever referred to Edwin John Sherborn, or any mystery surrounding him. The only things I have are his seamanship certificate, when he disembarked at Limehouse on 7 April 1859 on the completion of his voyage to Australia and back; a block of melted tin-tacks salvaged from the Great Fire of Chicago in 1871; the letters, and a photograph of Edwin John alone. Why one wonders, did the letters cease in 1863 when he had 17 more years to live and his mother 27? His death certificate, which has just been sent to me from Chicago, tells me that he was single without children, worked as a painter and died of bronchitis and gangrene of the lungs. His whole life was a fantasy with not a word of truth in any of it. A phantom, a rotter and a disgrace.

The eccentric Charles Davies Sherborn was the eldest of the children of Charles and Hannah and was born at what was later called No. 10

Gunter Grove, Chelsea, on 30 June 1861, and was christened at St Luke's. At the back of Gunter Grove were the Royal Exotic Nursery Gardens of Sir James Veitch, and as a small boy he used to be taken for walks by his father, sometimes to the old farmhouse which stood on the site of South Kensington Station (to which his father had been sent to stay for weekends away from his parents' home in Leicester Square) or to Walnut Tree Walk (now Redcliffe Gardens) to catch insects and butterflies or play cricket. Another farm, on the site of Earl's Court Station, was useful because there one could get mulberry leaves for silkworms, while nearby there was the former home of John Hunter, the great surgeon, who worked there on the preparation of the skeleton of O'Brien, the Irish giant. Charles could remember the captive balloon kept in the grounds of Ashburnham House in the Kings Road which used to give people controlled ascents for the benefit of the great view that could be had of London.

He was sent to school at the very early age of three, the establishment being run by a Miss Foy in the Fulham Road. At six he went to another school run by Miss Rowley in Limerston Street, where the master employed had the habit of running his pen through his hair to dry it. How long he stayed is not clear, but his next school was that run by a well-known and clever educationist, Elizabeth Rye, before he finally went on to St Mark's College School, an establishment run in conjunction with the teacher training college founded in 1841 in a handsome Stuart mansion called Stanley Grove, fortunately still standing now. He was at school with the old Savoyard Cowtree Pounds, and another old boy was Sir Henry Lytton, much admired for his interpretation of Gilbert and Sullivan parts. In the upper school Charles won certificates for drawing, geography, acoustics, light, heat and geology – then his favourite subject. Taken away from school at the age of fourteen because of his parents' financial difficulties, Charles was found a job in a shop in New Bond Street called Stockleys the Stationers at a wage of seven shillings a week, but he left there about eight years later for a job at thirty shillings a week at Fosters the tailors, in Waterloo Place.

All this time he spent as many moments as he could in the Museum of Practical Geology in Jermyn Street. Not only did he take a keen interest in geology, he also took up photography, and with his friend W.

Low-Sergeant, paid a visit to Exmoor with the first hundred celluloid photographic plates made by Thomas of Norwood. A volume of them, labelled *A Camera Round Exmoor* belongs to the Royal Photographic Society. It was at about this time that he became friendly with and worked for Professor Rupert Jones, who had then just retired from the Chair of Geology at the Royal Military College at Sandhurst.

In July 1884 he had scraped together eighty pounds and went off to see the Continent and learn French and German. He spent eight months in Lausanne, three months at Strasbourg and Vienna and visited Brussels and Paris. In Easter 1885, back in England, he left his parents' home at 540 Kings Road and moved into a house nearly opposite, lived in by an undertaker called Bultitude – Charles used to help him when he was busy by polishing coffins! It was not until 1888 and after various minor jobs that he first got a part-time job at the British Museum, in its geology department. He retained his connections with the museum until the end of his life. As a geologist he became famous, and those interested in this aspect of his career should read J.R. Norman's excellent biography of him, which has a long list of his published works at the end. The greatest of these was, of course, his *Index Animalium*, begun in his rooms over Bultitude's shop in 1890, which took forty years to complete and contained 44,000 references. During the time he worked on his *Index Animalium* he also found the time to complete indexes to no less than 28,000 works. As an index maker it is unlikely that we shall ever see his like again.

It was about this time that he embarked on a history of the Sherborn family and rediscovered four members still living in Bedfont – thus ending the family civil war.

The year 1912 was to see not only the death of his father, but also the death of William Sherborn, his distant cousin, and last of the Sherborns then still remaining at Bedfont.

A considerable number of letters from Charles Davies Sherborn written in his later years have survived, and I feel that a few of them would be appropriate here to show the extent of his interests and enthusiasms and to give some indication of his great work. Great Uncle Charlie was not noticeably artistic but had a manic interest in the theatre and got together a large collection of theatrical memorabilia, photographs, autographs and letters. He seems to have had no aesthetic sense whatever and the fact that he had many works of art on his walls was an accident of inheritance, not taste. However, he did collect ancient coins and admired them for their design and beauty. As he wrote to his great friend, Agnes Arber:

'To Agnes Arber, August 8 1920, B.M. (N.H.)
'The Spirit (non-alcoholic) moves me to write to you, that you may not think I forget but life is much harder & years slip by & the cheap hair will come off & teeth decay as well as intellect.

'But you will be glad to hear that last I see daylight at the end of my tunnel & I now on my last thousand volumes – all at the B.M. I have exhausted every other library in London before going there. It is a fairly easy job for books but Lord help me on periodicals! There are over 300 of them many running over 30 years & many in vile German script on vile paper. I have been to the oculist as a precaution & he says that my right eye is unaltered from 10 years ago, but the left beginning to develop a fold in the lens the same. So I said "Give me 5 years more & the devil can have 'em both" & he has done so to the best of his ability & I feel I can attack the B.M. in peace for a six months campaign ought to do it. AND I have sorted *A* lexicographically already. Merciful Heavens, while in my 1758–1800 vol. there were 53 "affinis" there are in 1801–1850 NINE HUNDRED. Do you wonder at the cheap hair? If you were only a Bug instead of a plant, I might hope for some help in some insect papers I want.

'I am full of rage & fury. I got today from Rothschild a *separate* of an 1849 Bird paper, only to find that the Vile author had *reset* the last pp & inserted 2 new *genera* – think of the iniquity of it! But you've got to get up early to take in C.D.S. . . . I have shelled out all my new types of Byzantine coins to the B.M., 150 of them – a jammy lot . . . They call it a "splendid gift" but I've had my pleasure in working them out. Also given them the pick of the R. Owen literary letters 350 + 100 letters of the Clift family. Superb letters of Livingstone, Jenny Lind, Carlyle, Dickens etc. etc. which cost me a pang but they are safer there than in my rooms. I shall gradually part with everything now & see it safely housed before I pack up.'

'To Agnes Arber, 15 May 1921, 49 Peterborough Road

'I really believe Science would benefit from a Labour Government after all. The present people simply scoff at science & are completely ignorant of its aims & uses.'

'To Agnes Arber, 18 July 1922 [After the death of his mother.]

'I am getting free. I have sold the house: divided the goods: moved my two brothers & myself: put my sister's stuff into store & got her away for some months: found the staff a room (heavens what a job) & a new place at double wages to sleep out – so she is in clover. Another fortnight will I hope see an end of the terribly monotonous $2\frac{1}{2}$ years of alphabetic sorting. Then I go AWAY ... to Norfolk to look for Roman pottery far away from humans & indexes & museums ... I have done little outside the regular grind for months but managed to get a perfect pre-Dynastic pot (Egyptian c.4000 B.C.) with paintings of humans, ibexes, trees & boats on it, a most rare object & interesting for the fact that the drawings are identical with those on the early pottery of Susa in Mesopotamia of same age. Also a little gem of a glass vase, highly decorated, Egyptian 300 B.C. I am sorting my stuff out & fitting it in, but as I was crowded out before my prints & pictures came from home, it is not an easy job.'

'To Agnes Arber, October 1922, 49 Peterborough Road

'I had a holiday (the first whole month since I was a boy) & despite the cold & rain, enjoyed it. I collected many hundreds of flint implements, some coins, 3 Roman fibulae, fragments of pots from neolithic times to Geo 5 & found a Roman villa.

'The family affairs are now all closed. My sister goes to the U.S. on October 5 for 2 years, one & a half of which will be spent in Pacific Grove, Cal. & this will be rest & recompense to her for her long nursing & confinement. I fear she will find it very expensive but have told her not to spoil her ship for a ha'porth of tar. As for news there is little.

'We have a most beautiful Myolosaur skull from the Oolite & a gorgeous Dinosaur from Alberta showing skin all over the back. He came during the War, but we have only recently been able to dig him out.'

40

'To Agnes Arber, October 14 1928, 49 Peterborough Road

'Our phenomenal summer has now come to an end & now comes rain, cold & fog. Still it is years since we had such a treat. I went up to the Derwent Valley for 3 days to get local colour & came back & finished the pedigree I have been working at for years. It remains for the family to print it & then I shall do an index linking up all the Yorksh[ire] S[herborn]s who do not fit into the main story. A great flood of annoying work has been let in upon me by the Berlin "Nomenclator" which has recorded hundreds of *merely obvious* misprints & therefore compels me to list them in my suppl. tho' I had refused them admittance. I wade through 10pp each morning from 10–11 before starting on my own suppl. which is a fearful labour in itself ... I recently bought a superb gold brooch of Graeco-Roman period (Augustan) head of Persephone in ¾ relief in a hemisphere size of a 5/- piece ... a lovely thing. The B.M. have never seen anything like it & say "Whatever its date you have a wonderful work of art". We have no history so I had to buy on my own judgement. Couldn't let it go!'

'To Agnes Arber, July 18 1930

'Several times have I thought of writing but time has passed as usual. I am well; have had a wretched spring and summer so far & have not been away. I shall be content with the inside of a week at Kings Lynn & the village of Shernborne nearby where I believe the S's had a castle in Saxon times. I want to see what the place is like now. Glad that you are busy & at work. It is the greatest of all things this continuous drudging. I have lately had through my hands the very last of the great rarities in books of my period, Martyn's *Psyche*, a butterfly book for which I paid £18. The only other known copy is in Washington. And when I got my hands on [it] I found inside a letter from myself over 30 years ago asking for them, they having disappeared ever since. They are now safely housed in the Entomological Society & safe.

'My ledger records over a thousand volumes nearly all the rarest of things which have passed through my hands into permanent safety for future students. *Laus Deo.*

'I have recently purchased a few bits of Persian pottery from the Sale after the London Exhibition. One a deep blue bowl deeply scalloped & grooved round the edge, the other a delightful bowl of lustre with three

41

saints in brown inside. The first was 13thC. the latter 11–12th. No more for a long time as the Index does not permit of extravagances like these! Coins seem to have vanished off the face of the earth, scarcely a dozen have come my way in twelve months, except a magnificent Roman AS nearly a pound in weight & of the early period of Etruria which lately fetched £14 at the Samborn Sale & entered my hospitable home at 7/6 . . .

'But I get old (70) & most of my cronies have gone home & it seems foolish to magpie any more. I have sent all my gems in literary books to the B.M., my Chinese coins have gone & my other collections will follow suit as I make up my mind as to those who will appreciate & care for them for my sake. For I will not sell a thing after all the joy I have had in finding & possessing. As Varro says, "it is time to pack up" and so be it.'

'To Agnes Arber, March 3 1932, 49 Peterborough Road

'At long last, after three months of horrid cold this morning the thermo rose to 50 & I breathe again. The hideous brutality of cold weighs heavily on my soul & has done since I was a boy. I hate & loathe it. I have finished the main work, the last part containing Z came out a few weeks ago. Now we are printing the last thousand pages of index, corrections, & add to Bibliography. Will take a full year of typing & press reading all the time as one has to feed the printer continuously. *Laus Deo*. I now hope to live to see it through despite the daily holocaust of motor victims, for that is as serious as disease in these days. You will have heard that I have given the Fitzwilliam my complete collection of my Father's work, a magnificent series second only to that in the B.M. & in some respects finer for I reserved many proofs & prints to the envy & hatred of all good collectors; & survived all their wheedlings & bribes of open cheques etc. My MSS are gone to the B.M. & fill nine volumes. So I feel all is safe now & the threat of fire greatly removed.

'For years I have had my eye on a superb collection of kitchen utensils in bronze from a villa in Pompeii which belonged to Dr Sambon. He died suddenly a while ago & I feared they were lost. Though I mentioned my friend to the exors they did not communicate with him. But curiously enough another dealer who was called in told him he did not want some bronze stuff that had been offered to him & if he liked he would take him round and introduce him. He did and to his joy found they were the Sambon things that I had to look out for & he immediately bought the lot. There are saucepans, spits, graters, jugs, spoons, ladles, & a fine steelyard – magnificent & unique outfit, as well as a set of surgical instruments found on the field of Trasimene & therefore actually dated to the time of Hannibal. I went last night to identify them & was overjoyed that at last they were safe. Where they will go I don't know, I can't afford them.'

'To Agnes Arber, December 12 1934, 49 Peterborough Road
'God is good to little Sherborn. About a month ago my good friend Lawrence, knowing I was interested in the history of the elephant before AD, told me of a wooden figure of that beast to come up at Sotheby's in an Egyptian collection. He did not get it as Welcome bought it. But a few minutes later a little bronze bust came up wearing an elephant's scalp which he bought thinking it would do for me. I at once recognised it as the portrait on the coins of Alex IV of Egypt which were prepared for the boy by Ptolemy I. But this was his *father*'s portrait & thus a contemporary & unique portrait of Alexander the Great! I took it at once to the B.M. & had a real reception. So gave it to them as so precious & historical a piece was safer there than here.'

Uncle Charlie was a determined mysogynist: 'As regards my relations with women a great deal of misapprehension has arisen in various quarters. I never liked women and never chose them as companions. They never interested me in their ways or ideas. With few exceptions and they are mostly foreigners. I found them ignorant, unread and with little desire to learn. Possibly this is due to the rotten kind of education provided for them. But I had many friends among women and many a woman can testify to my consideration and helpfulness in times of trouble. I once esteemed a woman very highly and engaged to marry her, she was highly intelligent and well read, but as I could not give up my career and make the sacrifices needful, and had no prospect of ever being able to keep her in comfort, we parted after ten years and she wisely married another. After an interval of many years we met again and she and her husband and I were excellent friends and correspondents. Little children up to about ten and elderly women are often attractive to me.'

Charles' long labours were rewarded with an honorary degree of Doctor of Science from Oxford University in 1931. The day for the ceremony, 10 March, was an exceedingly cold one and he wrapped himself up well and wore a flannel apron under his shirt and trousers. The ceremony was in the Convocation House and he stood there shaking visibly, not just with cold but with Parkinson's disease which affected him in his later years. The public orator's speech, delivered in Latin, commended to those assembled that day 'the author of an immense enterprise, who, of his own accord and free will, has carried out a truly Plinian plan with truly Plinian industry. He has carefully searched out the names which investigators have from time to time given to animals during the period of one hundred years after Linnaeus, has traced every name back to its source in separate short rubrics, and finally has arranged the whole in alphabetical order, and with singular zeal and diligence committed it to print. In order to complete this index he has exposed and digested well nigh numberless volumes, pamphlets and the transactions of learned societies, all written in many languages, and such has been his perception and judgement, that among students of natural science both at home and abroad it is agreed that no author of a zoological bibliography exists of greater skill than he. Thus I know not whether to compare him to Atlas, seeing that alone for nearly fifty years he has carried so great a burden on his shoulders; or to Argus, inasmuch as not even the minutest shreds of evidence seems to have escaped his eyes; or to Ariadne, in that he has provided all zoologists and those who derive the material for their studies from the storehouse of zoology with most trustworthy clues amid the many labyrinths of literature ... As for the father of the index himself, now that he has happily completed his self-imposed task, more mindful of the needs of others than of his own profit, him we gladly honour with the laurels of this University, as the author of a work most worthy of any academic writer and of any University. And so I present to you a most watchful servant of Zoology – Charles Davies Sherborn – that he may be admitted to honorary degree of Doctor of Science!'

I cannot better J.R. Norman's description of Charles' house at 49 Peterborough Road, Parsons Green, where he lived for forty-five years, taken from *Squire Memories of Charles Davies Sherborn* (Harrap, 1944):

'It would take an abler pen than mine adequately to describe that well-known room – half a study, half sitting-room, with a strong flavour of a museum. The newcomer obtained a mixed impression of simplicity, order, antiquity, overcrowding, and above all, plenty of what Squire was wont to call "good honest London dust". The room would have been the despair of any conscientious housewife, but to his friends it was so much a part of the man himself that none would have desired a single feature changed; the ceiling, black with age, was fretted with cracks, and such portions of the original wallpaper as could be seen between the bookshelves, pictures, framed prints and engravings, and other treasures with which the walls were covered, had taken on a nondescript neutral shade. Shelves from floor to ceiling on either side of the fireplace, were loaded with books, and above the mantelshelf a shallow, glass-fronted cabinet held miscellaneous smaller antiquities, which also overflowed onto the shelf itself. On the opposite side of the room were tiers of home-made bookshelves with additional books, pamphlets and specimens, and a many-drawered wooden cabinet held further treasures of all kinds. A low desk, its top fully loaded, occupied the centre of the wall facing the window, and was flanked on the fire side by a rocking chair and on the other side by a safe. Under the window two or more tables placed together provided support for small cabinets and larger antiquities, leaving a clear space for writing. Two simple wooden chairs, one of which had an old cushion tied to its seat, and one or two further cabinets for specimens, completed the list of furniture, and little free space remained in the room. Among other familiar objects which caught the visitor's eye was a marble statuette of the Venus of Milos (by John Gibson) under a dark hood, for many years topped with a man's Tudor cap, a plaster cast of the face of a large gorilla, Squire's favourite microscope under a glass shade, a fine chained book, and the sardonic-looking death mask of Richard Parker. The room had certainly not been decorated during the forty odd years of his tenancy, and he always told me that it never would be in his life time. Moreover he had little or no use for duster and brush, and certainly none at all for more elaborate cleaning. "It's only dust," he would say, blowing a cloud from a book taken off

45

the shelf "and it soon settles again; if you flap around with a duster you only stir it up." In the days when long skirts were fashionable, he was in the habit of watering the floor to lay the dust whenever lady visitors were expected. The place, in a word, was filthy, but undeniably intellectual.'

It seems a shame that the things were so neglected. It matters little to me that the foot of the mummy in the wall case over the fireplace was embellished with living green mould, because this was an object of revulsion rather than art, but the books all had brown, red, mouldering and snapping spines, even the ancient chained copies of the Bible and Jewell's *Apology* and – and this cannot have been right – the pictures inherited from his father, which included two Constable landscapes and a Wilson, and a pair of rather charming small early eighteenth-century oil portraits based on Vertue engravings in their original carved frames, were all dark, dark, brown. For food, he seemed to exist on dates – the kind one once could buy packed hard into largish wooden boxes. He was extremely disagreeable to most people, avoiding all company, especially that of women, who he once was heard to describe as 'all cheats', but this did not include either his mother or his sister Ada, nor one or two others. For his brothers' wives, or his nephews' wives or any other female relatives he could spare no time. I was still only 16 when he died in 1942 but he had taken a remote interest in my collections of stamps and coins, and on his death I was to inherit both, although, alas, the important early gold coins he intended for me were stolen after his death before I could receive them; I had seen them once, for just a second. My own grandfather had pinched them all and sold them within the hour.

The greatest treasure he possessed was his father's magnificent collection of old master etchings and engravings, which I discovered had been given to London University. The family Engleheart miniatures had also gone, this time to the British Museum. His three houses were left to the family: my father inheriting Bedfont; his brother (my funny Uncle Leslie) inherited Aunt Ada's house; and his niece Joan (his brother Sidney's daughter) inherited his own house. Neither of the Peterborough Road houses survived the war, both being destroyed together by a single bomb.

Uncle Charlie outlived his sister Ada by two years, dying on June 22, 1942, but let us now address our attention to her and not race on too far.

46

Ada Mary, Charles and Hannah's only daughter, my great aunt Ada, was born a year later than Charlie in 1862 and like most eldest girls was expected to help run the family, the house, and later to care for her ailing parents until their deaths. Aunt Ada travelled quite a bit, going to Norway in the 1890s and climbing horrifying hills.

A friendship dating from 1899 with two American girls, Bessie and Annie Cutter (great nieces of a relative of the Sherborns, Dr J.C. Reeve of Dayton in Ohio) was to be valuable to her. Reeve got the best medical education available in America at the time, but when he graduated in 1849, at Cleveland, he had never even been taken to the bedside of a patient. It was all books and lectures and theory, and an occasional operation seen from a seat in an amphitheatre. Once he had enough money he went to England and Germany to complete his studies. A few letters survive from this time – writing to his wife from London on 31 January 1854, he regretted that it was his last day there: 'I have stayed several days longer than I should for the purpose of seeing the Queen proceed in State to open Parliament. This I have seen and had a fair view of her and Prince Albert and some of the Royal babies and of the Lords and Ladies, and as I waited on my feet three mortal hours, I am somewhat tired. On Saturday p.m. I went to the *Dreadnought*, Professor Partridge told me there would be an amputation at the hipjoint, an operation not often performed, even in London, and he was going down, so I made bold to go, and was kindly received. I had a fine opportunity to see the operation – indeed assisted at it and got covered with blood. I tell you it was a great operation, it was like a battle!' On 4 February he wrote again, this time from the *Dreadnought*: 'At ten the physician and surgeon go around their wards, and such a mixture of diseases and nations you never saw! Everything but women! Everyday there was a post mortem. After dark I go to the dead room. We live on the second deck – I go to the deck below and in the office open a trap door which leads me down a pair of steps to the Museum, in which are skeletons, skulls, and all those horrid things which medical men delight in. Down another pair of steps through another trap door and I am in the dead room . . . its furniture – one table, one stool, a bench, a sink and three plain black coffins; its company the coffins' inmates. It is a gloomy little, low room, lighted by day by a single three-light window; by night I use a candle, and here I stayed each night till 9 o'clock, dissecting and operating; beautiful subjects, quite fresh, nothing unpleasant about it. I only want company. This is a great school I assure you. I am now at Mrs Charles Sherborns. Left the vessel at noon and came to King's College Hospital and there saw Ferguson amputate a thigh, and perform several other operations.'

No anaesthetics were used, of course, they had not been invented. The *Dreadnought* was originally one of Nelson's ships at the Battle of Trafalgar, a second-rate 98-gunner built at Portsmouth dockyard in 1801. She became a hospital ship in 1827 and was moored off Greenwich in 1830 when she became the Seaman's Hospital, an office she performed until replaced by another old ship, *The Caledonian*, in 1856. The poor old *Dreadnought* was broken up the following year, and it was not until 1870 that the hospital was transferred to shore buildings.

Going back to Bessie and Annie Cutter, these two young girls were not of any particular interest or importance at the turn of the twentieth century, but the friendship lasted for years and eventually Bessie married Dwight Morrow, a senator and ambassador (1873–1931) and it was their daughter Ann who, in 1929, married Captain Charles Lindbergh. When Aunt Ada went to America after her mother's death in 1922, American society was there to welcome her and she made a kind of royal progress through the States. Her long visit was a great success.

Five years later great fame descended on the family. In 1927 Charles Lindbergh was the first man to achieve a solo flight across the Atlantic, landing at Le Bourget, his plane, the *Spirit of St Louis*, having been in the air for 33 hours. The event made him the idol of the world and at this time his position was equal in popularity to that of the Prince of Wales in Britain. The tragedy of the kidnapping of their eighteen-month-old baby son from their home in March 1932 was a world sensation at the time, and the subsequent discovery of the baby's murdered body was unspeakably awful. Aunt Ada was not alone in the world in being deeply shocked and upset.

After the case was over (a man called Bruno Hauptman was found guilty of the crime and sent to the electric chair) the Lindberghs decided to leave America for a while to escape the attentions of the police, public and press, and in 1935 took a two-year lease of a furnished house called Long Barn, at Sevenoaks Weald in Kent. It was an ancient timber-framed house to which a wing made from the timbers of an old barn had been added, and it had the first garden created by Vita Sackville West and Harold Nicolson, this before they moved to Sissinghurst Castle. The house was lovely, with a thousand luxuries and Aunt Ada greatly enjoyed her visits there. It was from there that they sent me their autographs in June 1935, on writing paper headed 'Next Day Hill, Englewood, New Jersey'. I was only eleven at the time and I fear I never met them. It was while living there that they took a suite at the Ritz Hotel in Piccadilly to view the funeral procession of King George V. Aunt Ada and Uncle Charlie were both invited to the Morrow – Lindbergh's apartment at the Ritz – for the funeral. They had an intense dislike of crowds, but in Charlie's words, 'Had no end of a beano at the funeral. Was invited with my sister to breakfast at the Ritz. Left here at 7.45. Howling mob at Earl's Court, pushed my sister in train, and said I would follow on the next. Did so, stopped at Knightsbridge, next stop Piccadilly Circus. So got out and went to Hyde Park Corner. No chance, thirty deep, so went home and phoned the Ritz to look after Ada. Not yet arrived. (At 3.30 she turned up home.) She was taken to the Circus, walked along Jermyn Street, no chance of crossing St. James' Street, so stood by railing. Felt faint, woman next to her shouted "Ambulance come and take away this old lady". They did and put her in the road. After a bit they asked if she could walk. Said: "No my legs won't work". So they made a cat's cradle and instead of carrying her round to Jermyn Street took her right across the road and put her into Arlington Street. When she felt better she walked into the hotel and they gave her a couch and sent for her friends. She had breaker, saw the funeral, had a good lunch and came home comfortably. She was the only one of nine guests who got there. "Never again"! Downstairs from where she was in the Ritz was her brother Percie with his wife, my father, my mother and myself. We were watching from the windows of Roberson's Gallery which then, for years before, and for years after, occupied shop premises in the arcade there.'

It was sad that Lindbergh damaged his reputation in later years by expressing approval of Fascist and Nazi regimes. He had visited Germany in 1936 and had been greatly impressed by German airpower, and then put his energies into encouraging friendship with Germany and headed an organisation for this purpose. In a speech at Des Moinestown on 11 September 1941, he accused the British and Roosevelt administrations, and the Jews, of pushing the United States towards war. The fact that in 1938 he had accepted a medal from the Nazis, the Service Cross of the German Eagle, was further indication of his pro-Nazi sympathies. Aunt Ada was obviously unhappy about all this but never mentioned it. His career was not ended by his political speeches and he was eventually promoted to the rank of general by President Eisenhower. He died in August 1974.

Aunt Ada's new house had been furnished entirely from the family home. Her artistic bent had been encouraged by her parents, and she became quite good with watercolours, pastels and oils and particularly proficient with coloured enamels on copper and silver, and at the creation of the original metal bases for firing them in her own kiln. She was keen on music also and cherished a rather fine piano.

The house chosen for Aunt Ada by her brother Charlie was No. 55 Peterborough Road at Parsons Green, three doors away from his own. I suppose the houses must have been built about 1880. They were fairly narrow fronted with just an inset door and a tripartite sash to its right to light the drawing room. Above this was a wooden balustraded balcony; the frontage was of fairly elaborate brickwork with a gable top and there were rather nasty, over-elaborate cast-iron railings and squeaking gates in front. The paint was dark green; but the most striking feature was the drawing-room window, not for itself, but for its curtains which were formed of lengths of cigarette-thin bamboo punctuated by glass beads which hung on strings from a closely-punctuated wooden bar halfway up the window. I never saw any anywhere else but recently have seen some modern ones for sale in a shop. Inside, the whole house was utterly gloomy, and smelt of cats! The hall was a very narrow passage leading to a stair up and a stair down. On the right was the drawing room, a grey-brown room with a multicoloured marble chimneypiece, cast-iron grate and double doors opening into the back half, probably originally the dining room with matching fireplace. On the chimneypiece was a garniture of five, cracked, Canton vases and above it a period-style bronze mirror wrongly thought to have been copied from Cellini. There was a rush-backed winged chair from the

Orkneys and a large wicker one too. A rosewood-cased, good, upright piano with a finely carved rosewood stool, six early Victorian rosewood hoop back parlour chairs, a narrow and fairly tall rosewood china cabinet (full of mixed bits from Roman and Egyptian times, to black Wedgwood objects and Belleek baskets), a Sheraton cross-banded card table in the window, and a birdseye maple and ebony Louis style Davenport with gorgeous inlay work and magnificent ormolu handles and mounts – the finest such thing in existence anywhere I would think. There were also two very good work tables dating from her grandparents' time, one a splendid inlaid rosewood trumpet shaped example with carved cabriole legs, fine carving and boxwood floral inlay, and a rectangular walnut one of quality. Elsewhere there was a very small Chippendale-period glazed bookcase, a bigger Victorian one, a kneehole desk, a folding campaign chaise longue from Sir Chandos Wren Hoskins, hundreds of bits and pieces and gloomy pictures, hung by wires in tiers from the picture rail. One is very much reminded of this type of interior at the Linley Sambourne House in Stafford Terrace. The paint was drab, the curtains drab, the carpets drab and the frieze above the picture rail was decorated with a wallpaper covered in tangerines and oranges.

Upstairs (the stairs incidentally were carpeted and then most unusually covered with a linen damask drugget) was a landing, with, on the right, a combined lavatory and bathroom which must have been quite a rare feature in houses built then. The lavatory was mahogany cased and on the Bramah principle – a long chest with lid, which when exposed revealed a china handle in a bowl-shaped container. The actual loo was a decorated china bowl with a fall-away trap at the bottom. It fascinated me; I have not seen a working one at any other time. The bath was similarly cased and lidded. The bath itself was of painted tin, plumbed in and drained. At the back of the house was Aunt Ada's bedroom, an ordinary enough room that I think I only saw after her death. It had a tripartite Victorian wardrobe of considerable size. Upstairs again was a small back bedroom furnished with not much at all, and in the front was the largest room in the house which went right across the front and opened onto the balcony; whether it was thought of as a drawing room or a bedroom I do not know, but Uncle Charlie retained this for his own social occasions and used it just once a week.

Curiosity overcame me one afternoon when at tea at Aunt Ada's, and I crept upstairs, knocked on the door and walked in. Uncle Charlie was there within a smoke fog of learned old fogeys. I was given two pennies and a sticky bun and ordered downstairs. I just wanted to see the place; but I never did! Down the stairs I went – it was all half-flights and mezzanines – right to the bottom where the kitchen-cum-dining room was. It was an old fashioned kitchen with a cast-iron range, shelves along the walls as a dresser decorated with a pretty old porcelain tea service with seashell necklaces festooned on the dresser hooks. Below the shelves was the haybox, to one side was one of Sir Chandos Hoskyns' mahogany military chests, and in the centre was a heavily-draped dining table supporting a rumbling Lazy Susan stacked high with pills, peppermints, preserves, pickles, peppers, sugars, salts, sauces and a fern in a brass pot. The kitchen range had been curtained off and a small gas cooker installed, while wooden stairs led down outside to the brick-walled small back garden. I suppose this type of house is now admired and in demand but to me it was a nightmare of stairs, bad planning and everything that was utterly dismal.

Aunt Ada was both quite well off and extraordinarily mean. Winter visits to her house were of excruciating painfulness with the miserable gas fire turned down so low that only half an inch of blue flame showed, while her younger, but elderly, brother Sidney sat nearby complete with greatcoat, gloves and hat absolutely shivering with cold. Unkind relatives, like ourselves, said that Ada could live on a fourpenny hambone or a farthing kipper for a fortnight, and one of the jokes we always enjoyed was the fact that when making her own jams, chutneys etc. she would bring them to the boil on the gas ring and then bury the pan, lid on tight, in a box packed tightly with hay and with a hay-stuffed green baize cushion over the top. It is a perfectly sound system scientifically and they were much used at sporting events and shoots, but the eccentricity of Aunt Ada's haybox and its hidden contents bubbling away just reduced us to helpless giggles.

Aunt Ada's pet cat, a black one called Sambo, of which she was inordinately fond, predeceased her, the vet saying tactfully that the poor thing was undernourished, if not starved. Not even the haybox could save *him*. Ada died at home on 22 January 1940 and was buried at Highgate. Sidney Newton Sherborn, the youngest son to survive infancy, was a dear old man as I remember him, very fond of woodwork, making wool rugs and carrying out bits of family research. I did not know until recently that he never forgave his mother for not providing the money so that he could train as a solicitor and for the whole of his life he suffered the indignity of having to be a solicitor's clerk for Beale's. Messrs Beale & Co. were solicitors to the Great Western Railway and out of their fortune built themselves Standen at East Grinstead to the designs of Philip Webb. It now belongs to the National Trust. I remember Great Uncle Sidney telling me how he had visited Cremorne Gardens and seen a 'tableau vivante' (a kind of real-life nudie show) and an ox roasted whole, had called at Disraeli's house as he lay dying, and how as a boy the horse bus drivers at South Kensington carried loaded guns to stave off robbers. He married Helen Rushworth of Berkhamstead, and had two sons, both killed tragically: Geoffrey Robert in France in the Great War, and Hugo in a motorbike accident in 1936. His daughter Joan, Mrs Moore, lived until the age of 92 at East Grinstead, not so very far from the Beale's old home at Standen. Uncle Sid died on 7 July 1959. Geoffrey was the only man in the history of the family since Crecy to have been killed on War service.

We have left to the last, Percie Coates Sherborn, because he was my grandfather and thus a direct link in this story. I think the least clever of the siblings, he nevertheless had a respectable, but badly paid, job with Charles Robersons, the artist's colourmen and picture and sculpture dealers in their shop in the Ritz Hotel in Piccadilly. Robersons sold not only paints, brushes, canvases and picture frames but watercolours, paintings, etchings, miniatures, engravings, French carved ivories by Preiss and others, Lalique glass, reproduction Greek and Roman bronzes, Dresden porcelain figures and their monkey bands, and even, for a while, antique panelled rooms and marble chimneypieces removed from historic buildings. Percie managed the shop for untold years and sometimes told stories of the customers he had met, some of whom did little sketches for him while they spoke to him in the shop, like Muirhead Bone, Count Grixoni and Lord Leighton, and others like Queen Ena of Spain who merely shed her hairpins on his display table.

He married Annie Greener of Hampstead, the daughter of George Dobson Greener and his wife Mary Elizabeth Tooley. Here I think we find something rather odd; something unexplained. For they were quite rich by the general standards of the day and there has to be a reason for it. My father was born at their home, No. 12 Beauchamp Place, just by Harrods, in a house bought for the Greeners and partly furnished by Sir William Eden (1849–1915). He was just a little older than my grandmother, who was born in 1862. He was the father of Anthony Eden, prime minister and first Earl of Avon. Why? There is no doubt that Eden was something of a scallywag, and the only reason I can think of for him doing this was that he must have had an 'arrangement' with my grandmother. There is something odd, too, about her father, George Dobson Greener, who hailed from Northumberland and whose first job was as lamp boy to Lord Ravensworth at the great palace John Nash designed for him called Ravensworth Castle. He spent most of his life there, and must have been a pretty youth for he earned the name 'The Golden Boy of Ravensworth Castle'. I can understand the testimonial and the gold watch given him when he left his service, but perhaps he had a more intimate acquaintanceship with his lord and master. The Greeners subsequently came down to Hampstead. I remember being taken as a boy to see an old lady of some ninety years in bed in Holly Mount in Hampstead, and she was a connection of the Greeners called Mrs Gander. In the census of 1871, the Gander family is given as William, born in Tunbridge Wells in 1840 and employed as a waiter in a hotel, his wife Ann, a year older. They had three children, all at school, Alice being the eldest and born in 1863. I never heard anything about the four sons, but they also had in the house another family and two lodgers.

Sidney Colvin, writing in 1902, says that in June 1874 he and Robert Louis Stevenson both occupied for a while lodgings at Abernethy House, Hampstead. Abernethy House was the home and property of the Ganders; Colvin was then Slade Professor of Fine Art at Cambridge and was later to become keeper of the Department of Prints and Drawings in the British Museum. I still have two photographs of Stevenson that he gave to Aunt Goosie; one of the time he was staying there, and the other from the 1890s when he was in Tusitala, in Samoa. He must have kept his connections with the Ganders for many years. He died at Tusitala in 1894 and was buried on a mountain top that he particularly adored. How long his connection lasted with the Ganders I

Charles William Sherborn the engraver 1831-1912 and his wife, Hannah (d.1925)

The rogue great uncle Edwin John Sherborn 1837-1880

Dr Charles Davies Sherborn 1861-1942 at his desk in the Natural History Museum

My uncle Leslie Farrows yacht *Zaza* built for the first Lord Beardmore

Lost - Bedfont Lodge, Bedfont, Middlesex

© M. Engleheart, English Heritage N.M.R.

Home - Fawns Manor, Bedfont, Middlesex

© The Author

Lost - Stand Old Hall, Lancashire

Lost - Silhill Hall, Warwickshire   © Stanley Jones, English Heritage N.M.R.

Lost - Rushbrooke Hall, Suffolk   © English Heritage N.M.R.

Saved - West Bromich Hall, West Midlands

Lost - Hoppyland Hall, Durham

Lost - Marple Hall, Cheshire

Lost - Shavington Hall, Shropshire

© English Heritage N.M.R.

have no idea, but Aunt Goosie remembered the author of *Treasure Island* and *The Strange Case of Dr Jekyll and Mr Hyde* with real affection. I still have the tea china that they used. Tremendously old-fashioned their house was, but with many lovely things. It is the only time I have ever seen a piece of seaweed hanging on a wall as a barometer. When damp, it was wet, when dry it was sunny. Poor Aunt Goosie became very hard-up in later years and lived out her last days in a single room at 12 Gayton Road, Hampstead. We helped her a bit but she did not live through the last war.

Annie Greener, Percie's wife, died in 1924 (soon after I was born) of a tumour on the brain, aged 64. She was not wanted and my grandfather had already dropped her down the stairs! The family suspected attempted murder but had kept quiet about it. Percie had had a long-standing affair with a very handsome charming and attractive neighbour called Mrs Louise Cool, who suddenly found herself a widow when her husband died very conveniently in a chair at Percie's house, 27 Gleneldon Road, Streatham, whence the Sherborns had moved from Beauchamp Place. The Gleneldon Road house was much bigger and rather grander than Beauchamp Place. Percie married Louise almost immediately after his wife's funeral and they moved to Wyatt Park Road at Streatham Hill. I remember visits to Wyatt Park Road as awe-inspiring and uncomfortable, with electric doorbells clanging down a long corridor to the distant kitchen. As a little boy I much preferred to creep off to the housekeeper, Mary Fox, and to be allowed to play with her box of buttons and thimbles in the kitchen. It was a good Edwardian semi-detached house with front and rear gardens and substantial rooms and passages. There were the usual extensive domestic offices, four bedrooms and one 'good enough for a servant'. And servant there was. We called grandpa's second wife Auntie Louie instead of grandma. Born Louise Backwell, strangely enough, in Hatton Garden, London's diamond and jewellery quarter, she had a grand manner and was extremely interested in the theatre. I found her to be oppressive and formidable.

My father and his youngest brother Leslie Rupert (always known as funny Uncle Leslie, because he *was* funny, to distinguish him from rich Uncle Leslie, a connection through the Allman family, who, of course, *was* rich), was my favourite uncle, and his wife Auntie Dorrie, the former Dorothy Shearer, was also great fun. Their daughter Jean (always called 'Biddy' by them) was also my favourite cousin and it was a great treat to meet them at their houses in Selsdon and Sanderstead, and latterly near Worthing. They used to visit us a lot too, and occasionally shared holidays, like the occasion when I was 12 when we went to Heyst-sur-Mer in Belgium, and Biddy and I shared a long double-bedstead-like reclining bicycle and went out in the main road in it and tore the wing off a taxi, causing complete uproar. Biddy married later in life and lived happily with her husband Leonard Terry at Aldsworth in the Cotswolds. I have always greatly admired her for her artistic talents and the very capable way that she tackled everything. She and I were now the only surviving Sherborns, she dying on August 23rd 2002 aged 81.

My father, Ronald Thorne, born at Beauchamp Place in 1893, was a handsome man uncommonly like Anthony Eden, quite clever with photography and watercolours, and a dabbler in oils and pastels. Never strong, he suffered for years with deafness, and it always surprised me as a boy how he was able to hold his job with such an obvious disability. The deafness increased as years went by until it was virtually impossible to speak to him at all, and made his latter years a misery and a cruel burden for my mother. Father hated Beauchamp Place and was sent to Brompton School, instead of St Paul's at Hammersmith which he always bitterly said his parents could have got him into. The area must have been vastly different when he was young, but he preferred to remember little of it, merely recalling that he was so shy as a choir boy soloist at Holy Trinity, Brompton, that he had to be stood behind a palm tree to prevent his high notes from warbling.

He remembered too the parties at great houses in Belgrave Square and Park Lane with the powdered flunkies, the tigers, the awnings and red carpets, and the magnificent carriages used by the nobility at that time. It was thought that only the very vulgar had such things as motor cars, and these were considered a passing phase! My father waited until 1919 to become a car owner. He remembered few holidays, but his stay with the Shaftoes at Beamish Hall in Durham was made memorable by his falling fully-clothed into a tub of pigswill soon after arrival. The stinking, dripping child had to be taken indoors and scoured. He seems to have spent most holidays with his uncle, Harry Staples Thorne (called such after his godfather, Sir John Staples, who was supplier of turtles to the Queen and sometime Lord Mayor of London), who had married a cousin. The Thornes were considered very rich as the family had a distillery, Thorne's Whisky, in Scotland. They originated from Barnstaple in Devon, and it was Robert who broke loose from his family and founded the firm of Robert Thorne & Sons, Wine and Spirit Merchants, at Greenock in 1831. The firm owned Greenock distillery in the 1890s, and extensive warehousing, blending, and bottling stores – not just in Greenock, but also in London, Dublin and Liverpool. Thornes no longer exists. The Thorne family business connections ended in the 1920s, but they must have been rich once; Uncle Harry was always believed to be so.

I have always understood that the Thornes were pioneers in free gift advertising and sponsored artefacts, and certainly there was a pack of branded Thorne's playing cards as well as a miniature barrel-shaped dice shaker, a plated oval tobacco box, a stoneware flagon, a plated corkscrew and penknife, a splendid two-handled large oval tea tray engraved with the Thorne's crest and monogram, and once I saw a typical multi-coloured stoneware water jug made for them by Doulton. All these items were clearly for advertising. Maybe one had to collect the labels off a hundred whisky bottles to qualify!

Uncle Harry was fond of fishing and shooting, and had been sent to Africa after big game. Later he generally went with his wife and my father to Aberffraw in Anglesey, where they took rooms at the Prince Llewellyn Hotel and spent most of the time fishing. We went there once in 1939 just weeks before war broke out, and again later, which must be the subject of another story. But we digress from Uncle Harry, a very grand, old-fashioned English gentleman, a product of Lancing (like his brother Edwin Ludlow), and the owner of a substantial double-gabled house called Heathfield, at Hassocks, with a belvedere on the roof (from which one could see the Jack and Jill windmills at Clayton and even Brighton) and a trusty old housekeeper called Nellie, who remained till he died. He was quite a collector, and formed collections of specific things like old ink bottles which he sold to Stephen's Ink, match-boxes which he sold to Bryant & Mays, and stoneware gin bottles with political or rustic motifs on them, which went elsewhere. My father used to buy things for him on his travels and I particularly remember a large multi-sided lithophane metal-framed glass gas shade he found; surely a very rare object. Uncle Harry later gave up Heathfield and went to live at Wickham Villas, Hurstpierpoint, but worry over money caused him to drop dead in the bathroom when my father was staying for a visit in 1943. His wife Annie had died long before and had been a trial to him and a secret drinker, and his brother Edwin Ludlow (they were descended from the Cromwellian General Ludlow) fared even worse, for his grand house at Rogate and grand wife and grand way of living dissolved when Eddie's wife eloped with their chauffeur. We, of course, never heard any more of them.

We were all terribly distressed about Uncle Harry's death and the circumstances of it, and we made the wartime train journey to Hassocks, bedevilled by minor air-raid inconveniences, the great viaduct at Preston Park having been bombed on 25 May. Uncle Harry died totally penniless, his declining years having been provided for by his housekeeper, who had not been paid for eleven years, and who, of course, was rightly entitled to everything. The sale of the contents, already organised by Uncle Harry, was held on 30 June 1943. But it was all very sad. The little Victorian stucco cottage was the scene of the sale and we, as family, sat in the front garden while the other bidders stood in the private roadway outside. Much was sold that one would now have liked to have, but that is the way of things. We could not afford very much.

As a boy, my father was quite naughty and egged on by his brother, who was two years his junior, used to get pennies and halfpennies and make them red hot in the drawing-room fire and then throw them out from the balcony windows in Beauchamp Place to beggars, to hear them scream. One day at his grandfather's house, 540 Kings Road, he got hold of their cat and tried to flush it down the lavatory shouting 'drown you bugger, drown'. Father had wanted to be an architect and started work in the studio of Lanchester and Rickards and worked on the drawings for the construction of the Central Hall in Westminster, but the Great War interrupted his studies and being unfit for active service he was put into the Admiralty, where he remembered working all night and all day on the occasion of the sinking of fourteen ships on 31 May, 1916 in the Battle of Jutland. The next of kin had to be informed and 6,097 men had been lost. On another occasion he remembered Winston Churchill, then First Sea Lord, flying into such a rage with a telephone that he tore it off the wall and threw it out of the window into the Admiralty courtyard.

My mother was a considerable beauty, played the piano well and sang very well indeed, and had other artistic accomplishments. As a young girl in a large family she was apprenticed in the millinery trade – not a very respectable job for a young girl – and for a time worked in a hat factory at Tooting. Wages were quite scandalous, with one shilling a week followed by half a crown a week being the going rate, and things like piecework with more money for being an improver, were an added encouragement. Having learnt the trade from the bottom, she found herself a job in the Court Millinery showroom of Miss Spray in Knightbridge, and there had to deal with Ladies in Waiting whose carriages waited for them outside while shopping. One of the customers she never forgot was the actress Mrs Patrick Campbell, who she once went to see with some hats and bed jackets in her house in Kensington Square. She was shown up to her bedroom to display them to her. Her daughter was there at the time, and my mother handed one of these bed garments to Mrs Campbell, whereupon she took off all she was wearing and sat up in bed stark naked. 'Oh Mother!' protested her daughter, 'Not in front of one of Miss Spray's young ladies.' To which the reply was, 'Nonsense, dear, just everyone has seen Scraggy like this.' Mother, with her strict Methodist upbringing never got over the shock even to the end of her days in the 1980s. Mrs Pat is also credited with the remark about gays, that she did not care at all about what they did as long as they did not do it in the streets and frighten the horses! With the outbreak of war, Mother tired of grand ladies and great hats, and sought her fortune in the City, for some years working for the Hearts of Oak Building Society, where she had the nasty experience of being caught in one of the Zeppelin raids on London.

Father's inheritance of the Bedfont property took place at the height of the War, in 1942. Uncle Charlie, although owning Fawns from 1912, had never lived there and it was let, but we knew that Father was to inherit, and to some extent this influenced me in my collecting. One day we would need all the furniture we could possibly lay our hands on, so large was the house compared with our own. My father and mother knew that when they had married. Bedfont was their horizon –

and mine from 1950 onwards. Bedfont was also their grave. 1950 had seen the return of the prodigal sons in the shape of my father, mother and myself. And no one ever noticed the fact. Father was at last a gentleman. Mother had crossed the factory floor to be the squire's lady. I think that they quite liked it and I hope they did. My tenure, however, was to be terribly fraught.

3

The Poor Allmans

My mother's family arrived in Streatham in about 1885, her father having been for an early part of his adult life in the Metropolitan Police in Harrow, Middlesex. He was born in Staffordshire, at a place called Wolstanton, Tunstall, on 20 March 1849, the son of Charles Allman, a potter of Pittshill and Ann Clews, his illiterate wife whom he had married nine months before. There were to be two sisters and a family of four, and before them a family of unrelieved poverty of whom William Allman, or Almond, had been baptised, of all places, in the House of Correction, in Middlewich, Cheshire in 1772, son of an illiterate pauper called Hannah Heton. They could not have been poorer or more unfortunate!

The Allmans not only lacked a hidden fortune, they also lacked a respectable background. Their supposed descent from the great potter Josiah Wedgwood was just a load of pretentious nonsense with no basis in fact whatever, nor was there any truth in the family connection with William Clowes, one of the founders of Methodism. It was just put around as a fact in the hope that it would be accepted. Even more worrying is the fact that Grandma Allman's parents were alleged to have been landlords of the Sir Robert Peel, a pub in Bishopsgate in the City, and that she had been married 'in that dear little church', St Ethelburga's, nearby. We visited both with grandma, but neither story had any truth in it at all! I found her marriage in the register of the large Georgian St Botolphs nearby and I can only think that she wanted to conceal her long-standing pregnancy before marriage, and that the Sir Robert Peel sounded respectable to her.

It says something for the social mobility of the English that the Allmans were eventually to make good and earn some respectability.

William first came to London in the 1860s. In March 1876, aged 27 he married the 24-year-old Mary Ann Savage at St Botolphs church in Bishopsgate. She was already several months pregnant. She was the daughter of Henry Savage, a publican born at Walkern in Hertfordshire in about 1812, who died the year before his daughter's marriage. Savage forebears have proved impossible to unravel. Anyway, they were duly married at St Botolphs and I still have the little lilac silk dress, with corset, lace sleeves, lilac silk parasol and the ivory prayer book used by her then. He was described as a policeman from Harrow, she 24 of 4 Crosby Square. One of the witnesses was Martha Savage, who was perhaps a sister. Mary Ann had been born at 14 Bakers Buildings in Bishopsgate on 18 September 1851, her parents being Henry Savage and the former Lydia Andrews, his career being described at that time as a gentleman's servant. What happened in the after years is not known but long before the respectability of a Methodist grocer was pronounced acceptable by Mrs Thatcher, they came to have a grocer's and off-licence in Sunnyhill Road, Streatham, about 1890. The house and premises were just sufficient and here some of their eight children were born and their one maid housed.

The first child was Maud Martha, born at Harrow in 1876. She was followed by William Henry Charles and Arthur Leonard in 1880, Ethel May in 1885 at Cumberland Lodge, Streatham Hill, then Elsie Beatrice in 1887 at Sunnyhill Road, Daisy Gertrude in 1888, Edie in 1890 and Evelyn May in 1893. For a family in such poor circumstances it was perhaps unwise to have had so many children, but Victorian families were large and family planning hardly existed. It might have been better for me to have had fewer domineering aunts in my life. The children were strictly and cruelly brought up to non-conformist beliefs on a very modest income, and their manners and behaviour were severely drilled. Father was a real Victorian parent, a Bible-punching humbug in top hat and tails on Sundays, preaching total abstinence, selling alcohol in his shop in the week and running up the road, whenever occasion suggested it, to his mistress Mrs Sangster in Farm Avenue. In May 1915, as the result of an accident through straining himself, he became very ill and the hospital could not save him. He had twisted his gut, they said. He had narrowly escaped death before, on Tuesday 3 September 1878, when seeking to board the *Princess Alice*, an ironclad saloon pleasure steamer, for a voyage down the Thames. He arrived just as the boat had left its moorings and within hours, on its return from Sheerness, she was in collision with the *Bywell Castle*, a large iron-screw steamer of 1,376 tons, against the tiny *Princess Alice*'s 251 tons. It was one of the worst disasters in English shipping history and the nation was appalled. Between 600 and 700 people were drowned, the collision taking place just by a major sewage outfall in the river at Woolwich, the victims dying in the stinking waters. He often missed the boat in other ways.

I have little sympathy for my grandfather because he was dead years before I was born. I can only work out his character and beliefs from the memory of others. I think, although his daughters all adored him, his sons William and Arthur hated him. They fled to Canada while still in their very early teens.

The Allman sisters all lacked vision and curiosity and were really very limited in their aspirations, but managed for the most part to marry respectable husbands. Elsie married a very bright, up and coming chartered accountant called Leslie William Farrow, who made a great name for himself in the City and was showered with honours of various kinds. He was a most generous and kindly man, and I was his godson. He can hardly have liked me very much (as a child I think I was pretty horrid), but he never really complained.

The Allmans had the minds of asset strippers, always worrying about cost rather than quality, reliability or long-term advantage. I suppose a rather hand-to-mouth existence encouraged this, and I imagine it helped my grandmother to keep the house exactly as it was when her husband died in 1916. An example for widowhood had been set for the nation by Queen Victoria that nothing should ever be altered. The nation should be kept as Albert had had it. How foolish Victoria always was!

Until recently I had no idea that any relations of mine were involved in the Gold Rush at all! There was more than one such at the end of the nineteenth century and not just gold either, because diamonds, silver and precious stones of various kinds might be found which would lift people from poverty to an acceptable lifestyle. It was the Victorian National Lottery. South Africa now poured forth diamonds by the trainload and colossal fortunes were made overnight. On the Canada-

USA border vast deposits of gold were found in the neighbourhood of the Yukon and Klondike rivers.

Arthur Allman is supposed to have arrived first, but I find this hard to believe as a William Allman is recorded as working as a labourer at the age of only twelve at Nanaino – could this be possible, I wonder? William lived for some time with a Percy Allman, who might have been a distant cousin from Staffordshire. Arthur, whom I have some feeling for, had a rather tragic life, and a completely misguided one. I guess that Arthur and his brother may have arrived just in time for the great Gold Rush of 1896, when rich deposits were found on Bonanza Creek and a wild rush to this inaccessible region followed. A population of 30,000 came within the next three or four years, the climax being reached in 1900 when the output of gold reached 22 million dollars. The area sounds absolutely terrible to me – the ground is frozen hard all year round and the roads are terrible. In the winter, when the sun never rises above the hills, the cold is incredible. Communication was via dog teams or horses, the overhead telegraph wires between Dawson and Vancouver being frequently broken down. The area was a homing ground for all the misfits, malcontents and disappointed sons in the world, and their prostitute followers, but there was only a little crime, they said. It was a rough way to get rich quick and an appalling scenario living in tents or wooden huts, muckraking in river beds or burrowing underground. The Comstock Lode further south was particularly ghastly: they lived in horrid shacks or boarding houses, and mined in complicated wood-strutted underground workings.

Using one of the envelopes and two slivers of thin wooden 'paper' from Japan, Arthur wrote to his mother and father from Last Chance, Hunters Creek, Dawson in the Yukon in July 1907. He was worried about his money demands in England and about his future in Canada: 'I don't know what I shall do this winter. I expect there will be some ground open for staking up here presently, and if there is I shall stake and then stay in here this winter. Will will be going down to Vancouver anyway.

'I was up Henry Gulch (that's about half an hours walk from here). I got a Mastodon tusk and two horns supposed to be buffalo, but they differ from buffalo in the way they sit on the head. The Mastodon tusk was taken out of the ground three days ago, and the horns a couple of days previous. They were eighty feet down in solid frozen ground and the tusk isn't thawed out yet; I shall keep the tusk and also a piece of the tusk which isn't very good as it's old and badly cracked up! The tusk is only about five feet long. They found a pair over on Quartz Creek, which when stood up on end make an arch six feet high.'

Another letter written by brother Will to a friend has also survived from 1907. He was a builder for a time but what is illuminating is the letter he wrote to cousin Tom Taylor in April 1907 about Arthur: 'Heartiest congratulations to Beaty and yourself; delighted to know that there is one more member of our race and who will perpetuate our memory. Let me express the hope that Beaty is well and strong again and that Babs, Her Majesty, is thriving for now my lad you require more vigour and vim for that mighty business which you are striving to establish, you ask whether we want a man of your business. Canada could not hold you *now* I am sure, what would you think of coming out here for say three years, *alone*. Eh? Arthur is away in China now. This is the second trip he has made since I came to Vancouver. He prefers it to staying here, it must be fine from the way he describes the places and the customs of the people in Japan and China. He was out there at the time of the war a year or two ago; he saw the smashed battleship, heard the firing and saw the places burning and while he was in Nagasaki, Japan, he saw Gen. Stoessol of the Russian Army at Port Arthur, a prisoner with his officers. I think when he gets back he will go north again for the summer, we shall get our letters forwarded wherever we are. I have been lucky to get into the best choir in town. There are several Welshmen in it and I often hear about the Welsh singers but it sticks in them when I remind them of how they were licked several times by the choir in which I had several cousins! That is something I am truly proud of.'

Arthur's end came in January 1917. He had wanted to return to England to his family, but William, probably unsure that the loan would ever be repaid, refused to lend him the money for the journey. He died in a shack in White Rock, British Columbia, having come down from the Yukon. He had been without food or heat for days, and died of pneumonia. The family was shattered. Uncle William never forgave himself and nor did his family at home, it was just so tragic. Maybe it had been a better life than in Sunnyhill Road, but I find that difficult to believe.

The Allman family business and the house were so incredibly old fashioned when I was a boy that even then I was astonished by it all. As no such thing has existed for a great many years it may be interesting to record what it was like. To start with, the shop occupied a corner site with a large window to Sunnyhill Road and double doors on an angle with Farm Avenue. It was a tall, yellow brick building with a gable top, standing three storeys high, very plain, very utilitarian and typical of its date. The floor inside the shop was of boards strewn with sawdust, so one had the back of the shop window on the left and two counters at right angles facing one as one entered.

Ranged along the left were round bundles of firewood, six inches long and tied with tarred string, heaped as high as they would go. In front of the left counter were arranged stacks of biscuit tins, square in shape with printed coloured labels covering them completely. The top range all had their solid tops replaced by glass hinged lids, so that madam could taste them before agreeing to make a purchase. The counter was topped with white marble and here the huge cheeses were kept to be cut up with wires stretched on the board. Butter was patted up out of barrels and served in greaseproof paper on china platformed scales. Bacon was sliced by hand to madam's order, and York hams, boiled in the kitchen and sprinkled with brown crumbs, were displayed on china stands. The walls behind were shelved to display the ranges of wines and spirits and other goodies, and such things that were tinned or packeted (and there were far fewer then than now), were displayed there. Breakfast cereals I remember and 57 varieties were piled in decorative pyramids almost touching the ceiling. The counter on the other side had stools for madam to sit down at and this contained a drawer with fixed wooden bowls to contain the money – there was no such thing as a cash register then.

In the large drawers beneath the remainder of the counter were kept figs, sultanas, dried apricots, dried apples, currants, demerara sugar and other things that were kept loose and weighed up individually, while behind the counter was a massive mahogany fitment, I suppose of the 1850–60 period, with small drawers at floor level for boot polish, Bath brick, Wellington knife polish, hearthstone, metal polish, matches, candles and such like. The next tier provided spaces for packeted sugar, cube sugar and castor sugar, by then being packeted by the manufacturer, each packet being inscribed 'Pure Cane Sugar; untouched by human hand'.

Above all this was a double range of small drawers containing things like tapioca, almonds, candied peel, cloves, peppercorns, turmeric, nutmegs, chillies, pearl barley, gelatine, essences in small bottles and even ground pepper, sure to give everyone a fit of sneezing. Above this stood a range of green painted tea canisters all with their numbers on, far too many for the varieties of tea stocked, and above these was a handsome mahogany cornice. The order desk stood at one end of the counter, concealed by piled tins and packets; at the other was another screen of stacked merchandise concealing a short vestibule and the door through to the living quarters. Electric light had been introduced into the shop after the gas lighting had set fire to a display of brushes and mops, but a gas fitting was retained in the centre of the shop, with its green and white enamelled coolie shade.

If the shop was old fashioned, the house was even more so. The principal living room, which lay behind the shop, was gas-lit with a two-burner incandescent fitting which popped and flared as it was lit. In the corner by the fireplace hung a Vienna wall clock with knobbly columns, a plate glass door to show the pendulum and weights, and a porcelain dial. The fire, virtually always alight, winter and summer, burnt in a cast-iron grate with splayed reveals of apple blossom tiles. On the mantelshelf was an immense mantelboard covered in blue-grey festooned repp, decorated with ball fringes, and above it was an overmantel mirror with balconied shelves displaying bits of porcelain. The chief ornaments, however, were (horribly): a pair of large polished brass shell cases from the Great War, brass griffin candlesticks with bejewelled eyes and a pair of good bronze candlesticks with brass nozzles.

To one side lay a rather pretty mahogany chiffonier with yet more shell cases and on the other side was a mahogany upright piano which my mother could play so much better than her sisters. Apart from the usual mid-nineteenth century spoon-backed dining chairs (they were not considered properly wax polished until the dusters squeaked on the film of wax on their legs), a reeded-legged table covered with a plush cloth and a rather overpowering scroll-ended couch, the chief things that stick in my mind are the starched Nottingham lace curtains beneath a valance to match that over the fireplace, and the pictures – some huge, some much smaller, which all hung very formally from immensely long cords attached to brass-capped nails near the ceiling, but which rested on nails at their bases so that their whole being was thrust forward overhanging the people seated beneath them in an unattractive and menacing manner. To crown all this, over each doorway was a trophy of the chase. No Allman had ever shot the deer whose great antlered head and moth-eaten eyes hung over the door to the kitchen, nor the lesser deer that hung over the door to the stairs, nor the elk which hung over the door back into the shop.

Upstairs was equally quaint, with a fishtail-jet gas bracket on the landing complete with ground glass globe and glass consumer, constantly burning as if it were a sanctuary lamp. In my grandmother's bedroom everything was extremely old fashioned. There was a valanced chimney piece to match the window valance and starched lace curtains. The dressing table had a starched lace skirt and there was a swing toilet mirror with a hundred things on the toilet table. There were maple-framed prints and photographs, and a really beautiful 'plum pudding' tall chest of drawers, with the most gorgeous polish on it. On top of this was a marcella cloth, with an arrangement of work and other boxes inlaid with mother-of-pearl or coloured woods. There was also a marcella bedcover on the piled up feather mattressed brass bed with a box pleated dimity lace valance, an embroidered watch pocket and a truncheon for protection. In the fireplace was a steel fender and fireirons, all gleaming like silver, and a pair of big, gold spotted Staffordshire poodles – an odd place, surely for such things. There was no light, just a chamber stick and candle on the pillow. The fire risk was dreadful. Oh, and a marble topped washstand of course, with all the bits, and a coal purdonium. Off the bedroom was a dressing room with another starched lace dressing table, chest of drawers, built-in curtain hung wardrobe, and a really rather horrifying looking bamboo jardiniere stand, the three crossed over poles bound in the centre and supporting a large brilliant blue pot with aspidistra, and the top brass ends of the poles each carrying three chains each with its own smaller, matching pot, to carry lesser varieties of vegetation. There was no bathroom or anything like that of course. There were further bedrooms, naturally, and I well remember being reduced to tears when about thirteen in my Aunt Maud's bedroom, because on her gas bracket hung a dainty receptacle for burnt matches consisting of a tiny tumbler hung in a specially crocheted bag with tassle and everything, all in pink. I, being nosy, lifted the thing up to look at it, and on letting it down again the cord snapped and the thing crashed to the floor and shattered in bits. The tears were as spontaneous as the crashing glass, and I was comforted and made to feel all right by it being discovered that the heat of the gas pipe must have gradually scorched through the cord and it was not really my fault after all.

The working part of the house was the kitchen, where the hams were boiled for the shop and everything else was prepared. A large iron Kitchener, roaring away even in the height of summer, stood next to a great brick-built copper for boiling clothes, hams and Christmas puddings. Apart from a yellow stoneware sink with a brass tap and some large open shelves, I remember little about the other details. At the back was the business yard, where a great covered cart beneath a roofed structure stood close to the stable where the horse and all its harness was kept. Store places abounded, and in all of them were stock items waiting their turn to be needed in the shop. Everything was delivered by horse and cart to wherever it was needed in Streatham, generally speaking to the larger houses near Streatham Common or Tooting Bec Common, where the richer, and therefore more valued, customers lived. Housekeepers who did the ordering expected the occasional present, and when it was known that a new owner had taken a house it had been the custom for Allman's Stores to send round a hot roasted joint with vegetables etc., on the day they moved in, in the hope thereby of getting madam's custom in the future.

Grandma Allman's house had only one living room. For a family of eight or nine the whole place was hopelessly overcrowded, even in the bedrooms upstairs. The surviving daughters eventually rebelled against the preserved Victorian interior of the house and one Christmas when grandma was away at Kenley the whole place was gutted. The gas light was the first to go, then the lace curtains, the brass beds and the maple-framed pictures. Sandersons fabrics, electric light, mahogany beds and a strong whiff of modern ordinariness, which Auntie Elsie paid for. Everyone was in favour of it, but when grandma came home she slumped down in her chair, overwhelmed with tears and anger. She did not like her house being interfered with behind her back.

And so the house and shop remained until after the war ended. Abandoned to their fate, the Allmans soldiered on through the Blitz, the house often falling victim to nearby bombs, V1s and V2s. They had no air-raid shelter whatsoever, nor any modern heating, let alone a hot water system or bathroom. I remember one occasion when we rushed up by rail from Reading to London, picking our way through the broken glass from the roof of Paddington Station which had itself been hit, to go to Streatham to see what we could do to help. The place had been very severely damaged with holes in the roof, ceilings down and all the windows blown out. There was Grandma Allman, black from head to foot with soot from down the chimney, with still no shelter nor any facilities for washing to speak of. Curiously enough they felt that they had to stay and see the War through. As if they were defending an important part of the Empire in a way. They were being patriotic.

Our own house had also been damaged in the raids and so we had to go and look at that and make it secure, but we could lock it up and leave it and return to Mapledurham and yet still be part of the War. We would all come through it alive in the end.

Grandma Allman died in March 1947 and Auntie Edie's husband died in 1950. Auntie Maud and Auntie Edie soldiered on in the house and shop until 1953, (we had left Streatham in 1950), and they were given a house in Burnham-on-Crouch by Uncle Leslie Farrow for their retirement. Ultimately they moved into Dengie Manor with them. Maud lived until she was 97 and died in 1973, Edie to 84, dying in the following year. They had had a rotten time. Auntie Maud had worked for years in a very old fashioned milliner's shop in Upper Norwood. The business was a double fronted shop with live-in staff over, and was run by a man called Frank Grimes who had an alcoholic and useless wife. Auntie Maud was expected to do everything for him in the business, including on one occasion the totally uncalled-for task of sewing on one of his fly buttons while he was still wearing his trousers. Auntie Maud used to walk all the way each day to and from Sunnyhill Road down Knollys Road to Grimes' shop and back. She did it for years and years and on one occasion she fell over a paving stone, flat onto her face causing immense distress and disfigurement. She also had a horrid experience in Germany in about 1936 when she fell again and broke her wrist. She had found the Germans all wonderfully kind and considerate and could never understand the preparations for war.

Daisy was not very well blessed financially by marriage, but she had a loyal and devoted husband called Walter Dennis and a fine son, Peter who married Barbara Boyling, the daughter of a respected Methodist minister. They had a son, an airline pilot who lived in Bedfont whom we were unfortunately never to meet.

The dominant characters in the Allman family were Elsie and her vastly successful husband, Leslie Farrow. Where they led others had to follow. There are now no Allmans left on this side of the Atlantic.

PART TWO

MY FORMATIVE YEARS

4

Childhood

My parents were timid about everything, even starting a family, twelve years after they first met and five years into marriage, but that was the way it was in those days. There was to be only one child: me. They had a copy of Marie Stopes' book, *Married Love*, and another book on gardening. It is a great shame that some people never study married life and bringing up children. My parents could have been much better informed than they were. As the youngest in a large family my mother had practically no domestic instruction at home. There was never time for her to learn basic skills.

Mother always used to walk with me to the Busy Bees School, in Ambleside Avenue, because it was quite a long way and involved crossing Streatham High Road as well as walking along a busy shopping street. When the time came to change schools when I was eight, it involved a greater distance to travel, and one had a briefly exciting period when the rival private enterprise bus companies Thomas Tilling and the London General Omnibus Company drove their open-decked buses in competition with one another. Soon after there was another exciting time when the new completely enclosed and magnificent London Passenger Transport Board's buses replaced them. This must have been about 1932.

After Busy Bees, the school chosen for me was Streatham Hill College, another private establishment, housed in two large Regency mansions at Streatham Hill next to what mother insisted on calling the Tram Stables, although electricity had long since replaced horses. Mother thought the boys looked so nice with their red blazers, white flannels, red caps, white caps, quartered red and white caps with or without tassels and 'boaters'. The college was primitive in its facilities, but tried to point the public school way with its cadet corps, tuck shop and occasional beatings. It was going downhill fast, but its education was excellent as far as it went. The lower form was presided over by Mrs Fairbrother. The headmaster, Mr Harper, was well into his seventies and was a dry and wily Scot who paraded the classrooms saying, 'Wurk, Wurk, Wurk!' and whacking the desks with a ruler. The chief unorganised game in the playground was sexual, where all the smaller boys were lined up against a wall while the bigger boys charged and attacked their private parts.

Being young and innocent I told mother and father, who complained to the head, but after an interview he took no action, not being personally involved in games of that kind. The school kept retrenching on its activities until finally masters left, and we ended up being taught upstairs in a bedroom where a master was lying in bed too ill to come down. Another master was something of a boozer, and had a drunken accident one day, breaking his leg by tripping over his dog on a lead when out for lunch!

The school closed in 1936, and much against my parents' will but in accordance with my wishes (there was to be no Dulwich or St Joseph's for me) I went to Streatham Grammar School, a rather downgrade thing after Streatham Hill College, but with some willing masters teaching way behind what I had already learnt. The school was housed in Mitcham Lane in a motley collection of detached buildings of various dates, built within the grounds of a Victorian mansion lived in by the principal, Mr Large. I was far more interested in this house and its contents – its handsome Chippendale chairs and Cromwellian brass lantern clock – than ever I was in the school itself, the only exceptional feature of which was the copper war memorial plaque polished on Wednesdays by boys in the fourth form room. Little did I know how soon it would be that yet another war would be on our hands, but I probably feared it more than most, and several of the boys I was at school with were to lose their lives in it.

The most frightening thing about ordinary schooldays at this time were the terrible winter fogs which were so dense then that it is difficult now to describe them to people.

I once saw, and only once, a horse-drawn furniture moving van, a great thing drawn by a team of eight horses, while trams, traction engines, brass-helmeted firemen and the like were commonplace. I am grateful that my mother always wished me to see everything and go everywhere, and I was always carted off to jubilees, state funerals, coronations and events of that kind; exhibitions and fireworks at the Crystal Palace (and the fire that destroyed it in December 1936), and to museums and art galleries.

Our seaside holidays were always very simple: two weeks in apartments run by Mrs Ferguson at Walton on the Naze, or up near Scarborough, or on a farm at Abererch near Pwllheli, or in a boarding house at Watergate Bay in Cornwall, or at a pub in Aberffraw in Anglesey. There was just one trip abroad, to Belgium and Holland, which was all that could be afforded. The only occasion that I actually stayed in what might be termed a hotel was when we stayed at the Hotel de l'Univers in Heyst.

My mother encouraged me to go to the cinema from the age of four, and occasionally to the theatre, and I well remember silent films like Charlie Chaplin in *The Circus* and *City Lights*, and the early talkies like Al Jolson in *The Singing Fool*, Matheson Lang in *The Chinese Bungalow* and with Constance Cummings in *Channel Crossing*. There were also the Hollywood spectaculars like the Busby Berkeley musicals, westerns galore, and lots more. In those days one had to be over fourteen to see most films, or if under this age to be accompanied by someone, and the shows in the super cinemas like the Davis at Croydon, the Gaumont, the Astoria at Streatham, or the magnificent Granada at Tooting, would cost about sixpence for admission. They consisted of an organ recital on a great Wurlitzer organ which rose magically out of the floor, two major films, a newsreel and a stage show in the interval consisting very often of a great dance band under the direction of Jack Payne, Jack Hylton or Ambrose, or occasionally a variety programme. One interval show, which my mother insisted I should see, at the Gaumont Streatham Hill, was old-time variety with Charlie Coborn topping the bill, singing 'The Man who Broke the Bank at Monte Carlo'. Coborn must have been incredibly old then, because he had made his name with the song in the 1870s!

My mother also encouraged me, even when small, to go to auction sales. There seemed to be very many more house sales then than there are now. We went to house sales quite often and they almost always had good things in them. I remember one sale in Leigham Court Road because of its splendid Louis XV commodes; another in Streatham High Road for the gas globes in the house, round and white and all hand-painted with Chinese figures. There were others: a house in Effra Road, Brixton, with some marvellous bits of eighteenth-century furniture including a stunning large Georgian bracket clock which played several tunes. Another, I recall, was a 'country house' hotel in Dulwich, with fine Boulle furniture in the drawing room and the most terrible sleeping conditions for servants in the attics and basement that I have ever seen. Many of these houses were demolished soon afterwards and one went to the sales to see the houses and their contents rather than to buy. We were supposed, correctly, to be unable to afford anything.

Another thing I used to enjoy was to be taken to a shop run by an old chap called G.F. Lawrence in West Hill, Wandsworth. He dealt in antiquities rather than antiques and I loved going there and buying silver pennies from the reigns of Henry III and Edward I, and others, for just sixpence each, and also ancient Roman bottles and other glassware for a mere half crown. My expeditions there ended with Mr Lawrence's death in February 1939 at the age of 78. Known as 'Stony Jack' he had made a point of being friendly with building contractors and their workmen who knew they could always sell their finds to him. It was due to this odd connection that the great hoard of Elizabethan jewellery found in Cheapside was saved for the London Museum.

One of mother's very scrappy diaries has recently turned up, for 1936, but all her others seem to have gone. The diary notes that the King was reported ill on 10 January and died on the 20th; my mother went out the following day to buy mourning clothes and she went to the lying in state in Westminster Hall on 26 January. On the 28th we got up at 5.30 to secure our places in Roberson's window in Piccadilly to see the funeral procession. On 1 March we listened to the new king's first broadcast, and on 9 April Streatham Hill College closed its doors. Sadness filled the family when cousin Hugo Sherborn was killed on a motorcycle two days after his twenty-sixth birthday. On 29 March I sat for an entrance examination to Streatham Grammar School and came out top. Then came Hugo's inquest and his funeral with its crowded church, fifty letters of condolence, and seventy-two wreaths.

In February we knew that Streatham Hill College had been sold for development and the handsome Regency stucco houses were to be replaced by a large block of flats and I needed a new school. The parents' first choice was St Josephs College, a large Catholic establishment, near Streatham Common, but I took an instant dislike to the Fathers in long 'dresses' to the ground, their crucifixes and religious statues all over the place. No! No! I would *not* be sent there. I was really quite frightened, and was not in any sense religious. How can children be religious if they have had no sex education and cannot imagine what Immaculate Conception and virgin births can be? Mother had told me that babies were bought in shops and that was that. One of the major problems with homosexuality lies in the word itself and its interpretation. The first part of the word is 'homos' and is derived from the Greek meaning the same and not from the Latin 'homo' which means male. There is nothing wrong with homosexuality. Indeed there is hardly a word about it in the Bible and one just takes it for granted in the Book of Genesis where men greet each other by grabbing each other in the groin, the current form of greeting. In the greatest schools in Britain homosexuality is a compulsory subject as part of the study of the Classics.

In June there was a garden party at Elmwood at Kenley, Uncle Leslie and Aunty Elsie's house, and it was a glorious day. The following week we went on their yacht, the *Elfrida*, for the weekend. In August we went on holiday, leaving Victoria at 10.30. We were at Dover at 12.20 and arrived at Ostend four hours later. it was a terrible crossing with hundreds sick all over the place. We stayed at Heyst, visited Zeebrugge, Blankenberg, Knocke, Ypres, the Menin Gate and actually went in the trenches and visited battlefields. We also saw Bruges, managed to get lost in Knocke, and returned at the end of two weeks.

In September we went to the Crystal Palace to see the fireworks display, but mother forgot to note in her diary that on 1 December, just weeks later, we went there again and watched the entire Palace burn to the ground. I still have a piece of Osler's great central crystal fountain from the Palace. My best friend, Rowland Kayzer, was mentioned constantly in mother's diary up until May, but is not mentioned thereafter, and I remember that once I had started at his school at a lower level, because he was older than me, we ceased to enjoy the close friendship that we had previously had.

The year ended, as had become usual, with Christmas at Kenley. I often stayed on after my parents left and returned home in the New Year.

When I left Streatham Hill College I had to change from taking a bus from Streatham High Road to Streatham Hill and instead had to walk down Angles Road by myself and without mother. It was a street of rather dreary Victorian houses, with squeaking cast-iron gates. I then went down Pinfold Road, with its rather grander Edwardian houses, rather like those in Gleneldon Road and Wyatt Park Road, past the Edwardian public library donated by the sugar tycoon Sir Henry Tate, then past Zeeta's, an offspring of Barker's of Kensington, famous for its enormous real cream merigues in pink or white which cost as much as three pence each. As well as being a bakers and pastrycooks, Zeeta's had a restaurant and café too. I loved those sticky merigues! Next door was Mence Smiths, an oil merchants, ironmonger and hardware shop, which always smelled strongly of paraffin. Only a few doors away was Fullers, another pastrycooks and restaurant, who I remember always lit their shops with white glass coolie-hat shaped lampshades draped with square, centrally-pierced coloured handkerchiefs with tasselled edges. Fullers were very highly regarded, particularly for their iced walnut cake, which I hated. Here I crossed over the road by a Belisha crossing to Pratt's Stores, until lately the largest department store in Streatham. It was all 1930 art deco with hideous artificial stone fascia boards and window spaces with corridors and island windows all along the front. Next there was a great Edwardian pub, c. 1900, called the White Lion (the smell of beer blowing out of its doors rather fascinated me), and a large old-fashioned drapers and haberdashers called Tyrell's, with a Maynards sweet shop jammed into its middle part. I hated Maynards, particularly their famous wine gums which certainly tasted of gum but hardly at all of wine and which pulled the stoppings from one's teeth. They did, however, do rather nice sugared almonds, and particularly nice white or pink mice made entirely of sugar with real string tails, which our hypersensitive contemporaries would now say children might swallow and be choked by. Across Prentis Road one found

80

Beringer and Strohmenger's pianoforte warehouse and music stores. A few more doors took one to Dorothy Perkins, whose plate-glass windows had individual old tile gabled roofs on them with 'beautiful' carved oak Tudor style grey oak bargeboards and finials, and a crazy-paved stone entrance walk.

I just about remember a handsome Georgian mansion standing here its front drive planted with laurel bushes which I assume were responsible for the house name of 'The Shrubbery'. For many years it had been a rather posh girls school which I remember my cousin Joan Farrow attending. The point I remember particularly was that the girls had to walk about in the school with their heads piled high with books to improve their deportment and posture!

Just past here was a shop called Harvey's. This was a double-fronted establishment with the whole of the shopfront made of polished brass and dating from about 1890–1900. The shop had two matching shopfronts, with deep entrances and was terribly old fashioned with thin poles with adjustable brass branches awkwardly displaying unfashionable merchandise. The whole shopfront had to be polished every day, and the entrances to this shop and, indeed, to all of the shops, were scrubbed by hand each day by a special kneeling breed of white-haired seventy-year-old ladies who had buckets and scrubbing brushes, plenty of soap, an old sack to kneel on and a sack tied around their waists. I wonder where their equivalents are now, and how, if ever, these shop entrances are kept clean today. Harvey's described themselves as Fancy drapers, blouse specialists, milliners and ladies outfitters' and when they closed down I remember that hand-knitted woollen bedsocks were marked down to three pence a pair!

After passing a number of other shops and banks, one got to St Leonard's church and its large graveyard, which had played a big role in my parents' life and my christening, and here one had to cross over Tooting Bec Gardens, where I just remember seeing Russell House, an early eighteenth-century mansion of the Howlands, later becoming Bedford property and latterly a convent. It had a good staircase in it which is illustrated in the Royal Commission on Historical Monuments volume. It was pulled down before the war and a new house was built there.

Once across this rather dangerous road junction one found the

Roman Catholic Church of the English Martyrs, with its spire outdoing that of St Leonard's and with a matching electric power station, designed in full Gothic style with decorative windows, buttresses and roof as if it was a chapter house or really part of the church. Mitcham Lane was a bit dull after the High Road, but a few yards away was the fire station with its brass-helmeted firemen and polished brass fire engines – all just about to lose their polished brass, their bells and some of their fascination for a child. Nothing else of importance remains in my memory save for the Thrale Hall Hotel, a very large, grey brick building, originally a house dating from the 1830s or 40s, I would think, lace curtained and very respectable. Mummy could not satisfy my curiosity about what it was really like or what kind of person would stay there. It had quite a drive in front with trees and it always intrigued me. Next door was the Grammar School.

What on earth did one ever learn at school? Algebra, geometry, logarithms, calculus, German, Latin, games, French, elocution, singing, Swedish drill, physical training, general maths, scripture, English, etc. etc. but never Art. Only English and French did I really want or need, and I should have liked more, but the other subjects seem now to have been a waste of time. What is the use of teaching the scriptures to children? The hymns were always nice to sing, particularly the bit in 'All Things Bright and Beautiful' where the rich man was in his castle and the poor man at his gate – that seemed just right and fitted in with the story about the Church of England being the Tory party at prayer.

My parents never encouraged me to go to church; it was no doubt a reaction to their own youth when they were compelled to attend church twice every Sunday. What I probably needed to be taught about was art and architecture; no, I could not stay in the art class because I had no ability, they said. I remember very few school visits anywhere except for a country ramble one day in Surrey where I seemed to be hit on the head all day by larger boys carrying big enamel mugs, and a visit to Australia House which seemed to have an enormous display of tinned fruit and absolutely nothing else. Armistice Day was celebrated by a wreath-laying at Streatham War memorial, and Empire Day in some other way which I forget. History was entirely right wing in its attitudes; it was right that the British owned half the earth and the suppression of the populations of these countries by explorers, missionaries or guns was what this great country was all about. The great Clive and those horrid Indians with the Black Hole of Calcutta! Nelson was our greatest hero, in spite of being insubordinate, disobeying orders and living with another man's wife. Cromwell was everything that was beastly, cutting off the King's head like he did. The sun would never set on our great and glorious Empire; the Church of England, founded by a lecherous murderer and glutton, had been a great blessing, although it was a pity all those fine abbeys had had to be demolished and some of their priests executed. I am afraid I never believed in history as taught at school and consequently was extraordinarily bad at it. Homework from school was always 'horrid' and often reduced me to tears.

On the way home from school one crossed over the road to the south side where there was a long row of very ugly Victorian houses with two storey (or was it three storey) porches rising from the pavement. Only one house was lived in, I think, the others being semi-ruinous, and they all went eventually. I well remember Shakeshaft's furniture shop where my first purchase of antique furniture was ever made when I was thirteen or fourteen. I bought a Georgian thirty-hour grandfather clock in an oak case for 12/6d. Yards further on and across another road was Streatham Green, a rather featureless rectangle of grass, once the village green and where my grandmother Allman thought that victims of the plague were buried in 1665. Back across the High Road, now, to the top of Gleneldon Road where I was born, where on one corner stood the showroom of Maxwells, the funeral furnishers and undertakers, which is chiefly memorable to me for a life-size Italian marble angel with wings outstretched, which was the main item in the window display. It was there for years and years and when the shop was bombed there stood the marble angel, complete and unscratched, the building gone. Auntie Maud saw in this a symbol that Right would prevail and that the Allies would win the war. It is marvellous what a little faith sometimes achieves. But the war has not begun and the journey home must be finished. The Wykeham Studios, I remember, and I was photographed there as a boy, its windows full of heavily retouched sepia or coloured pictures of local ladies and weddings. George Pratts was next: a large Edwardian, gabled red brick building. It was a tailors and gentleman's outfitters on quite a grand scale and highly respectable, and Auntie Elsie had an account there. Behind George Pratts stood a large and handsome classical-fronted mansion called Bedford House, used as a furniture depository, but with a long history of occupation by the Russells, Dukes of Bedford. The Prince Regent had been entertained there and it was said to have splendid marble chimneypieces. It was, however, destroyed by fire in August 1936.

Then there were shoe shops and a shop bearing an LCC (London County Council) blue plaque recording the residence of George Dyce, the Victorian artist. Montague Burtons, with the inevitable billiard hall and dancing school upstairs came next, then the local police station, brown brick and stone and Edwardian, and McLaren's the butchers, all sawdust and wood blocks and marble, where I would often stop to buy a pig's kidney as a present for Grandma Allman's very dreary tabby cat. It was a real torture for me to go in there; I have never been able to stand the sight of blood or the essential odours of butcher's or fishmonger's shops! Round the corner and down Sunnyhill Road one passed Dowsett & Jenkins, the undertakers, with their splendid horse-drawn cut-glass panelled hearse and fleet of black horses, drawing closed black carriages. Mrs Knapp's sweetshop was there too, with her home-made custard ice-cream cornets, and down the hill was an awful old clothes shop which I once entered into and bought a pretty Regency picture on glass in a rosewood frame for 1/6d. My mother was quite annoyed that I had been in there at all. After calling in at Allman's Stores with my pig's kidney (not a daily occurrence) it was either up Farm Avenue to Angles Road, or straight up Sunnyhill Road to the top and then left and back home.

Other bits of Streatham I remember were the great United Dairies bottling factory in Valley Road which one could visit and be taken over in parties and given tea; indeed the bottling process and interior of the factory could be seen from a viewing window for passers-by in the road. The United Dairies factory has long since gone. The cinemas were the Empire, down near Streatham Station, where I had seen the first talkies and which fell victim to one of the first V1 rockets in the war; The Golden Domes, a pre-first war 'flea pit' as they were called; and the Paramount Astoria, a magnificent cinema built in 1930 with Egyptian columned foyers all painted in authentic colours, marble staircases with glass fountains showing varying coloured lights through the jets and cascades, and a restaurant on the first floor with gold Lloyd Loom easy chairs and tables, and waitresses serving delicious teas with bridge rolls filled with egg and cress, meringues, chocolate eclairs and other treats. The enormous auditorium had a great Wurlitzer organ rising out of a pit and the curtain, I remember, was of gold cloth with art deco panels above the fringed bottom, fitted with triangles and squares of what looked like glittering mirror glass. The Granada at Tooting was even more magnificent. The Gaumont at Streatham Hill (1932) I can remember little about, nor can I recall the inside of the Streatham Hill Theatre designed by W.G. Sprague. I do remember that it had a white ceramic exterior and a foundation stone laid by Evelyn Laye. The theatre was bombed in the war, and people actually used it as a kind of air-raid shelter, but the side wall went and the building had to wait years to be restored and reopened as a live theatre, but it did not survive as such.

Streatham had, and has, two splendid commons: Tooting Bec Common and Streatham Common, and gardens at The Rookery. A little further off is Norwood Grove, which had a charming Regency stucco house. Streatham Park, the home of the Thrales and resort of Dr Johnson, had gone in the 1860s. Coventry Hall, a seat of the Earl of that name and designed by James Wyatt in 1810, survived in a Victorian mutilated form. Leigham Court, designed by J.B. Papworth, has long since gone, as has Mount Nod, The Rookery by Michael Searles and a hundred lesser citizens' 'country' houses. Streatham's population exploded during the mid-nineteenth century, already in the early nineteenth century a number of elegant stucco villas had appeared at Streatham Hill, all but one or two vanishing as a result of War damage.

Despite my vivid memories of it, I suppose I never liked Streatham; it was the choice of my grandparents on both sides. We left in 1950. It was an impersonal place; no one ever knew anyone else, or was ever likely to get to know them, but with its open spaces, its cinemas, theatres, ice rink, Locarno Ballroom, pubs and other facilities, it had all that a man could possibly want.

Streatham dominated most of my early life and schooldays; my relatives dominated the rest. Try as I might, I find it difficult to recall very much more of my childhood and I cannot now say how it was that

I was taken on board a submarine and shown around it; nor can I remember now how it was that I was shown over the *Olympic*, the great liner and sister ship of the ill-fated *Titanic*. I remember being bought a monkey glove-puppet on board and how eventually it was eaten by moths. I remember a little of the ship's size and magnificence and a few years ago, was rather delighted to find the decorations of one of its grand saloons recreated inside the Northumberland Arms Hotel in Alnwick in Northumberland. The IRA was busy even before the war and I recall their trick of setting fire to the contents of postal pillar boxes in streets in Streatham, then leaving their signature IRA on them.

Scholastically undistinguished, I had once won a second prize at school and a silver cup for my efforts in a tug-of-war. September 1939 saw the end of my formal education with the outbreak of the war. Hell was to take over.

Here I must break off to talk again about mother's sister Elsie and her husband, Uncle Leslie. While the Sherborns had always been a reasonably respectable crowd, the Allmans and the Farrows came from a rising stock of humble non-conformists – bible pushers, lay preachers, total abstainers etc. A surprising number of them became successful in business, a number even becoming millionaires and peers of the realm. Uncle Leslie was the son of a capable and successful official at the London County Council and dated his service there from when it was the Metropolitan Board of Works. He and his wife Elfrida were great workers at Tooting Central Hall and the High Road Methodist Church. Such places were, in those days, often packed to overflowing. They were particularly active with choral and organ recitals which drew great crowds, and the cantatas had to be heard to be believed. Uncle Leslie studied very hard as a young man and was sufficiently brilliant to carry off the Institute of Chartered Accountants Gold medal. He joined Sissons & Co., where the ageing Mr Sissons was in virtually sole charge, and built the business up until he succeeded Sissons himself, while the partnership there expanded as the business grew. My parents ambitiously chose him as my godfather in the hope that I might get lifetime favours or a bequest from him, but his own family and descendants were enough.

Uncle Leslie must have been incredibly rich in the mid-twenties and thirties. Sissons was renamed by him as Farrow & Co. He was on the boards of the Royal Exchange and of Wiggins Teape and Co., the paper manufacturers, and later chairman. He was also a director of Burmah Oil and Wakefields. He was much admired in the City. He was a Commandeur de l'Ordre de la Couronne (Belge) and was made a CBE in 1947, and had numerous other positions and honours.

In 1956 when he was chairman of Wiggins Teape – then a £31 million company, he wrote a letter to the head of the firm, whoever it might be in 1,000 years time, which was enclosed in a lead casket in the entrance hall of the firm's new Watling Street building in the City of London. He told his successor about the Wiggins Teape business that year and the paper-making techniques then in use. He enclosed samples of the paper, contemporary newspapers and other documents, and wished his successor in office similar prosperity, A nice historical gesture, but the firm has already abandoned the City for Basingstoke and I cannot imagine whether the box really has a chance of being found on the appointed day. Very interesting it will be, no doubt, but it is hardly likely to survive.

Leslie Farrow married my mother's sister Elsie in 1915, and their first child Joan was a bridesmaid at my own mother's marriage in 1919. Joan went to the Shrubbery School in Streatham followed by Farrington's, the Methodist Girls School at Chislehurst, married Guy Wilsdon, then a corporal in the RAF at Cranwell where I was stationed, and he subsequently became an officer.

Uncle Leslie Farrow was the only son of 'Grumps' Farrow and his wife Elfrida, towers of strength at the Methodist Central Hall in Tooting. He had a sister Daisy, later to marry John Catterson and to have a son David, later to become a Methodist Minister. Uncle Leslie was invited to be my godfather in the hope of future benefits and certainly there were numerous invitations to stay at Christmas and a few invitations to stay on his yachts. He had started off with a small motor yacht called *The Doff* and progressed to have an absolute flotilla of steam yachts, motor launches, sailing boats, speed boats and dinghies. On the *Zaza* and *Elfrida* all the lesser craft were located on davits and they swung peacefully from them as we steamed away on our trips. It was a charmed existence.

5

A Collector's Lot

All children are supposed to like collecting things. Not necessarily things of value; they could be moths or butterflies or marbles or stamps or foreign coins. As a child, I graduated to bits of Roman pottery and glass or ancient coins dug up out of the ground or anything that kind uncles and aunts should give me. I had accumulated stamps and coins and bits of Roman pottery, even birds' eggs, butterflies, moths and minerals and a stuffed armadillo in a glass case and a free standing half size alligator.

Eventually I adjusted towards Staffordshire pottery figures and Sunderland lustreware but was stopped from taking a closer interest in Staffordshire figures by the complete absence of any literature on the subject. One simply had no idea what dates they were or who the figures represented, nor had the manufacturers either. Strange notions existed of who the subjects might be and they were quite capable of labelling a statuette of Franklin or Washington or vice versa, not that one's pennies or half-crowns would have bought such grand pieces. Tuppence or fourpence could only buy a pottery sheep broken in half or one shilling and sixpence, a badly cracked and dirty Sunderland lustre jug with a view of the Cast Iron Bridge over the River Wear. Anyway, the Sunderland lustre jug was a non-event as my mother forbade it leaving the cobbled pavement of the Caledonian Market then at Highbury in North London, whether cracked or dirty, its loss was ever to be regretted by me. Street markets were early introductions to collecting and many were the trips on Saturday to the markets in Surrey Street, Croydon. I still have most of my childhood finds there.

An early purchase that earned another firm rebuke was a Regency period painting on glass in its original rosewood frame entitled 'Rural

Courtship' which I had bought in an old clothes shop for one shilling and sixpence. I should not have gone in there, Mother ordered. I could have caught a dreadful disease from there and, true enough, the decomposed corpse of a bed bug was found inside its worthy frame.

Street markets have never been for me a primary source for my purchases but they were far more rewarding half a century ago than now. The Portobello Road need never have existed for me for all I ever found there.

My first venture into pictures was encouraged by the interest all the Sherborns had then. Charles William Sherborn, the artist, etcher and engraver and all their siblings all had houses with walls covered in pictures. They were never to go with the fashionable trend for plain walls and minimal decoration. They never followed trends of any kind.

'If a man isn't a born collector, you will never make him one.' This was a favourite dictum of my Great Uncle Charlie. Only a week or so before his death, he was heard to remark to a friend, 'I've been a magpie all my life and next to my work it has been my greatest comfort.' He certainly had every claim to the title of born collector. By the time he was fourteen, he had amassed collections of shells, fossils, minerals, stamps, coins, books, autograph letters, historic and other documents and even collected a few prints and furniture, some of which I still have in my house in Brighton. The Sherborns have long been collectors. My great grandfather Charles William Sherborn's house must have been quite exceptional because he was an artist, engraver and etcher and he had several hundred pictures in his collection. Pictures are seldom things that one finds ordinarily. For a start, ordinary antique dealers do not understand them any better than ordinary shoppers and it was a waste of time searching for them there. Ordinary houses do not have them at all, except by accident, and the only source for them is at auction sales at private houses or public auction rooms.

My first purchase of a portrait was at a country house sale at Roselands at Bucklebury, Berkshire during the War and it was a portrait of Edward Fairles, a late 17th century Mayor of Durham, for three shillings and it was coupled with the purchase of old four poster bed posts and other survivals of obsolete ages.

With the War over and our return to Streatham, we had to find places for our inherited family things from Great Uncle Charlie, Aunt Ada and Grandpa Sherborn as well as our wartime purchases. Most of this had to be stuffed up in the loft over the house. An early post-war holiday was taken to Sidmouth, a charming Regency seaside town, which was to give birth to the first ever Civic Society in the world, The Sid Vale Association, in 1846. There I added to my picture collection by buying a continental harbour view some way after Vernet and kept it for years never discovering anything about it in its favour.

In the later 1940s, I discovered the auction rooms of Messrs Robinson & Foster in Harrington Gardens, South Kensington, an established firm that specialised in 'rejects' from Christies. I got my mother to bid for me and my first purchase there was a large three-quarter-length portrait in a massive gilt frame. It was of a grumpy elderly man of the late 1750s and, when getting it to Streatham and out into the garden to brush it free of spiders and cobwebs, the back revealed an engraved brass label. 'Was there an artist called Gainsborough?' my father asked. However, the portrait is now identified as being by Reynolds of William Dawtrey of Doddinghurst Place in Essex and of More Place at Petworth in Sussex, and actually not by Gainsborough at all. It now hangs in my drawing room in Brighton. Having made an interesting find, there was no stopping me and within a few months I had discovered a portrait of Capability Brown by Nathaniel Dance, for thirty five shillings and a fine portrait of Edward the first Lord Montagu of Boughton by Marcus Gheeraerts in splendid costume. It had come from the great collection so admired by Horace Walpole at Wroxton Abbey and had cost me just four pounds.

Although one could buy works of art very cheaply, one still had to pay for their restoration and quite often their framing as well. The downside of the Gheeraerts portrait was that the restoration was costed at £300 and the result was that I could not afford it and had to sacrifice it to the restorer.

Robinson & Fosters were to produce numerous treasures down the years, not all of which I now remember. In their furniture gallery, I discovered a Regency chaise longue which had been part of the original furnishings of Brighton Pavilion which I offered to my colleague, Antony Dale, then running the Regency Society but he rejected it, incorrectly thinking it not genuine. I managed to buy it for myself and it remained in my collection until recently I sold it to Brighton Pavilion. All good things come to an end and sadly Robinson & Foster was to close, but in their final sale I found and bought a pair of whole length state portraits by Highmore of Lord and Lady St John from Lydiard Tregoze which had come from the house in 1943. I was delighted to give them to Swindon Corporation for return to the house and was even more delighted when I discovered that my gift had inspired the restoration of the house and its furnishing as a country house museum. Not that Robinson & Fosters were the only auctioneers selling treasures from houses at knockdown prices. Even Sothebys and Christies sold lots for just one, two or three pounds. The general public were not interested in collecting fine things in those far away years.

My chief sources for portrait busts, apart from important London auction houses [where I recall buying for a mere ten shillings out of a six pound bid a splendid marble bust of 1843 by William Behnes, complete with a yellow scagliola column] were the personal columns of *The Times* and the wanted columns of *Exchange & Mart*. It was from them that I got a pair of extremely fine marble busts of the Great Duke of Wellington and Marshal Blucher by Peter Turnerelli, identical to those at Windsor Castle and dated 1821, plus a marble bust of Napoleon and a set of three blue scagliola columns. They were packed carefully in crates and delivered to my house in Bedfont for a mere twelve pounds and ten shillings. Later they were to be followed by a bust of John Bridge, the famous royal silversmith, and associate of Paul Storr. It is by Edward Hodges Baily, best known perhaps for his less good statue of Nelson on his column.

My passion for portraiture was all embracing and although my collection never included the major European names of Rubens, Van Dyck or Zoffany, it otherwise embraced works by numerous artists, many of which have now gone to other collections. Friends used to ask me to buy things on their behalf, the house was often overwhelmed and at times domestic bills forced the sale of things that would otherwise have been kept. My collection nevertheless included works by: Peter Angelis, Mary Beale, Sir William Beechey, John Constable, Nathaniel Dance, Michael Dahl, William Etty, Hans Eworth, George Engleheart, Daniel Gardner, Sir George Hayter, Joseph Highmore, Hugh Douglas

Hamilton, James Holland, Charles Landseer, Sir Thomas Lawrence, Sir Peter Lely, Jan Mytens, Peter Nason, Alan Ramsay, Sir Joshua Reynolds, George Romney, Jonathon Richardson, George Richmond, Sir Henry Raeburn, John Riley, George Stubbs, Gerard Soest or Zoust, Charles William Sherborn and other members of the family, Henry Scott Tuke, Charles Towne, John Wooton, Benjamin West, and Joseph Wright of Derby.

Sculpture also was important to my early teens onwards and I remember during the war buying from a junk shop in Hosier Street, Reading for seven shillings and sixpence, a fine marble bust of Voltaire which I was to meet again half a century later in a Treasures of French Art Exhibition at the Royal Academy in Piccadilly. After the War was over I purchased again for seven shillings and sixpence, a Regency period white marble bust of a young man in classical pose in a shop in Queenstown Road, Putney.

Busts represented in the collection included two by Peter Turnerelli and others by William Behnes, Peter Hollins, Joseph Nollekens, Peter Rouw, John Cheere, John Gibson, Mathew Noble, and Richard Cockle Lucas.

6

The War Years: 1939–1945

The Second World War finally broke out on 3 September 1939, but was long expected after the invasion of Abyssinia by Italy in 1935 and the annexation of Austria by Hitler in 1938. There was no certainty at all that one was safe, even in remote areas, and one of the first bombs to fall landed on the Orkney Islands, killing a rabbit. The early days of the War were full of rumours, false alarms and scares, but once the Nazi armies had invaded Norway and Denmark in April 1940, followed by Holland, Belgium and Luxembourg, they overran the whole of Europe except for Britain and Russia within just eight months. The War seemed almost completely lost. The ragged remains of our armies were rescued from Dunkirk in late May and early June 1940, but still some troops were later landed by us in France, including a friend of mine, a Captain in the Gunners, Cyril Plant. France surrendered completely on 22 June. Germany had an alliance treaty with Russia dating from 24 August 1939, but they may have suspected attack by Russia, for instead of invading or even trying to invade Britain, they did their best to bomb our towns and cities flat and then turned their wrath and military machine on Russia. We were practically helpless here from any army point of view because all our equipment had been left in France, but we dressed up some cars in cardboard boxes to look like tanks, and had them exercise at seaside places where the enemy might see them from the air.

If it had not been for our fighter planes and pilots we would certainly have lost the Battle of Britain. Handguns, pistols and sporting guns were appealed for, tree trunks were laid across minor roads, signposts and milestones were defaced or removed and church bells which had been rung to call people to prayer were suddenly silenced because it was ordered that the bells in future should only be rung to warn of invasion.

Elmwood, where we lived at this time, is a nice comfortable house in Kenley, standing in extensive pleasure grounds, and the air-raid shelter was large, but away on the edge of a football field and after a while it was thought better that we should take shelter in the empty wine cellars beneath the house. Elmwood was to come through the war unscathed but the Air Ministry was alarmed about our proximity to Kenley Aerodrome and the Royal Air Force station and notified all house-holders that if they did not need to stay they would be sensible to leave because of the perceived dangerous situation we were living in.

Uncle Leslie had been appointed Deputy Controller of Paper in the Ministry of Supply, then housed in the Great Western Hotel in Reading (a stuccoed station hotel built in 1844). He decided it would be sensible to take a furnished house near Reading so that he could live at home, and that we should all go with him. A suitable and rather delightful house called The Fishery was discovered on the River Thames at Mapledurham, just outside Reading, and everyone was packed into it. It was a pretty house with lovely lawns going down to the river. Three islands belonged to it, and we remained there until the War in Europe ended in 1945. Mapledurham and Reading had their own war troubles. The house had no mains electricity or water and everything had to be run off a petrol engine in a shed, which was constantly breaking down. The boiler-house had a smelly and temperamental anthracite stove. The gardens were looked after by the owner's gardener, an old boy called Oliver, who kept the stove going and the gardens and the chickens looked after. I was just sixteen in May 1940 and had been removed from school as soon as the War had started. Once at The Fishery I enrolled with a correspondence school, but it was a hopeless idea. The bombing of England began. I well remember the bombing of Coventry in November 1940 when Nazi bombers flew immediately over the house on their way to their destination, and how it lasted for hours and hours, with us crouching in a narrow corridor for safety.

Uncle Leslie had by now been transferred to Warwick Castle to work for the Ministry of Supply there, having as his office the Countess of Warwick's bedroom. He had the misfortune to be on fire-watching duty on the roof of the castle during the whole of the Coventry bombing.

After a little while I had to find a war job and got myself one in the Paper Control office in the Great Western Hotel in Reading as a temporary clerk (Grade III) for nine months prior to service in the RAF. I was placed at a trestle table in the ballroom of the hotel, the bedroom accommodation having been requisitioned. Adjoining the hotel was the Berkshire Club, an 1880s red-brick county club of the kind once common. This was requisitioned also, holes for doorways being knocked through the walls to unite the two buildings. My table was part of an emplacement of seven, headed by an old boy called Mr Palmer, egg-headed, pipe-sucking and smelling of tobacco smoke. The others I remember were Mrs Keir from Beckenham, a jolly and pleasant soul, a very left-wing lady who did not like me, and a very much grander lady known to us as Mrs Ward. Mrs Ward and I became great friends. She had great charm, signs of early beauty, an infectious laugh and some of the most gorgeous diamond rings ever seen in wartime. We often went out for lunch together and it was then that she quietly told me one day that her name was actually Mrs Dudley Ward, and though she would never admit it, the grim foreign-looking gentleman who used to call for her in the office was her husband, the Marquis de Casa Maury. She had not been 'Mrs Ward' since her second marriage in 1937. Born in 1894 she had been the intimate friend and lover of the Prince of Wales in the thirties, but more of her anon.

Father's war work was to do with criminal photography for the Berkshire Constabulary and he was always being called out to photograph drowned or murdered bodies, suicides, burglaries, fingerprints on furniture and window panes, stolen property and suspected or convicted criminals. I still have a mildewed leather case full of these grisly mementos, and I still have my father's peaked cap and uniform with his sergeant's stripes. He was quite highly thought of among the police in Berkshire, and was awarded two medals.

At this point in the war I volunteered for RAF aircrew, but was turned down on medical grounds. Eventually I was accepted at the age of seventeen, but with no great enthusiasm on my part. Duly reporting at the recruitment headquarters in October 1942, I walked to the station for a train to London and from there to St Pancras for a train to Cardington, a large RAF station just outside Bedford. I had never heard of Cardington then, but others knew of its great airship hangars for the

R100 and R101. I had never enjoyed being despatched into the unknown, and at seventeen, never having been away from my parents, it was all a bit worrying, rather as though one was going to a death camp or prison. I was only at Cardington for a few days for kitting out. I was then sent, hardly able to stand up under the weight of my uniform, gas masks and all the other necessaries of death, to Skegness, a remote Lincolnshire seaside resort, once marketed for its bracing seaside air.

There is not much I can say for the good of Skegness; it was bitterly cold and while I was there the sand-dunes and the sea actually froze over. I had practically collapsed on the road on the way there, my equipment being so heavy, and I suffered dreadfully from complete loss of the use of my fingers from cold, and acute sinusitis. The snow was heavy, the barrack yard drill excruciating and even worse was training with Sten guns, hand-grenades and handguns on the rifle range and among the sand-dunes, and bayonet practice. Being short of weapons after Dunkirk, we could not have real rifles with bayonets, so bayonets were welded onto lengths of scaffold pole to make two weapons out of one. Anyone who has handled a scaffold pole in cold weather will understand that there is nothing colder. My frozen fingers made it absolutely impossible for me to fasten any buttons on my clothes, and I was the subject of criticism when I was improperly dressed on parades.

Illness was a recurring factor. I suffered regularly from boils in the ears, which created such intense pain that I could not eat and was then taken into sick quarters. Also extremely agonising was the pain from my sinusitis, which sent excruciating pains across my face, preventing me from bending down and closing my eyes completely so that I could not see a thing. The biting winds in Lincolnshire from the North Sea are incredible. At one time I was attacked by frostbite and the edges of my ears fell off. It was all most uncomfortable.

Skegness itself was slightly bomb damaged and architecturally unspeakable. The whole town had been taken over by naval and RAF units, Butlins holiday camp belonging to the Navy and various requisitioned boarding houses and hotels belonging to us. We were housed in No. 12 Ocean Avenue, and we did our square-bashing in the roadway outside. We ate in a requisitioned hotel called the Seacroft and attended lectures *en masse* in the mornings in the Arcadia Cinema.

There were thousands of servicemen in training there and if the weather had been warmer things might have been tolerable. We were only there for six weeks, and it should not have made too much of an impression on me, but the truth is that I have never recovered from the experience and when people are being told, when being sent to prison for the first time, that it is not too bad after the first day or two, one soon gets the routine and that it is rather like being in the services, I can understand this. From my side of the fence and my own experience, prison could not be worse.

My feet were soon in agony from blisters caused by the hard and unfamiliar thick leather boots and my parents, worried about their feeble and over-petted son, came up to Skegness to spend Christmas at Hildred's Hotel. The highlight of the holiday for me was the opportunity to sleep in a comfortable bed for once which I did, I recall, completely wrapped up in my RAF greatcoat. I also remember walking out with my parents to look at the marvellous fifteenth-century church at Winthorpe just outside the town, the very first time that I had actually seen a church of that date still retaining practically all of its original screens and seating. My parents were interested, no doubt, but I am sure that other concerns and worries were uppermost in their minds.

I knew I was going to Cranwell. Christmas over, my parents returned to Mapledurham and I was detailed to march through the snow, laden down with kit, to the station for the train to Sleaford. I never got there that day, collapsing in the street and being carried into a house and then by ambulance to some place called a sick quarters. Nothing much was found to be wrong, but the medical officer detected possible tachycardia and I was then detailed to Cranwell with the benefit of some physical assistance with my kitbag and belongings. Cranwell was pretty ghastly too, hardly a degree warmer, but it was a permanent station and had slightly warmer accommodation.

At Cranwell the Arctic weather continued, but much of the time I was placed in the huge technical stores in the camp which dealt direct with everything from petrol to guns and bombs, and the then secret radar equipment. Cranwell was also to receive one of the very first jet-engine planes, and everyone was told over the tannoy system that it was all extremely secret. All we knew for sure was that it had no propellor! Barrack huts and beds were tough to cope with, but the station had a decent camp cinema and a large dance hall which doubled as a chapel. One could, when off duty, travel to Newark, Lincoln and Boston by bus. I fell in love with Newark at once and also with the Lincolnshire country churches round about.

I had arrived at Cranwell on 1 January. On the 4th I was told to help others manhandling and shunting trucks on the station railway line. On the 6th it snowed all night and I lost my voice completely. On the 22nd came my first leave and I remember going up twice to the City of London with my mother and touring around looking at the bombed remains of the (then unknown to me) medieval and Wren churches by taxi. At the end of the week, having seen both families of grandparents in Streatham, I returned to discipline. On 1 February I developed a boil in one ear which made me feel desperately ill, and was put into sick quarters for six days. Months later the performance was repeated in the other ear but in the meantime I had attended my cousin Peter's wedding in London. The second boil was much worse, delirium set in and I was in sick quarters for about two weeks. On 11 April I was sent to a hospital at Rauceby in Lincolnshire to see a specialist, and was put on a coarse of injections I suppose now to have been penicillin, the cause of the boils having been detected as acute dandruff clogging the pores of the ears. The injections went on through April, May and June, visits to the cinema to see *Mrs Miniver*, *In Which We Serve* and *The Road to Morocco* were briefly noted, along with the weekend visit of my mother and father to stay at the Bristol Arms in Sleaford following the death of Uncle Harry Thorne at the end of May. I was able to have leave to go to Uncle Harry's sale at the end of June, but still being unwell the RAF sent me to Blackpool to convalesce for nearly two months, which was sunny and summery but with wind for much of the time.

Events which cannot be placed in time were those many occasions when I cycled off with friends to see the beautiful Lincolnshire churches round about, and those times when we went into Lincoln, Boston and Newark. Newark, then totally unspoiled, struck me as having the most marvellous ancient market-place in England, and I still believe I was right. Boston enraged me because Sir Charles Nicholson, the eminent architect, had restored the church and destroyed all the unique medieval wooden vaults and ceilings to the nave and chancel – and this with the approval, subsequently retracted, of the Society for the Protection of Ancient Buildings (SPAB). The quality of the carved oak ceiling bosses was of the very highest and the excuse that the ceilings were thought to be eighteenth century merely indicates the level at which eighteenth-century art was understood and appreciated. Sir Charles Nicholson obtained his title through inheritance by being a second baronet and was not knighted for his services to architecture. He had a successful practice and was surveyor to several cathedrals, leaving as his hallmark bell-shaped lampshades for his lighting schemes. His work at Boston must be regarded as a gross piece of vandalism and several other things he did would now be considered questionable.

Other things I remember were the weekly, band-accompanied, colour-hoisting parades – an absurd exercise in military nonsense. There were occasional fire-picket duties in an unheated mid-airfield bunker, occupied by two duty firemen all night who failed to arrive. I did not know it then but my time in the services was drawing to a close; an overseas posting turned down by the medical officer would ultimately lead to my discharge on medical grounds the following March.

The only good thing that came from my RAF experience was the curing of the boils in my ears and the dandruff – two scourges that had bothered me constantly for about four years. Sexually both blind and deaf I knew nothing about the French letter that was inflated and burst in front of my nose in Skegness and very little about sex apart from what others told me about weekends in Nottingham which was then one of the naughtiest places on earth! An old friend from school called to see me at Cranwell but alas I was not there. He was Roland Kayzer from Streatham who was by then a pilot officer and serving at a nearby station on active service on bombing raids in Germany. I never did see him and the poor fellow was killed not long afterwards. I have a strange feeling of personal responsibility as if, if I had only been better at my job, I might have made just that difference to the War and that he might have been saved. Silly of course, but there it is.

I had lasted in the RAF from October 1942 to March 1944 and then what was I to do? Uncle Leslie thought he could get me an opening in the Gaumont British Studios at Shepherd's Bush, as he was then Arthur (later Lord) Rank's right-hand man. I visited the studios when filming was in progress on a number of sets, met James Mason, Stewart Granger, Margaret Lockwood, Patricia Roc and a host of others, and was offered £3 a week. As this would not even cover my travelling expenses I was pleased to turn it down and soon afterwards the flying bombs began to fall and it looked as though the second front was near and the War nearly over. Flying bombs were terrifying things, airborne like small aircraft and jet-propelled, they would be launched towards England from bases in Nazi-occupied Europe. One could see and hear them in the sky and suddenly the motors would stop and with that they would plunge to the ground. Attempts were made to shoot them down from the ground or from aircraft but the majority got through and their landing would cause considerable devastation. An alleged first one demolished the old Regal cinema near Streatham Station where I had originally seen Al Jolson in *The Singing Fool*. Hundreds were to follow, one descending on houses in Farm Avenue in Streatham, destroying or rendering uninhabitable every house in the road and doing serious damage to my grandmother's house. People became used to flying bombs and knew the times at which they would arrive. We always made sure that we were not caught in the street.

Once out of the RAF my parents decided that a holiday was needed to put me back on my feet. People did not take holidays during the war; most of the seaside resorts were half fortified, requisitioned for something, bombed or deserted – or all four – and it was not really patriotic to go away for a rest. Women were fond of shrieking, 'Don't you know there's a War on?' at the slightest provocation, and the suggestion that someone was to take a holiday would have been quite enough to start a row. Despite this, in 1944 we decided to go to Aberffraw in Anglesey for a two-week holiday, a repetition of that we had had in 1939. It turned out to be quite a funny experience because one had to advise the station master by letter in advance so that the driver could stop the train at Ty Croes railway station where we could be picked up by taxi. The only taxi available was a funeral hearse and there we were, loaded in with our baggage and lying horizontal in the back like three dead corpses. The hotel itself had blacked itself completely, and paraffin lamps and candles were the order of the night. The toilet out in the garden was still just the same, with its ivy clad crumbling walls, deal seat, Jeyes fluid in a bucket and a hen's wing on the seat. We never did discover why this hen's wing should be there! All was peace except for a lost bomber which flew over the beach one day. The idea of food rationing had not really been absorbed by the local shopkeeper – we got a pound of jam there without any coupons once.

The second front opened in June and I shall always remember it because I was at home at The Fishery on that day and had gone out in a boat on the river. Although we were hundreds of miles away from the French beaches, the sound of gunfire and bombs was loud and the leaves of the trees trembled all the time.

Once out of the RAF, I decided that it would be interesting and useful to investigate all the buildings of architectural interest in the town of Reading. I really had no idea how to set about it but, anticipating what was to be my future career, I prowled the streets and roads of the town in search of buildings of quality or antiquity. Not content with that, I was to do what I could to research their histories and on occasion to photograph features of importance generally internally. Reading was then a nice old county town with numerous buildings in its centre and on its outskirts buildings of a more rural character. With scholarship at such a low level at that time, it was quite a tough assignment.

At the same time I had made the acquaintance of an elderly architect called C Birdwood Wilcocks who enjoyed the friendship of, and was able to introduce me to Frederick Etchells, the artist and architect, a friend of John Betjeman and inspiration for the Omega Workshop so closely involved with the Bloomsbury Group and with Charleston at Firle near Lewes in Sussex. Educated at the Royal College of Art and in Paris, he did much church work throughout the country. He had translated Le Corbusier's *Vers Une Architecture* and *Urbanisme*. I was very friendly with him at the time he was writing his great study of the *Architectural Setting of Anglican Worship* with his friend Cannon Addleshaw, for which I supplied two illustrations. I used to love my visits to him and his wife and beautiful daughter in their restored timber framed cottage at West Challow in Berkshire. Regrettably, I never met John Betjeman through him, nor indeed ever, and once the war was over and we moved back to London, visits to see him proved impossible. He was a great character and true friend. It was at this time I was put on the formation committee of the proposed new Reading Civic Society.

Life at The Fishery had been difficult because of shortages of fuel and food and other things. And so it came about that as soon as the war in Europe was over, we returned home. My uncle and aunt were glad to see the back of us, I'm sure. My mother and her sisters were all domineering women lacking in sense and sensibility and somewhat enjoyed rubbing each other up the wrong way and taking offence. We returned to Streatham where our house survived, although it had been quite uncomfortably damaged. It had no windows at the back at all, holes in the roof and ceilings down. However, it was home and we were glad to be free. We would be there for the next five years.

7

Picking Up the Pieces: 1945–1949

Back in Streatham, our bomb-damaged house was only habitable in the front rooms. I had bought a great deal of furniture at sales around Reading, and this had to be stowed away up in the roof space of the house. I remember when it was being delivered that the situation was so desperate that I gave the removal men my beloved American organ because I simply could not get it through the front door that day.

Everything they unpacked was pushed up into the roof, together with hundreds of pictures that had come from Aunt Ada's. An early Broadwood grand piano, dated 1801, that I had bought in a draper's shop in Devizes for £10 could only be housed in my bedroom, and the remainder was stuffed into the spare single bedroom. It tried the patience of us all but with father's inheritance in 1942 of the Bedfont property we had only to wait until such time as we could move in there. All these things everywhere were a trial for the time being, but it would all be vital in our anticipated new home.

Job hunting went on apace but I thought that I knew what I wanted and I was fairly bloody minded about it. I had started and continued my researches into buildings in Reading, and architecture in general, and I decided it would be a good idea to travel regularly to South Kensington and go through the whole of *Country Life* from its inception in 1897 to the present day. I did several other things too, like going through the Buckler drawings of English buildings from the early nineteenth century onwards in the manuscripts department of the British Museum, and going on numerous other wild goose chases. In some of them actually catching geese. In the Egmont papers I found an early eighteenth-century travel journal for Sir John Perceval, First Earl of Egmont, and in the library itself, pursuing records of the South Sea

Company, I came across a valuable source of information in the shape of two books published by the Government after the collapse of the South Sea Bubble and the total loss in confidence of the institution and its directors. The discredited directors had to reveal all their assets and accounts, and inventories had even been compiled of the contents of their houses. Using these as my source of reference I sent material about Carshalton House to Arthur Oswald at *Country Life*, who knocked it up into an article with additions of his own under my name that I was never quite happy about. I gave Mrs Esdaile details of payments to masons and sculptors, wrote to Lord Aldenham at Briggens Park in Hertfordshire about what I had found, went to Purley Hall in Berkshire, a really remarkable old house, and sent details of my discoveries to Ralph Edwards for his book *Georgian Cabinet Makers*.

I also wrote to the Ministry of Town and Country Planning, saying that I had done a survey of Reading. I had in the meantime, at the age of seventeen, joined the Society for the Protection of Ancient Buildings, the National Trust and the Georgian Group, and used to travel to town from Reading after my release from the RAF and sit in the bomb-scarred premises of the SPAB at 55 Great Ormond Street and listen to committee meetings with Lord Esher in the chair. I was very impressed by the SPAB and remember quite well such people as Maresco Pearce, Lady Worsley Taylor, Dame Una Pope-Hennessy, Marshall Sisson, Richard Stewart-Jones, J.E.M. McGregor, Jim Lees-Milne and the secretary, Miss Soppitt (later Mrs Dance) at their deliberations. Incidentally, I was quite amused to read in one of Jim Lees-Milne's books his version of the discussion about Fountains Abbey. He says that he pointed out the inconsistency, as he saw it, of the SPAB's benign attitude to rebuilding Chelsea Old Church and Holland House in Kensington, and their attitude to rebuilding Fountains Abbey. But the real point to me was that these London projects concerned only recently ruined buildings and no conjecture would be needed in rebuilding them, as opposed to the case of Fountains Abbey, which was a medieval building of the greatest importance and on which full information was not available, it having been in ruins for four centuries. Jim left soon after when Lord Esher turned to the committee and said, 'The trouble with these Catholics is they cannot disassociate their religion from anything they discuss. Obviously we cannot allow Fountains to be rebuilt as a modern abbey.' And it wasn't.

I continued my researches on Reading, visiting it often. One of the pressing things that had to be done was to find space at home in which to move about and the collected accumulation needed sorting and disposal. The National Trust announced that it needed gifts or loans of furnishings for Montacute House in Somerset so all my domestic bygones, kitchen equipment, country chairs and long-case clocks were sent down there on loan in February 1946.

There were flutters of excitement when George Langley-Taylor telephoned one day in 1946 to ask if I would like to become the secretary of the Council for the Preservation of Rural England. The grapevine had become twisted, and he must have been led to believe I was an older and more sophisticated man. All I had from this was tea with an elderly lady called the Hon. Mrs Graham Murray in her house in town, who gave me a book on old cottages and a lecture on self-improvement. Learn to type, she said. Mr Clifford-Smith, the great furniture expert, friend of Queen Mary, historian of Buckingham Palace and retired Keeper of Woodwork at the Victoria and Albert Museum, came down to tea to select things for the National Trust and also invited me to tea at his house in Campden Hill. He offered me a job with the National Trust, saying that I was just the sort of person they were looking for. Perhaps I could telephone Mr Lees-Milne to get things fixed up? Mr Lees-Milne's response was abrupt, unexpected and very much to the point. he was very angry with Clifford-Smith for offering me a job; there were no jobs available with the Trust and that was that.

Crushed, but still on my legs, I pursued various other ideas. The Victoria and Albert Museum perhaps. Sir Leigh Ashton said no. The Geffrye Museum. Again, no. The Royal Commission on Historical Monuments. No, again. But the Ministry of Town and Country Planning was impressed and responsive. Mr Garton, known as Sammy or Dick to intimates, was not the intimate kind. A sort of wreck of a man, he had been an architect (LRIBA) with the Ministry of Works, and had subsequently worked with the Ancient Monuments Section with Bushe Fox and O'Neill. They had all been sent to Rhyl in North

Wales for the War and at the end of their stay there, Garton was seriously injured in a car driven by Bushe Fox which overturned. Garton was crushed in the passenger seat and with concussion and various serious injuries was to have poor health and partial deafness for the rest of his life. He received my manuscript list for Reading with amazement and delight, and I visited the then regional office set up in Reading and was driven round by the top brass there on a tour of the buildings I had selected. Clearly, he said, I must come and work for them; not permanently, of course, because there could be no permanent posts, but there would be a vacancy in Nottingham for eighteen months and then all the survey work for the whole of England would be complete and the staff dispersed. Frankly, I was not keen and I let the matter rest.

Our post-war holidays were firstly at Lowestoft in Suffolk, chosen by my parents for no better reason than that they had spent their honeymoon there. I thought it unattractive and uninteresting but I was able to try out father's cine-camera and made a good amateur film in colour which showed to advantage the beauty of the trawlers in the harbour, the delightful streets, churches, alleys and buildings in the great medieval cathedral city of Norwich, the then still standing, blast-damaged but unique medieval rows of Yarmouth, the charming, and then still complete, early Georgian church of St George, the burnt-out over-rebuilt great parish church and the delightful Fishermen's Hospital. Journeys had to be by bus and train, for there was no petrol to spare for our car. My enthusiasm for country houses had now been awakened.

That year was to see the loss of the very large and wonderful house, Garth, at Welshpool, sold for £1,475 for the sake of the lead on its roofs. Garth was a marvellous house in the Gothic style, designed by John Claudius Loudon in 1809. It was a kind of *ferme ornée*, with an enormous circular stable block likened to the one at Brighton, and of the same date and with the unique feature of an overshot waterwheel being purposely designed so that it was visible the moment one entered the main hall of the house. A magnificent staircase hall with Gothic vaulting was the centrepiece of the house, and no expense had been spared in the building anywhere. There was a slight hint of Indian influence in many of the features and the Mytton family seem to have

106

been more closely connected with India than Wales. Seldom had such lovely craftsmanship been reduced to such useless rubble. What remained of the ruined walls was blown up in October 1952.

Also to go, as a result of a great fire, was Studley Royal in Yorkshire, the centrepiece of the great gardens which incorporated the ruins of Fountains Abbey. Studley Royal was probably basically Tudor, but it was greatly enlarged and rebuilt by John Aislabie who was Chancellor of the Exchequer at the time of the South Sea Bubble and made a great fortune from it. The work evidently stopped in 1721 when the scandal burst, to be started again in the years 1740–51, when things had settled down. Studley Royal had magnificent rooms and contents, most of it having been designed by Colin Campbell in the late 1720s, evidently with the subsidiary help of Roger Morris, but other architects as yet not known may have been involved with the buildings in the park and gardens. The gardens are absolutely outstanding and are kept in wonderful condition by the National Trust, but the house itself was completely destroyed by fire on 13 April 1946 and demolished. A house was then created for the family in the great stable quadrangle, and then they moved to Fountains Hall. The estate was sold to the West Riding County Council who after a lapse of years, passed the property over to the National Trust.

Hillington Hall in Norfolk also went just after the war in 1946. An enormous house in Gothic style, it had been built for the Ffolkes family in 1824–30 to the designs of W.J. Donthorne.

The following year, 1947, saw us on holiday in Sidmouth in Devon, where the charming Regency terraces and villas made the place a memorable delight. Bomb-shattered Exeter was explored, and also Dartmouth, with its Elizabethan Butterwalk, harbour and fine old houses, Totnes with its marvellous old main street with the town gate spanning it, its nodding gabled houses, their scrumptious Elizabethan plaster ceilings of the upper rooms sometimes just visible from the street, and its market pillared pavements.

Little bits of memory of these immediate post-war years come flooding back. The miserable rationing of clothes, food, bread, petrol and coal, and the bitter winters. Theatres and cinemas were open, but unheated. Christmases at Kenley were revived, but were to be limited by the burst central heating boiler and by a determination to sell the house and buy a farm in Essex.

At the end of the year my grandfather's health, which had caused anxiety for ages, eventually drove his second wife, Auntie Louie, out of her mind, and she ran screaming all over the house. Christmas was hell, thanks to this, but fortunately on 1 January 1948, she herself died. The twice-widowed husband, nurse supported, lived on for just a few more months. My mother's mother, Mary Ann Allman, had predeceased both, having died on 12 March at the age of 96. She was buried on 17 March, her wedding day.

December 1947 was an eventful four weeks because on the 1st I was interviewed for a job as a temporary investigator of historic buildings with the Ministry of Town and Country Planning at a salary of about £600 a year, and was later told that I had been given it at half salary and I would be investigating various counties near London. I started work on the very morning that Auntie Louie died.

The year was to see the loss of the large, early Georgian red-brick house Lockinge Park in Berkshire, the seat of the Loyd family, and Swarland Hall in Northumberland, a house once incorrectly ascribed to James Paine but probably actually by John Carr of York. It was a handsome place with recessed pedimented portico, built in 1765 for R.D. Grieve, and was for a time used to house the destitute unemployed of Jarrow. Damaged by army occupation in the war, it was demolished in 1947.

A serious fire loss that year was Sunninghill Park in Berkshire, a house built for Jeremiah Crutchley to the designs of James Wyatt in 1783, with a stone staircase by John Devall and elegant plasterwork by Joseph Rose. The house stood in a splendid deer park with a seventeen-acre lake. Sunninghill was often let in the twentieth century, including to the American families of Drexel and Mellon, and was eventually sold in 1936. The house was bought in 1947 as a home for Princess Elizabeth and the Duke of Edinburgh at the time of their marriage and destroyed by fire during building works.

Another loss for 1947 was Redgrave Hall in Suffolk, built for the bachelor MP Rowland Holt to the designs of Capability Brown in the 1770s at the vast cost of £30,000. It was one of Brown's finest and largest country houses, richly furnished throughout with a park and lake of his own designing. The estate had been the property of the Bacon family until 1702. Brown retained the great hall of Sir Nicholas Bacon's house with its open-timbered roof as a kitchen. Its curious entrance doorway had a relief showing the hand of the 'Divine Architect' reaching down to a survey table set among trees and inscribed with the Lord Keeper's motto 'Mediocre Firma'. Nicholas Bacon was Lord Keeper of the Great Seal and Lord Chancellor to Queen Elizabeth I. The Great Hall survived the 1947 demolition but was bulldozed later, a falling chimney doing £1,000 worth of damage to the vehicle. This second demolition was evidently performed without any permission being sought and the damage served as a kind of punishment. Finally that year, Morningthorpe in Norfolk saw the loss of Boyland Hall, a charming Tudor and Regency gabled house, the home of the Irbys, Lords Boston.

The first visit I remember when I started work was to Weybridge in Surrey where there was a threat to the Grotto in Oatlands Park. The great Tudor Royal Palace had long since gone but part of the Estate had been acquired by the then Earl of Lincoln in 1716 and he had built a new house there. But the feature of the greatest merit was the Grotto designed and built by Josiah Lane of Tisbury from 1747 onwards. It is said to have taken twelve years to finish and cost £40,000. It was on two storeys with three rooms on each floor which were decorated with vaults and huge artificial stalactites decorated with quartz, spar and tufa and shells. On the lower floor was a classical bathroom with a copy of the famous marble Venus of Medici. The Grotto was so splendid and so famous that it was chosen by a later owner, the Duke of York, to entertain the victors of Waterloo including the Emperor of Russia and the Duke of Wellington. There was a splendid celebratory supper which was decorated with crystal chandeliers and gold plate setting off the magnificent dresses and costumes of the guests.

The owners of the Oatlands Park Hotel had persuaded the Surveyor to the Local District Council to issue a dangerous structure notice requiring its demolition because one of their inebriated guests had fallen off the roof and cut his head. One third of the entire structure had been destroyed before I could get to it. The remaining part which I saw had already had the roofs, windows and doors stripped. There was really nothing I could do but watch in despair as this lovely building was wilfully destroyed.

My first year of work in the office was 1948 and I spent some time reading through existing lists and checking them against national building records photographs and other sources. One of the first places I was sent to see was Whitehaven in Cumberland, an early Georgian planned town, where I remember spending some time running through the eighteenth-century rate books to see if I could find the home of the American patriot, John Paul Jones, who came from there, but I failed in this, instead making the interesting discovery that the 'mansions' that were such a feature of the principal streets had originally been built as flats – surely the earliest flats ever built in England. No doubt the idea had managed to cross the border from Scotland. Other places I visited were Winchester, Hertford, Ware, Bishop's Stortford, Cambridge, Tenby, Huntingdon, Hull, Hereford, Ludlow, Ledbury and Southampton.

I was sent to Winchester to look at the model list that had been completed for the city by the husband and wife team, the Shepherds, and I was expected to learn from it. But I found it wanting in that they had omitted a great stretch of medieval walling near the Cathedral and had completely overlooked a splendid early Georgian mansion near the West Gate called Serle's House!

I had started my picture buying that year, purchasing at Robinson & Foster's auction rooms in Harrington Gardens, a three-quarter length mid-eighteenth-century portrait of a man in a splendid carved giltwood Carlo Maratti frame for £2.10/-. It was in good order, relined and restored within the last thirty years and on the back was the paper label of the frame-maker Edward Wyatt, carver and gilder to George III, and a brass gallery label which when cleaned read 'William Dawtrey, d. 1758, T. Gainsborough'. The excitement was intense; it had been sold twice at Christies as a Gainsborough I found in the 1930s, but thoughts over the years have required reattributions to others. In 1997 it was firmly attributed to Joshua Reynolds, and the semi-mountainous landscape background represents the countryside near his house, More Place at Petworth in Sussex.

That year was to see widespread demolition of country houses: Brightwell Park in Oxfordshire; Elmdon Park in Warwickshire, the late

110

eighteenth-century home of the Spooner family, one of whose number was to be the originator of Spoonerisms; Shipley Hall in Derbyshire, the enlarged Adam period home of the Miller Mundys; Foxley in Herefordshire, the home of Uvedale Price, one of the inventors of the 'Picturesque'. This house was probably designed by Francis Smith of Warwick and was altered by Robert Adam in a major 'Picturesque' park, where there was a summerhouse by James Gibbs of 1728. Gibbs had done work on the house as well. In the rather spoiled 'Picturesque' park we later found a Gothic 'ragged castle' designed by Robert Price in 1744, its original drawing being in Hereford Library. I also discovered a Robert Adam chimneypiece in Mrs Davenport's new house from Foxley and later Robert Adam's own drawing for it in Sir John Soane's Museum.

Bifrons at Patrixbourne in Kent, a Victorian stuccoed late eighteenth-century house occupied by George IV's Lady Conyngham, and Dyffryn Aled in Wales, one of the very few works in architecture by John Woolfe (partner of James Gandon in the production of the fourth and fifth volumes of *Vitruvius Britannicus*), with Joseph Turner of Chester, were also to go.

In March 1949 a weekend conference was organised at Oriel College Oxford for the investigators and the administrative staff. Just a few months later half the staff were sacked as part of a Government economy campaign and the idea of listing England and Wales in eighteen months received its final death blow. They said it would not matter when the survey was completed. In the meantime my uncle and aunt had sold Elmwood at Kenley and bought the Dengie Estate near Maldon in Essex, and the early eighteenth-century house, Dengie Hall, a seat formerly of the Fanshawes (renamed Dengie Manor). It was restored with my advice, nasty windows being replaced with appropriate ones; a horrid gabled trellis porch replaced by a handsome flat-canopied doorcase; and good chimneypieces found to replace the vile ones that had been installed in recent years. I went there to stay for the first time for a weekend in October 1949. In December we visited Bedfont prior to our removal there the following February, the tenants having found another house to go to, to make way for the Sherborn family's return.

111

Around this time, Grove Hall in Nottinghamshire near Retford went. It was an ancient house with a complicated architectural history which had been gone over by John Carr of York for Anthony Eyre about 1762. The park was laid out by Humphrey Repton in 1798. The interiors were splendid, particularly the library with its great bookcases. The contents had been sold in 1946.

The year also saw the end of the lovely Jacobean Marks Hall near Coggeshall in Essex, formerly the seat of the Honywood family with that rather eccentric Elizabeth Mrs Honywood, who had 367 descendants alive at the time of her decease, a figure which included 228 grandchildren and nine great grandchildren. Full of fine original panelling with a hall complete with a screens passage, it had been jollied up in the third quarter of the eighteenth century. Given by the Phillips Price family as a residence, oddly, for the director of Kew Gardens, it was given up by the Minister of Works for demolition in lots in December 1949. Curiously I was on that very day to buy at Robinson and Fosters the much celebrated double portrait of Mr and Mrs Honywood for a mere five guineas. No doubt the two sales were connected, but I knew nothing about it.

The greatly lamented Blatherwycke Hall in Northamptonshire was also lost that year. Angus Acworth, the Honorary Secretary of the Georgian Group, mistakenly thought that the house dated from about 1830, but it was only remodelled in the early nineteenth century from a house built between 1720–24 by that rare architect Thomas Ripley, designer of the Admiralty in Whitehall. Blatherwycke was sold for demolition for a mere £900. It was a handsome house and a great loss.

Gnoll Castle, near Neath in Glamorganshire, the remaining half of a house designed by John Johnson for Sir Herbert Mackworth in the 1770s and altered to the design of C.F.A. Voysey, was the birthplace of Hugh Dalton, and another unfortunate loss.

The tale of demolitions was to continue: Rollesby Hall, a large sixteenth-century house in Norfolk; Brixworth Hall, a square Georgian house in Northamptonshire; and Shustoke House in Warwickshire, another Georgian house. Easton Lodge in Essex, largely built in 1847 to the designs of Thomas Hopper for the third Viscount Maynard, and eventually the property of Daisy, Countess of Warwick, the girlfriend of King Edward VII and a Labour Party supporter, was pulled down.

Goodrich Court in Herefordshire, a Gothic castle-like structure designed by Edward Blore between 1828–31 for the furniture and armour historian Sir Samuel Rush Meyrick had been built on a very grand scale with splendid apartments, one of which contained a carved oak ceiling from Government House at Breda in Holland. It had not been used since being occupied by Felsted School during the war. For sale at £29,500 it was said to be wanted by London County Council, Herefordshire County Council, United Dairies and C&A Modes, and also that it was going to be exported to America, but in the end it was sold for demolition for a mere £6,000. The wrought-iron gates of 1889 now form the entrance screen to the College of Arms in Queen Victoria Street in London.

Campsea Ashe High House in Suffolk also went, the exterior being by Antony Salvin in 'Jacobean' style, but retaining two earlier ceilings, one of circa 1760 and the other dated 1620 with Jacobean strapwork. The splendid old gardens with their canal survive. The two lead figures of kneeling slaves and the statues of Prince Eugene of Savoy and the Duke of Marlborough went to Glemham Hall. The latter later stood on the terrace of Spencer House, overlooking Green Park. Flixton Hall in Suffolk, the seat of the Adair family, also went. It was an extremely large house, a copy by Salvin in 1846 of a Jacobean house on the same site that had been destroyed by fire. Sir Allan Adair's only son and heir having been killed in Italy during the War, the house had no foreseeable future. Also lost was Draycott Park at Draycott Cerne in Wiltshire, the old seat of the Earls Cowley, a mid-eighteenth-century house probably designed by one of the Bath architects of the day. What it was like inside I have been unable to discover, even after very extensive researches, but James Wyatt made designs for the ceilings there and a chimney piece surround at Barnsley House, Glos.

Also to go in 1949 was the lovely Seagry House in Wiltshire, burnt to the ground with its owner Clare, Countess Cowley, on 8 May. Her cook was also to lose her life. A beautiful house built for Nathaniel Houlton, in about 1740, it retained an earlier wing which escaped the flames. It, and some attractive eighteenth-century wrought-iron gates, still survive.

Foots Cray Place in Kent was also to fall victim to a destructive fire that year. A remarkable Palladian house designed on the basic principle of the Villa Capra at Vicenza for a rich pewterer called Bourchier Cleeve in late 1750s, it was about to be turned into a toy museum. The walls were demolished once the fire had finished its work.

Tickencote Hall in County Rutland, an important house of 1705 built for John Wingfield, which an Ancient Monuments Inspector of the time dismissed as a fake, also went. Little is recorded about the house but its closeness to the design of the Bishop's Palace in Lichfield is very remarkable. The house was a member of a distinguished group of stone-built houses in the Midlands which include the circa 1680 Belton near Grantham, the Palace at Lichfield (c. 1685–9) designed by Edward Pierce, and Burley on the Hill, Rutland, built between 1694 and 1705, the design being evidently shared between the owner the Earl of Winchelsea, John Lumley, and Henry Dormer.

Finally, Formosa Place on the Thames in Berkshire was built by Admiral Sir George Young in 1785 out of a fortune accumulated from prize money and his wife's inheritance. A curious looking house, it was given up by the Youngs in the 1930s, converted into a hotel, then sold to the John Lewis Partnership as a country club. But they never liked it, and it fell into ruins and disappeared, they keeping the land.

8

God, the Georgian Group and Other Stories

It's very boring, if not impossible, to be good as a child. I was regularly thumped and controlled by my parents, not allowed to wander off anywhere, not allowed a bicycle which would have given me some sort of freedom, and really rather strictly controlled in my choice of friends and acquaintances. I don't remember very much about parties or entertaining at home – my parents weren't interested in entertaining. They hardly ever had anyone to the house that I remember, and every kind of excuse was put in the way of anyone being invited. It was an introvert household. One was left to one's own devices, to try to find interests and contacts and things of that kind, if one can call them things. There were very few books at home and not many in Grandfather Sherborn's house, except for a long run of volumes of the *Connoisseur* and suitably bound sets of novelists like Dickens and other established authors, probably never read and all contained in the one Globe Wernicke bookcase. On the other hand, Great Uncle Charlie, the eccentric, was extremely concerned with books all his life. My great grandfather also was extremely interested in books. Great Aunt Ada was intellectual, a great lover of the piano, and interested in artistic matters of all kinds. She did etching, watercolours, leatherwork, beaten copper work, enamels on bronze, brass and silver and items of jewellery, but it was as an amateur and she didn't do a great deal of work, although she was able to get several of her pictures exhibited in prestigious London galleries. My Uncle Sidney Sherborn was interested in antiques and works of art, and greatly admired everything that had belonged to his mother or grandmother and in that way both sides of my family revered things that were old. Anything that seemed to be a hundred years old was to be admired. Everything that was new was horrible and everything that had come down in the family was to be treasured.

Books, books, books. I can't resist them and never have been able to resist them. I cannot go near a second-hand bookshop without going inside and buying books I really don't want and may never look at. I can't go in a new bookshop without buying books. I've bought thousands of books. I no longer have any of the best of them because I suddenly realised that the books were driving me out of the house; they were stacked here, there and everywhere and the more valuable the books were the less likely they were to be read. They just remained there for years, unopened. Sadly, I eventually sold all my books on country houses, like Kips' *Nouveau Théâtre de la Grande Bretagne*, Neale's *Views of Seats* (both series), Angus' *Views of Seats*, the *Copper Plate* magazine, Watts' *Views of Seats*, Hoare's *Views of North and South Wales*, Gibbs' work on architecture, *Vitruvius Britannicus* – anything that treated with houses or families.

I suppose I was a good child, although I do remember being chastised from time to time and being told to be quiet and 'be seen and not heard', and things like that. I remember on one occasion, for God knows what reason, my father went to an ironmongers and bought a cane so that he could thrash me with it. But he was a silly man in many ways, and although he probably meant well, he was terribly unsophisticated and his deafness was a terrible burden to him. It cut him off from all culture, civilisation and mixing with other people. In other ways he was actually quite clever. He did a few very good watercolours and became adept at drawing in pastels. His photography was considered very good indeed, although nowadays with cameras being so much better I doubt whether his work would be much admired. He once did a series of photographs from one of the Thames Bridges of Lots Road Power Station, a great big thing with huge towering chimneys, which was in Chelsea but no longer exists. He photographed it against the sun with clouds of smoke and real clouds billowing around, which made a dramatic composition.

Mother had a great fear of me going to church and being interfered with by some dirty old man, as she called it, and for the same reason she warned me against vicars and school masters, and would not allow me to have anything to do with boy scouts. She was a little reluctant, I think, for me to take part in sports, but that suited me because I had no great wish to kick a ball around a field in the mud or to throw balls or take wickets. It meant nothing to me. It was better for me to spend the time doing lessons in school which one had to do if one wasn't taking part in sport. Mother was also averse to, and hopeless at, cooking. She would ruin eggs by over-boiling or over-frying them, and burn joints to a cinder. The end result was that I grew up unwilling to eat anything which was not out of a tin. I remember at one time my favourite food was sardines (I hate the things now), and my other favourite food was baked beans on toast. I could eat these.

I think I've said enough about being good. It is thoroughly boring and I was far too good for far too long and missed out on a great deal. I try to make up for it now, but at my advanced age there is not a lot one can catch up with. The boat has gone.

I wasn't concerned with God and I'm not sure that God was ever concerned with me. My parents took me to church on the occasion of my christening in 1924, I don't remember that they ever took me to church again except after the War broke out in 1939 and we were all so frightened of what was going to happen that we all fell on our knees to pray, particularly as the King himself broadcast to the nation calling on us to observe a day of prayer. I don't think I ever believed in God. It would be nice to believe in a God in the same way that Prince Charles believes in an overall God and spirituality, but as one's prayers to Him seemed largely to go unanswered, one wonders what truth there is in it. If we all believed in just the nobility of man, and the humility of man and the greatness of man and forgot about God, maybe God would forget about us and stop us fighting each other. But a terrific lot of things need to be altered in the world, concerning the persecution of people, and the refugees that flee from poverty, violence and uncertainty. My mother was quite stupid at times and so was my father. I can't help feeling that mother was being peculiarly insensitive when she referred to the present Queen as being 'dressed like a refugee' because she wore a silk scarf over her head and thick boots. She seemed not to understand that refugees were fleeing from death and suffering and they weren't thinking about what they looked like in the fashion magazines when they fled their homes in fear.

I remember too how people were moulded in their beliefs by the

117

newspapers they read, like the *Daily Express*, the *Daily Mail* and the *Daily Mirror*. I think we had the *Daily Mirror* because I liked the antics of Pip, Squeak and Wilfred, a cartoon of animals dressed as people who had adventures every day and who were really rather appealing. They were politically motivated, I realise now, because the villain of the piece was a Russian Communist chap, always around with a bomb in his hands. he was called Witzkowski and was clearly designed to influence children to believe that all the Russians carried bombs and were dangerous. The fact that he was also representative of left-wing politics was probably the principal reason why he was in the cartoons. In the *Daily Mail* there was another cartoon about Rupert the Bear. Rupert was without any political purpose and therefore more acceptable. The Russians were under our beds. My Aunt Elsie strongly believed that we were ready to be taken over by Russia any day and servants who didn't behave properly were thoroughly 'Bolshy'. What were they thinking of, these people who feared not just for their lives, I think, but principally that someone was going to take away some of their surplus money, which they'd hardly have missed if they'd lost it, they were so extremely rich!

The other thing I remember distinctly in the daily papers of that time was the campaign run against the London Passenger Transport Board. It was an idea dreamt up by the socialist-inspired London County Council. The London Passenger Transport Board took over the London Underground and the bus fleets of rival bus companies like Thomas Tillings and the London General Omnibus Company. I remember when I was at school, these rival companies would operate on the same routes and would try to race each other to the bus stops to pick up as many passengers as they could before the other buses came along. They were very primitive buses, all open at the top, and it wasn't until the London Passenger Transport Board came into existence that we had luxury buses with a big tailboard which could take everyone who wanted to get on and off very easily. They were completely covered in, and quite generously upholstered inside. The trams were the same, and a great improvement on what had been done by previous private enterprises. I remember the London Passenger Transport Board invented a system of Green Line buses which would start in London and go as far as places like Windsor and Epsom, Hertford and Welwyn, Sevenoaks and

Lost - Wolseley Hall, Staffordshire

Saved - Cowick Hall, Yorkshire

Lost - Coleshill House, Berkshire

Lost - Syndale House, Kent

Lost - Scriven Park, Yorkshire

© Walter Scott

Saved - Lydiard Tregoze, Wiltshire

© Brian Leach

Lost - Garendon Park, Leicestershire

Lost - Tong Castle, Shropshire

Lost - Ashburnham Place, Sussex © English Heritage N.M.R.

Lost - Gopsall Hall, Leicestershire © English Heritage N.M.R.

Lost - Brockenhurst Park, Hampshire

Lost - Cuffnells, Lyndhurst, Hampshire

Lost - Bowood House, Wiltshire   © English Heritage N.M.R.

Lost - Badger Hall, Shropshire   © English Heritage N.M.R.

Lost - Egginton Hall, Derbyshire

Lost - The Oaks, Surrey

Tunbridge Wells. They would be more expensive than ordinary buses and they would do a country bus route. The Tory newspapers at the time were absolutely furious that this state organisation with socialist leanings should dare to operate a business like that, when private operators could do it so much better. Every day one was conscious of the fact that a London Green Line bus had scratched a car somewhere, or a London Green Line bus had been in collision with something, or a car or lorry had been in collision with a London Green Line bus, but it was probably largely untrue and merely part of a political campaign.

After meeting Cyril Plant in Edinburgh there was a Georgian group visit to Sussex in 1953, Cyril and I extended it by a night staying at the Spread Eagle at Midhurst and visiting some extra country houses, Uppark, Goodwood, Stanstead Park and elsewhere. We stayed at the Dudley at Hove, I remember. It was the beginning of my first gay affair.

I suppose I might never have recognised myself as being gay if I had never joined the Georgian Group Trip to Edinburgh in 1953, because there I suddenly found myself for a week with them going round the most marvellous houses and buildings in Edinburgh and the Scottish countryside, and meeting socially acceptable gays and intellectuals of various kinds. It was a marvellous experience. In Edinburgh I met Cyril Plant, who was to become a great influence on my life. We immediately struck up a friendship which lasted until he died of cancer long before he should have done. Cyril was a collector too. He had a collection of pictures by Joseph Wright of Derby, and objects made of Derbyshire Blue John and other lovely things such as Chinese armorial porcelain. He introduced me to friends of his who had similar fine houses with fine things. Through him I met Hugh Whitefield, who had a house in Somerset near Clevedon, called Nailsea Court. This was an important Tudor building with suitable furniture of various kinds that had been collected for it. Through Hugh I met Robert Cooke, then an undergraduate at Oxford, who eventually became Tory MP for Bristol West, and the owner of Athelhampton in Dorset, that marvellous medieval house.

The Georgian Group opened my eyes to many things and many people, and I was able to visit the most marvellous houses that weren't open to the public. In 1953, with petrol still rationed, the bus tours with the Georgian Group were pursued by otherwise vastly superior people who wouldn't dream of going on a bus tour anywhere, and people who one would regard as rich and intellectual – it was a real treat. They used to ballot applications for visits, but somehow or other the regular core of people always managed to be lucky with the tickets. Nowadays with the Georgian Group one hardly stands a chance of going anywhere, but the idea was a wonderful one and gave me the most marvellous pleasure. I saw Ireland and Scotland and the Palladian villas of the Veneto with the Group. It was a great institution which, like everything else, has changed over the years.

I had tried the usual route for a Deb's Delight on an imaginary social register. I became involved with numerous charities of which I had never heard. One would receive a letter out of the blue from the Duke of A, B, C or D or Lady E, F, or G or from a film, stage or broadcasting celebrity inviting one to serve on a committee for a ball, a gala theatre preview or a film premiere, and one would go along to a house, flat or hotel for a meeting, generally no more than a drinks party followed by the pressurised sale of tickets for an event, in which one felt of little consequence unless one was prepared to take a party of at least eight. I remember we were often asked to sponsor the flowers for the banqueting tables, to provide prizes for the tombola and on one occasion I recall Colonel G. being asked to purchase the entire gallery of the Theatre Royal Haymarket for poor unfortunate sufferers from some medical condition.

Quite flattered to start with by the attention I was receiving, I began to wonder how all these people could be living together in one small flat off Curzon Street and all be organised by the same person, Miss Irene Edwards. She had been trained in the charity organisers industry by the stately patrician figure of Tommy Frankland, who was proudly descended from Oliver Cromwell and the Franklands of Thirkleby Park in Yorkshire, and Chequers in Buckinghamshire. A large man with a Churchillian presence, Tommy had schooled Irene Edwards in the profitable calling whose only rival was the equally successful Mrs Madge Clarke. All charity events in London were organised by one or the other. But it became boring and expensive to remain involved and eventually I arranged that I would not longer go on ball committees but might still do occasional premieres or charity first nights at the theatre.

Looking back after fifty years I am glad I had the experience and met so many interesting people but it was all hugely expensive! I wonder what happens now?

Being gay in 1953 was to open oneself to arrest, prosecution, and even life imprisonment. This extraordinary state of affairs existed for years and years, but one managed to cope with it in devious ways. I became actively involved with the Homosexual Law Reform Society and the Albany Trust, two bodies set up at this time to campaign for acceptance and understanding. There were various kinds of clubs and pubs where gay men met. Any owner of such a club or pub laid himself open to extortion by protection gangs, or police who conceived it their duty to suppress places of ill-repute or whatever term they liked to use. It seems absolute nonsense now, but one was always looking over one's shoulder in those days to see if one was being observed or followed.

There were a number of gay clubs in London in the 1950s. The grandest, but perhaps also the stuffiest was that frequented by the nobility, the gentry and intellectuals: The Rockingham. It was in Archer Street, just off Piccadilly Circus, hidden in a basement. One went through a door, up a corridor, through another door into a reception area with a commissionaire where one left one's coats, hats and things like that, and descended to a basement. It was quite nicely decorated in vaguely Georgian style, with red wallpaper designed by Owen Jones, the famous Victorian designer, and decent mahogany furniture and comfortable chairs. There were copies of *Country Life* and *The Tatler* and similar magazines lying around for members to read. One was not allowed in with anyone in uniform, so soldiers, sailors and the like were barred, even if they were admirals. If you happened to visit the club without a tie or a jacket, which was sometimes quite possible in the middle of a heatwave, they would be provided from a stock of ties and jackets kept in the cloakroom for dressing stray visitors. It was extremely well run. Some of the bar staff were air stewards or people like that. Toby Roe, the owner, was a very kind and thoughtful gentleman, who ran the place impeccably until he retired. One could meet many of the famous people of the day there, and the nobility and aristocracy.

Also, there were lesser clubs, not necessarily lesser in that they had less appeal, but they were different. There was one called the Spartan

Club in Tachbrook Street, Victoria, which was extremely friendly. I remember Kenneth Williams being in there on a number of occasions, and the then sports correspondent of the *Guardian*. Of course, there were plenty of established figures like clergy and bishops in places like these. In the Rockingham there was always a Sunday night dance for men and women, with a live group playing, but there wasn't much room. There was enough room in the Spartan for dancing and there was always a chap playing the piano and singing. Other clubs I remember are the 50 Club, where Russ Conway was the pianist, the Two Decks, the A&B (Arts & Battledress), the Apollo, the Jubilee, the Witches Brew, the Rehearsal and the Boeuf sur le Toit, which had been founded by a member of the nobility called Evan Tredegar, the third and last Viscount, and had treasures from one or other of his stately homes. Well-known pubs were the Lemon Tree and the Paxtons Head.

Outside London were other pubs, which were interesting and fun to go to. There was one called the Marquis of Granby at Richmond, and in Windsor there was the Ship, near the Castle, and the Noahs Ark, which was quite good fun. Generally the pubs in Windsor could be quite interesting without confining oneself to just one or two. In Guildford there was a marvellous old pub called the Bull's Head, at which parties often started on Friday and Saturday nights. We used to get into our cars and drive off into the distance, not knowing where we were going, but they were great. I also visited pubs in Woking and of course in Brighton. There was a terrific selection of pubs and clubs in Brighton, none of which are gay any more now. There were pubs in the East End too, like the Watermans Arms, the City Arms and the Kent Arms. Provincial towns could be even more gay than London, places like Leeds and Blackpool particularly so.

I was far too bookish and interested in other things to ever take gayness seriously, although for some reason, no doubt caused by my family background, I knew that I never wanted a married life. To get married now is to be faced with a monetary penalty if all fails, and furniture has to be sawn in half between one partner and another. I think it is a disastrous move to put these penalties in, because it merely makes people think three hundred times before getting married, instead of encouraging marriage in any way. It is positively destroying marriage as an institution.

It's no great honour to be poor; and it's certainly no great honour to be gay. Mother used to say that homosexuals 'ought to be pitied rather than punished'. In those days, prior to the appointment of Roy Jenkins as Home Secretary under the Labour government in 1967, all homosexuals were liable to life imprisonment, but this did not apply to women who were thought incapable of such tendencies.

The great crime of this time was evidently being associated with the lower classes and being found out, and the fact of being found out and seriously punished was one of the real reasons why homosexual blackmail existed.

My gayness has remained with me to this day, but I doubt if it was ever obvious. There is no choice in the matter. I had reached the age of 29 in 1953 before I ever did anything at all. And that was through the Georgian Group.

I had the misfortune years ago to be posted to a detached duty station at Barnard Castle, 250 miles from home and was quite miserable and lonely there, isolated among acres of moorland. I sought solace for my loneliness in the arms of the waiter in the hotel one night, and stopping on the roadside on our return to the hotel from an evening out we were disturbed in our thoughts by a posse of police with torches knocking on the windows and wanting to know who and what we were. Another serious incident I recall was at home when I gave a garden and swimming pool party for office colleagues and their wives and others. One of the guests who was a royal prince jumped into the pool and at the top of his voice invited everyone to tear off their clothes so that we could all have an orgy! But it was simply not that kind of party at all! I was furious and embarrassed and no such party was ever any part of my life. Mother would not have approved at all!

PART THREE

AN INSPECTOR RECALLS

9

A Country House Obsession

I was not brought up grandly, in fact I was not brought up with anything envisaged at all. We got by in our little home in Streatham, we always had enough to eat and my parents quite vindictively reminded me on hundreds of occasions that I was being given a private education that they had to pay for, and if I did not behave better I would be taken away and sent to the former London School Board establishment in Sunnyhill Road. I was expected to be like every other suburban child and be seen but never heard. All my parents' siblings and their previous generation were joyless people who were more inclined to say NO than ever a welcoming YES to anything. It was even considered vulgar to run or laugh, and I well remember mother's sister Elsie giving me a tremendous lecture about having said 'Good heavens'! She said that my behaviour was appalling and that this was sheer blasphemy. The Sherborns were all stuffy too. But in other ways.

Many country house enthusiasts have been brought up in a country house background, and I had not. But at the same time my frequent visits to Uncle Leslie and Auntie Elsie's grand house, Elmwood at Kenley in Surrey, and to their steam yachts, gave me some kind of interest in a grander lifestyle. A peep through privileged fences, in fact.

The estate at Elmwood ran to eleven acres, mostly gardens and woodland, and with a large meadow converted for use as a local football field. It lay on a hilltop plateau close to a small aerodrome at Kenley. Essentially Victorian, the house had grand gravelled front and back drives, a stable yard with stables, coach houses, heated garage for a Rolls-Royce, other garages, potting sheds, apple and fruit stores and other buildings. Attached to the house was very large conservatory

127

growing calceolaria and other flowers for the house, plus heated houses for white and black grapes and mushrooms.

The lawns were extensive and beautiful, the rose garden with its pergolas a delight and all the beds in the kitchen gardens were bordered by diminutive clipped box hedges. Facing the house was the main lawn backed by the elm wood that gave the house its name and contained two rustic timbered summer houses. Beyond it was a weather-boarded and tiled laundry with wooden wash tubs and a drying ground. Among the improvements to the property made by my aunt and uncle were the addition of a hard court alongside the grass court and the creation of a very extensive lawn – the 'top' lawn we called it – with herbaceous borders and a brick summerhouse. Beyond that again was a Wendy house with its own garden.

The gardens were really lovely and that is why I have given them precedence over the house, which was large and square, vaguely Georgian-looking with brown pebble-dash render and ordered ranks of wood, mullioned transomed and leaded windows. It dated from the 1920s and was a remodelling of a Victorian mansion. The inside was also of the 1920s in various period styles, quite grand to the untrained eye but overdone and terribly overheated with its great boiler house. My aunt and uncle added two period-style panelled rooms and bought much antique and reproduction furniture. But I think Uncle Leslie was more interested in his yachts. Starting off with a small motor cruiser called *The Doff* he fell under the influence of his friend and business colleague, Colonel Wyndham Portal, later to be Lord Portal of Laverstoke, who had a magnificent steam yacht called *Star of India*. Soon Uncle Leslie had bought the first of a range of yachts, the *Elfrida*, the *Zaza*, followed by the *Aerolite* and the *Aldic* the latter two being favoured after the war was over. Grand living indeed. The *Zaza* was really big and had twenty-two crew on board.

When war broke out in September 1939 we were ensconced with Auntie Elsie and Uncle Leslie for the duration, first at Elmwood and then at their wartime rented furnished house, The Fishery at Mapledurham in Oxfordshire. Of ancient origin. The Fishery was a considerably altered house, possibly of sixteenth-century origin, with a modest Georgian sashwindowed front, flanked by projecting gabled wings in an unmistakable riverside Edwardian style. The gardens were lovely, with a tennis court and various outbuildings including an intriguing Georgian octagonal rotunda with a thatched roof, whose original purpose remained obscure. It looked nowhere. The Georgian bits I imagine had been built when John Abraham (or Braham to give him his professional name) had lived there. He was a very famous tenor of the Georgian period, builder of the St James' Theatre in London, and was also the father of Frances, Countess Waldegrave, a connection by marriage of Horace Walpole and inheritor of Strawberry Hill. It was Braham's country retreat from the glare of the footlights of the World.

Both The Fishery and Elmwood were minor country houses, but they were enough to excite my interest. Next door to The Fishery was the ancient manorial complex of Mapledurham Chauzey or Chazey Court, and a mile away right in the village next to the Parish church, was the Elizabethan seat of the Blounts – Mapledurham House. The church had a Blount aisle, and family monuments. The village was delightful, with its cottages, houses, manorial mill and Jacobean almshouses. It was an ancient estate still complete in every way.

One day in 1941 when I was still only 17 and at Paddington Station I picked up a copy of a magazine called *Country Life* which was a great revelation to me. Here was a learned magazine dealing with historic country houses, and from then on I was never to be without my weekly copy. Once the War was over, I started reading in the library of the Victoria and Albert Museum every copy of the magazine that had ever been published, way back to 1895. It was the greatest mine of information about historic architecture in these islands. My parents had always been interested in auction sales and I remember we went to view the sale of the contents of Mongewell Park, the Thameside home of a millionaire American, who, because of the war had decided not to return to England. Then there was the more rewarding but quite small old house called Roselands at Bucklebury, where there were the undisturbed accretions of generations of North Country ancestors, where we bought the remains of four-poster beds and other things. Mapledurham was just outside Reading and in those days was a nice old county town with lovely Georgian houses, and antique shops and one very good antiquarian booksellers called Smiths in London Street It was at Smiths that I bought my double series of Neale's *Seats*, published in the 1820s, and my passion for country houses was thereafter unstoppable. In those days there were no country houses open to the public at all. There was no *Dictionary of British Architects* and no *Dictionary of Sculptors* either. I therefore set about doing my own index of the biographical articles in the *Architectural Publication Society Dictionary*, begun in the 1860s, so that I could know what buildings were by which architect and from what date.

The Industrial Revolution with its explosion in the population had closed the doors of most houses save for the really great ones like Chatsworth, Warwick Castle, Arundel and Castle Howard. Murrays Handbooks published for the counties of England and Wales from the 1840s onwards still listed the houses and their owners and described the great ones, but by the turn of the twentieth century the archaeologists had ousted the travel writers and the age of the Little Guides was in. What was the point of mentioning country houses any more? Few were of archaeological importance. People could not visit them, their owners had withdrawn themselves from public gaze and left-wingers were beginning to question the right of people to have great wealth, great houses and great advantages over others. The long sunny days of the great houses and the aristocracy were now shortening fast. Not even in Betjeman's guides were great country houses much noticed; houses were all strictly private at this time, not open as in Georgian and early Victorian times to respectable callers who sent in their names to the owner at the front door, or had been introduced in advance privately, perhaps by letter. The grandest houses on show had their own printed guidebooks. Indeed, some like Chatsworth and Kedleston were so popular with visitors that they had their own inns (or hotels as we now call them) built on the edges of their parks to accommodate them. That at Kedleston also offered spa waters and a bathing pool. In other places like Blickling a substantial inn was conveniently sited by the park gates.

The War was to bring about the end of a great many houses. All usable property was liable to be requisitioned for war purposes of one kind or another and many people jumped the foreseeable gun by arranging for their houses to be used by schools or hospitals, rather than the forces. Not all were successful and when the War ended the country was littered with derequesitioned houses often in woeful disrepair. Not only were windows broken, roofs leaking and gutters blocked but lead had been stolen, ironwork was rusting away and inside, stair balustrades were smashed, treads worn away with hobnailed boots and chimneypieces scorched and burned by overheated stoves. There was unpainted woodwork by the yard, and neglect was rampant everywhere: dry rot, wrecked gardens and parks, disbanded staffs, spoiled, moth-eaten, broken or partially burned contents. It is little wonder that no one wanted them. What would one do with a wrecked house with non-available building licences, non-available fuel, non-available staff, non-available carpets, curtains and wallpapers, non-available petrol to drive to and from the house, and sometimes, through deaths on war service, no one left in the family to inherit anyway.

The first country houses I saw after the war, apart from palaces, were quite often through privileged visits organised by the Georgian Group, but a very few had started opening or reopening their doors to visitors. Penshurst Place in Kent had always been open, as had Knole, Warwick Castle and a few others, but one now knows that to a considerable degree it was Rupert Gunnis who was behind the later enterprises. I shall say more of Rupert Gunnis later. Blair Castle at Blair Atholl in Perthshire, a wonderful Scots Castle with almost unbelievable treasures; Godinton Park in Kent, with its unique Jacobean panelling; Parham Park in Sussex, then the home of the Pearsons, with a marvellous modern collection of historic portraits and furnishings; the magnificent Elizabethan Longleat in Wiltshire, seat of the Marquess of Bath with superb state rooms largely of nineteenth-century date groaning with great treasures; and in absolutely wonderful parklands, Chirk Castle in Wales, an Edward I Welsh Border castle with Stuart and Georgian interiors, the home of the Myddeltons. Gunnis had also inspired Lord Abergavenny to house Mrs Doris Langley Moore's Museum of Costume in Eridge Park in Sussex, the remarkable Georgian Gothic Eridge Castle having been pulled down before the war.

I became quite good at sniffing out interesting houses on my own. As I mentioned earlier, one day, being intrigued by the mention of the South Sea Company in the descriptions of various houses having been built by directors of the company, notably the handsome Eagle House at Mitcham in Surrey, and Carshalton House nearby, I searched through the indexes of the British Museum Library and found two volumes published in 1721 called *Inventories of the Estates of the Directors of the South Sea Company*. It transpires that after the scandal surrounding the collapse of the company, Parliament had ordered that the estates and possessions of the directors should all be seized, their moneys calculated and accounts compiled, and even the contents of their houses inventoried. Parliament ordered that all this information should be printed and published. What a discovery! All these houses could now be investigated and the accounts associated with whatever might still remain. At one stroke I found accounts for Sir John Fellowes at Carshalton House, for Robert Chester at Briggens Park in Hertfordshire, for Francis Hawes at Purley Hall in Berkshire (where I still wonder whether the words 'Cornwell the Painter' in the accounts could be a misprint for Thornhill, for there is a fine painted panelled hall here), and many others.

I was over the moon with excitement and could not wait to tell Mrs Esdaile, then in 1946, the best known historian of English sculpture, because she attended the Committee meetings of the Society for the Protection of Ancient Buildings. I wrote to as many owners as possible and also wrote to Lord De L'Isle and Dudley at Penshurst Place, Kent, because I had found an entry recording the payment to 'Mr Cooke the Painter for a picture for Lady Elizabeth Sidney' in one of the records and thought that the picture might be at Penshurst. It was through doing this that I was to meet Rupert Gunnis because Rupert had been informed by De L'Isle of my discovery immediately. Who Mr Cooke was has never been discovered regrettably, although the picture itself seems to have been safely identified as one still in the house.

Invited by Rupert to meet him for lunch at his house, Hungershall Lodge at Tunbridge Wells, one found a very formal Victorian house concealed from the roadway by an oak paled fence. The front door was guarded by a brass doorbell pull, with the engraved command 'Please do not ring the doorbell unless an answer is required', as if anyone anyway would ever do such a thing! Through the entrance vestibule was a large hallway stretching from east to west, with a conservatory at one end full of marble busts to a staircase at the west end, with a window containing old stained glass said to have come from Canterbury Cathedral. This was clearly a collector's home with all its portrait sculpture and other treasures of the past. Running the full length of the house on the south side were the principal reception rooms which were of some size and linked by double doors and the rooms opened onto a terrace leading to the garden. The gardens fell quite steeply away from the house towards The Common, The Pantiles and to the rest of Tunbridge Wells.

My visits to Rupert's house were to be frequent but irregular down the years. I never did see or understand it all. I was overwhelmed by its extraordinary contents and even the dining room had a remarkable shaped, hinged folding screen containing the mounted uniform of his much decorated cousin, General Sir Francis Lloyd. Chinese armorial plates and dishes jostled for attention with Georgian and Victorian wax portrait reliefs and busts. The staircase carried a series of small whole length portraits by Arthur Devis and portraits of Vicars of Penshurst who officiated as chaplains at Penshurst Place. Rupert was distantly related to the Perry family, cousins of the Sidney family through the Streatfields. The first port of call on arriving at Hungershall Lodge would be the cloakroom opening off the north side of the hall and this contained even more treasures including an antique toilet roll printed with portraits of the Kaiser, with a written instruction from Rupert 'NOT TO BE USED' and a Swiss musical box toilet roll holder, which played the National Anthem and commanded one to stand to attention immediately.

The pictures that hung at Hungershall Lodge were not especially distinguished, apart from the great Dobson family portrait of the Streatfields sold to America on Rupert's death, the enchanting Devis pictures on the stairs already mentioned, a trompe l'oeil of a notice board by Edward Collier, now in the Tate Gallery, a portrait of Matthew Brettingham, the architect of Norwich, by D. Heins, and a very fine portrait of Mr Justice Raymond by Jonathan Richardson that he was to leave on his death to Lincoln's Inn. One of the worst bricks I ever dropped in my life was to fail to recognise the identity of the sitter for the portrait of the exceedingly handsome young man hanging over the library fireplace by Kathleen Mann as that of my host himself!

Rupert's pride and joy was his great collection of sculpture, the number of busts seemed so great they tended to overwhelm the principal rooms and also filled the conservatory and a summer house in

133

the garden. One of the busts, a bronze of Charles I, had been found by me in a shop in Aylesbury, Buckinghamshire.

The series of volumes of drawings by John Deare were found by me in an auction in Hodgson's Auction Rooms in Chancery Lane. For the equivalent of a week's pay, I bought them and gave them to him as a present. I do not think that anyone knew at the time that the drawings initialled J P in the volumes were by the famous James Paine, nor the fact that they had shared a studio together in Rome. The drawings would now realise a small fortune. Regrettably the volumes are no longer intact but what remains of them are now in the Victoria and Albert Museum. Later I bought and gave to Rupert a portrait of his distinguished ancestor, Duncan Forbes of Culloden, by the Scots painter William Aikman but Rupert never valued it highly and it got lost when he died.

My visit to Rupert was followed quite soon after by an invitation to go on one of his church crawls and this I remember began in the Parish Church of Kentish Town which we found to be crammed to the roof with monuments and tablets. This was where I was able to see my first work by Charles Regnart. From there we struck up northwards via Stowe-Nine-Churches where we saw the great tomb to Dame Elizabeth Carey by Nicholas Stone. Normally on these tours we would visit seven to eight churches in a day, recording the monuments, and on this occasion we concentrated on North Buckinghamshire and Northamptonshire.

Rupert meticulously researched the itinerary for his tours, combing through the county histories in his library which included all of the scarcest and most valuable books of their kind, County Directories, Murrays Handbooks, great runs of the London and Gentleman's Magazines and others. His tour would embrace even town halls, hospitals and schools. No book that might indicate the survival of monuments and sculpture was overlooked. Record depositories, Estate offices and even banks he ferretted out. I remember going to Childs Bank and Hoares Bank and also going through the archives of Lady Every at Egginton Hall and finding there the payment in 1734, twenty-five years later, for the great monument to Sir Henry Every at Newton Solney who had died in 1709 by Thomas Carter the elder. In the estate office at Croome Court, we found the original contract signed by

Grinling Gibbons for the great monument of John Lord Coventry 1690 in Croome Church. In the library at Sudbury Hall, at the invitation of Lord Vernon, we found the payment to Edward Pierce for the monument to Margaret Vernon, 1675 in Sudbury Church which was hitherto unknown.

Country house visiting was an old established exercise. Celia Fiennes was one of the earliest inveterate sightseers who actually recorded what she saw. Horace Walpole left his often catty comments on places he visited. Sir John Perceval left (still unpublished) manuscript notes and there was quite a flurry of etchings and engravings of views of houses, both in books or produced separately for portfolios or for framing. Most architectural historians have their own card indexes for reference. What is astonishing is the vast number of these big houses; generally, one to each parish, but there were also manor houses, plus the homes of City traders out of London, and rectories and old vicarages. It is totally impossible to count the number of country houses that either exist, or existed, because there is simply no way of 'fixing the goal posts'. It is all very well saying that a country house only qualifies if it is a seat, or was a seat of some old family, because there exist so many important houses that were never such; and some very minor ones that really were. Thirty years ago when I was researching for a book on the lost country houses of England and Wales, I had the self-inflicted duty of touring the country looking at country houses that were no longer there, generally to get some idea of the setting of the house and to discover what, if anything, survived or could be discovered. Before this time, once I had started work at the Ministry in 1948, I was sent to see houses that appeared to be threatened with demolition and were sometimes, as in the case of Bifrons at Patrixbourne in Kent, deserted by their ancient families.

Owners of country houses faced the most awful problems. Years of wartime neglect led to widespread damage and water penetration, causing rot. Requisitioned houses did not embrace the regular clearing of valleys, gutters and downpipes of fallen leaves and other trash as was normal when the houses were lived in. There were acres of unused and unwanted kitchens, little or no modernisation and generally no heating at all, other than with open fires stoked by servants. The rot and damp experienced by hardy aristocrats in their own houses would be considered absolutely horrendous today. It might even have been considered selfish and unpatriotic to have wanted to save one's ancient home.

The Georgian Group was always élitist, believing in being on good terms with the very rich, seemingly whatever the cost or losses. Angus Acworth, the honorary secretary of the Group for years was a very difficult man and was known to upset people all the time. He also had a very limited view about houses for preservation, and had dismissed Blatherwycke Hall in Northamptonshire, built to the designs of Thomas Ripley in 1720, as early nineteenth century. He believed that the eighteenth-century Parbold Hall in Lancashire, rescued by the Moores family of Littlewoods, was not worth bothering about, and it was the Georgian Group who stood by and allowed Bowood House in Wiltshire to go without any protest. A fact that made James Lees Milne boil over with rage in a letter to *The Times*. It was a splendid house by Robert Adam.

I fear too, that although the National Trust has achieved miracles and will continue to be in the forefront of preservation in the entire world, it can probably be blamed for the loss of many of the country houses of England. We are not told what houses, collections and estates the Trust has been offered and refused as gifts. I suspect that probably the majority of lost country houses had at some time been offered as gifts to the Trust and rejected. Could they never have persuaded the government of the day to provide them with the necessary endowments? No doubt they wrote letters but did they ever campaign? One wonders whether, had their policies been different, many of these houses might have been saved. One knows too that the Trust has demolished country houses itself that have come into its ownership, like Ilam Hall in Staffordshire and Dolaucothi in Wales. The Trust made an application to demolish Tatton Old Hall in Cheshire, with its magnificent medieval Great Hall. And with its experiences of fires in houses the destruction of the uniquely important Coleshill in Berkshire which was coming to it, the total loss by fire of the delightful Dunsland House in Devon, one wonders why anyone was allowed to use blow lamps on the roof of Uppark in Sussex at all. They were unable to do anything to help save Boringdon at Plymouth in Devon,

136

the cradle of the Parker family before they moved themselves to the grander Saltram nearby.

I cannot count the number of houses I have seen. Some, once open have since closed, like my own at Bedfont and in most cases the contents have been sold. I remember the great timber-framed Pitchford Hall in Shropshire, the Queen Anne period seat of the Orlebars; Hinwick Hall in Bedfordshire; Acrise Place near Folkestone in Kent, belonging to the Papillons; Groombridge Place in Kent which had been bought by the Mountain family, complete with all the family portraits; and the great Elizabethan Cobham Hall near Rochester, the seat of the Earls of Darnley. At Chiswick House I remember objecting to the demolition of the wings added by James Wyatt with their Crace decorated and curtained rooms complete in all their details, but then we had no knowledge at all of how it was to be restored and changed or that half of one of Wyatt's wings was actually of earlier date and by Lord Burlington and would be kept. I cannot recall how many times I visited major houses on the edge of London but I bitterly regret the loss of the only surviving medieval courtyard house in London, Brooke House at Hackney, largely lost because purist medieval scholars found fault with it. Other sad losses were the unique scheduled ancient monument of Boleyn Castle at East Ham, with its great sixteenth-century red-brick tower; the Georgian mansion of Barns Elms at Barnes near Richmond; the Hampstead Well Houses in Hampstead; Wyke House in Isleworth, by Robert Adam; and many others. These losses were all in populous areas where other uses for these buildings might have been found.

Among the houses round London I visited for pleasure on numerous occasions are the Robert Adam masterpieces of Osterley House, Sion House and Kenwood House; Ham House with its unique Stuart period interiors and furnishings; Knole at Sevenoaks; Vanbrugh's marvellous Blenheim Palace, so splendidly enriched inside and out with all that Vanderbilt money; and Polesden Lacey, one of my favourites, being a Regency and Edwardian house tarted up with lashings of brewery cash.

Lamentably, where Rupert Gunnis might have been of use and value he failed to take action to save Ashburnham Place and its contents from its dreadful fate. It is a curious thing about people, either individually,

137

or as preservation groups, that they can see the importance of preserving a house or building where they do not know, or hate, the owners, but are quite incapable of taking action when a similar building happens to belong to friends, or even old school acquaintances.

It is not always the greatest of houses that one remembers most or likes the best – sometimes it is the people *in* the houses that one remembers. I was delighted, of course, to find myself invited by Philip Yorke to stay at Erthig when it was still semi-derelict, thrilled to visit Calke Abbey in 1949, years and years before anyone else had been there; frightened by a visit to a house where the housekeeper, with bloodstained and bandaged head screamed at me to go away, only to meet the demented owner who insisted that I went inside; saddened by poverty-stricken owners with their crumbling, worn-out houses with crumbling worn-out carpets, curtains and furnishings they could never hope to save. Later, when country houses were no longer falling like flies, I looked askance at the ghastly characterless furnishings that their new owners bought by the yard. There was no longer any historical atmosphere; instead a splendid kitchen, an enormous swimming pool, a regulation Regency sofa table, and a 'chandelier' bought from the nearest department store on a few inches of chain.

The most interesting houses were the unknowns, where nobody had said that the kitchen was the medieval hall of the house, that the plaster ceilings were by Paty, the reused hall chimneypiece from a design by Robert Adam preserved in the Soane Museum, and where one could name the painters of the family portraits for the owners because no one had been there beforehand to look. There were houses where naughty Georgian owners had contrived secret stairs in cupboards, so that they could go unseen into the servants' bedrooms above for sexual pleasures; there were houses with eighteenth-century French or English wall papers, splendid Elizabethan panelled rooms, and even more remarkably, a window surviving from a Norman structure on the site. Even a house of no antiquity or architectural pretensions can have the outbuildings or decorative gatepiers or other features from some long-vanished building, or a historic park or garden layout.

One of my greatest pleasures in life is in visiting country houses open to the public. Admittedly it is very nice to be invited privately by the owner but this can be time consuming and reduce one's conquests for the day from four down to one. The best houses are those that are really loved and cared for, where everything is in beautiful order and one feels as though one could sit down in them and feel at home. Sometimes it happens that these houses have been quite recently bought and restored. I remember Haseley Court, when Mrs Nancy Lancaster had it, Reddish House at Broade Chalke when it was Sir Cecil Beaton's (both alas since sold), but also rescued houses like Dunsland in Devon (National Trust and later totally destroyed by fire), Ston Easton Park (made into a hotel), Buxted Park (later sold and made into a health farm) and ancestral homes that have been restored like Weston Park in Staffordshire (Earl of Bradford), Deene Park in Northamptonshire (Edmund Brudenell, though the ballroom demolition was an unfortunate mistake and loss), Burton Agnes (restored by Marcus Wickham-Boynton), Newburgh Priory in Yorkshire (Captain Wombwell), Godolphin in Cornwall (the Schofield family), and Plas Teg near Mold in Flint (Mrs Bailey). Just think what a wonderful job the National Trust has done in restoring Erthig (adviser Merlin Waterson), the gardens at Westbury Court and the challenge it faced at Calke.

Then there are the depressing ones, often quite good houses, sometimes in the same family for centuries but without a stick of good furniture in them or any contents of any merit at all. They will not be named but I sometimes regret that they are able to entice visitors. Others that I dislike are the heavily restored medieval houses, with interiors more like Hollywood film sets than the real thing, and these include a few quite famous places. The public likes them, one understands.

I love the picture collections at Castle Howard, Somerley, Knole, Weston, Mellerstain, Mount Stuart in the Isle of Arran, Woburn Abbey, Althorp, Chatsworth and many more, and regret the lost ones.

After the war, things were still exceedingly difficult. Building works were limited to £11 without a licence and many people found themselves in deep trouble when exceeding this amount. I seem to remember that it was the second Earl Peel who got himself into very hot water as Lord Lieutenant of Lancashire because of work carried out at his home, The Hyning near Carnforth, in 1950.

Due to the crisis facing country houses, a committee was set up by the Labour Cotswold aristocrat Stafford Cripps, when Chancellor of the Exchequer, under the chairmanship of Sir Ernest Gowers, to look into the future prospects of buildings considered to be of outstanding architectural or historic interest. They only looked at historic country houses and for them I provided a draft list of potential subjects for their concern numbering about 2,000 throughout England. They were never concerned with industrial monuments, churches or great engineering structures like bridges, viaducts or railway stations, or town or village groups.

The resulting report has never been fully acted upon even to this day, and I very much question whether some of its recommendations are even practicable. However, its report did lead to the setting up of the Historic Buildings Councils for England, Wales and Scotland with powers to make recommendations.

Terrible problems were to continue for owners for thirty years or more until 1979, and it was too late to prevent the sale of Warwick Castle and many of its contents. Lord Brooke was condemned throughout the land for his actions, but he could not be prevented by law, nor can anyone be even now. The contents of Lord Rosebery's Mentmore had gone and there was the perceived possible threat to Castle Ashby in Northamptonshire, where the Marquess of Northampton claimed that it cost £8,000 a year to run the house, and where the lead roof alone covered an acre. He already had Compton Wynyates in Warwickshire, a perfect Tudor manor house of considerable size and he felt that he had more than enough on his plate.

Many country houses, my guess is about 2,000 or more, have been lost within the last century or so. Some were given up following the Wall Street Crash in 1930/31 and many that survived were requisitioned by the Forces during the War, most never to be occupied ever again. A small number were actually burnt long ago while occupied by the forces, like Park Hall, near Oswestry, a wonderful timber-framed house which was burnt in 1917, and Blankney Park in Lincolnshire, the seat of the Chaplins which was burnt by Wrens during the last War. Many other houses lost their owners or heirs as a result of tragic war deaths. Everything post-war seemed to be at an end; there also didn't seem to be any future for great ladies, grand hats and ancestral homes.

140

I was just in time to visit a house in Leicestershire owned by a very caring family and about to be abandoned and demolished: the lovely Burleigh Hall at Loughborough with its grand mid-seventeenth-century staircase and numerous interesting features. It was subsequently bought by Loughborough College (now University) and the architect drew up plans which totally destroyed the house. There was a house in Leytonstone I remember called Barclays which was plain enough outside, but inside had the most gorgeous Adam period decorated ceilings totally covered with gilding. This went, as did a nearby late seventeenth-century house called Goring House, possibly by Talman with a magnificent staircase and corner fireplaces with tiered china shelves over them. There was the house in Yorkshire which turned out to have Norman origins, to be the birthplace of medieval princes and to have an absolutely splendid Jacobean panelled room. All these were unknown, unrecorded, houses. Parks and gardens were often exciting too, frequently with much later and not very interesting houses standing on much older inhabited sites where one could find dovecotes, grottoes, temples, stables, lakes and cascades, gazebos, railings and gateways, and Tudor and Georgian garden and park layouts. Busbridge Hall at Godalming was one such, with amazing park features. I was one of the few who actually mentioned park and garden settings for listed buildings and fully explored them for items of architectural interest. Most list descriptions made no distinction between a house in a field and a house facing a street. Houses called 'Lodges' could be either big houses in parks, lesser buildings in their own grounds, or gamekeepers' or entrance lodges. Houses with funny names like Rats Castle would almost certainly not be anything more than a Georgian cottage; but Belmont Castle or Stratford Castle could be anything. The list descriptions left one guessing.

Interior features of great importance were occasionally to be found, like the superb Elizabethan staircase complete with dog-gate that turned up in a Victorian-looking pub in Ware, Hertfordshire. There was the Tudor heraldic plaster ceiling in a derelict house in the Mile End Road, which was taken by the London County Council for preservation, and the splendid Cromwellian staircase from Great Nelmes at Hornchurch. Staircases always posed problems and I doubt whether many were troubled about. Fine old ceilings in demolished houses were always destroyed, some of them much later, like the Adam glass drawing room ceiling from Northumberland House, which was acquired by Crowthers in recent years from its store place at Syon House. When the Victoria and Albert Museum acquired portions of the wall decorations, the ceiling was there to be had also. Unfortunately, that highly disagreeable man Ralph Edwards, author of the *Dictionary of English Furniture* and keeper of the woodwork at the Victoria and Albert Museum, seems to have had an argument about it, and I was told the ceiling was put out in the rain where it fell to pieces.

Sometimes parts of one house would end up in, on or attached to, another. For example, the chapel fittings and windows from Canons at Edgware had been taken to Witley Court in Worcestershire over 200 years ago, and when Hafod in Wales was rebuilt after its early nineteenth-century fire the materials and decorative features, such as chimneypieces were bought at the demolition sale of Beckford's Fonthill. Other materials from Canons went to building the mausoleum in Fawley churchyard in Buckinghamshire. When Nuthall Temple in Nottinghamshire was destroyed, parts were built into a house in Norfolk called Templewood.

With the post-war demolitions of buildings, the chief aim was often to get the lead off the roofs of Georgian country homes; anything else was extra. The greater part of the features of interest internally were thought of as scrap. Even good chimneypieces and panelled rooms of all dates were destroyed, and fine decorative plasterwork was only saved in one case that I heard of, and that was the decoration of the saloon at Halnaby Hall in Yorkshire near Darlington, which was taken to a restaurant at Walshford Bridge near Wetherby. The Adam interiors at Bowood were an almost total loss, but the decoration of the great room there was transported to London and installed in a mangled state in a room of the wrong size at Lloyds headquarters, from which Lloyds later rescued it. The great room and grand staircase went from Wolselely Hall in Staffordshire when it was demolished – they were the documented work of the great Stuart sculptor and woodcarver Edward Pierce. The great room was dismantled and mangled in its installation at Gawsworth Hall, near Macclesfield, and of the staircase practically nothing survives.

10

That Listing Job

Preservation is a difficult word when applied to buildings. One can preserve manuscripts, pictures or antique furniture, but buildings have to be altered in order to remain in use. They do not, however, need to be destroyed: this has been my position all my life. What is essential is modern plumbing, heating and ventilation, kitchens and bathrooms.

To preserve in aspic is an extreme form of retention, rather like Scott of the Antarctic in 1912 abandoning the prolonging of life by leaving behind food that it would be possible to see again and eat at the end of another generation. Aspic preservation is something that affects museum and gallery directors, where everything has to be available for all our grandchildren. Museum and gallery directors are often possessive and acquisitive squirrels, hiding away their nuts in secret parts of their nests, neither exposed in the galleries they control nor offered gladly to custodians of rival institutions. To them, I say that it is time they altered the whole philosophy of their ideas and that a fluid exchange of objects, like that available to libraries with books, ought to be forced upon them. It infuriates me to feel that there are millions and millions of pounds worth of pictures and antiquities hidden away from the view of the general public. How can they justify purchasing further objects when they so jealously keep from others collections they already possess?

While the urge of personal possession probably inspires many of those who feel that works of art and antiquities ought to be preserved in museums for all to see, it is not exactly the same for the preservation of buildings and landscapes, for here it is for the benefit of the public at large that the more intelligent among us strive our utmost. Fifty years behind the most advanced countries in the world as we are in England in so many fields, we are certainly half a century behind in the preservation of buildings. Nazi bombers did great damage to certain cities and their buildings but they did a certain amount of good in awakening the British public to the fact of architectural losses. If we had started thinking about losses of domestic architecture in 1900, so very much more might have been saved. However, organisations such as the SPAB were years behind the times, and unable to bring themselves to think of taking any positive steps towards the preservation of buildings in private hands. Indeed they only attacked public bodies like local authorities and the Church of England for their destructive ways. The great country houses were demolished without a murmur from them: their files reveal a total silence where private property is concerned, save only in the case of estate cottages which were being condemned as insanitary by medical officers of health. It was absurd, of course, and did great harm, but owners did not want to sell off cottages on their estates to others who would have preserved them. The Ancient Monuments Act allowed for the ownership and preservation of ruins and uninhabited structures, but the Ministry of Works were useless with regard to preserving the important seventeenth-century parts of Combe Abbey in Warwickshire, and helped to bring about the refusal of The Grange in Hampshire in its complete state as a gift to the nation. They were also worse than useless over the preservation of Marks Hall in Essex, bequeathed to the nation, and could actually be suspected by some of wanting to demolish complex buildings like Rufford Abbey and Theobalds Palace so that they could dig underneath to see what fragments of carved stone might be found in the walls of their basements. Historic ships, of course, were the concern of the Admiralty, or no one, and the Trafalgar relic *The Implacable* could be blown up and sunk at sea. The Ancient Monuments people were an outdated group of archaeologists without aesthetic taste or any sense of romance: bound occasionally to office desks, but with an incredible freedom to roam about England as their fancy pleased them. To a considerable extent I think they may still do this even now.

This unhealthy, unintelligent, situation still survived in 1945, in spite of the formation of societies like the Georgian Group. The war years had brought about the passing of the first effective Town and Country Planning legislation in 1944. The Nazis had bombed our lovely buildings and their further destruction had to be stopped. However, the legislation devised by the Georgian Group and its friends was just what the speculators needed. It certainly provided for the listing of buildings of special interest by the Secretary of State, with the obligation of two months notice being given to the local planning authority before works of alteration and demolition were carried out, but these works could only be prevented within those eight weeks by a building preservation order. Quite a few orders were made, but few succeeded, and many more were not made because it was believed that compensation would be payable if the owners were prevented from capitalising on the melting price of the lead on their roofs and in their pipes and the value of second-hand timber and other goodies. Listing became the vandals' charter and hundreds of listed or listable buildings were bought up because no one had the guts to prevent it. This absurd state of affairs lasted for years; it was far easier to destroy an old house of importance than to get planning permission for any new development anywhere. If a Building Preservation Order was made by a local planning authority and the owner objected, then a full-scale public inquiry had to be held under an inspector in a town hall. Sometimes the planning inspectors were good, and knew what they were doing, but generally they were not professionally briefed and reached crazy conclusions in their reports. The worst I ever remember was the published report into some houses on Market Hill, in Buckingham which the inspector concluded need not be kept, yet these houses were the only ones in England to my knowledge which retained all their original medieval paint-decorated oak roofs. What a fool he must have been and what an incredible loss!

Country houses fell like ninepins at this time, being offered for sale for figures like £900 upwards, £10,000 being excessive and scarcely ever asked. Agents did not bother to advertise them and a telephone call to a demolition contractor saved much time and expense. Several were given away to charitable institutions. For example, Oxo Ltd gave Ampthill Park in Bedfordshire to Group Captain Cheshire for the homes for the chronically sick that he was starting, and this approach saved several houses like Staunton Harold in Leicestershire. In other cases listed buildings were just bulldozed or had the match put to them. One could compile a list of these tragedies.

Things were tightened up a number of years later with six months being exchanged for the obligatory two months notice, but the cumbersome and unworkable Building Preservation Order system was retained and was not abolished until 1968, when listed building consent was slipped into the legislation. For the first time really effective control by local authorities was possible. It was indeed an uphill struggle from 1944 when I, on my own initiative in the War and without any thought of where it would lead, did a street by street and house to house investigation of the old buildings of Reading in Berkshire. I was just coming up to twenty at the time, no listing had ever been done there and one was feeling one's way all the time. There were a few volumes of the Victoria County History, some very incomplete ones by the Royal Commission on Historical Monuments (who one can now see had very little idea in fact how to date ancient buildings), a few Shell Guides to English Counties done by John Betjeman and colleagues of his, awful Little Guides which only talked about churches and only N. Perp E.E. or Dec. (even when the features described were actually Victorian) and the admirable picture books by Osbert Lancaster. There were no Pevsner volumes – they started by being based on our own lists, there was no real knowledge of the dates of simple ancient roofs – only decorative details were then thought datable, and no appreciation of Victorian and later buildings to speak about. Even buildings like the Natural History Museum and the Victoria and Albert Museum were to be graded III, but the latter could be graded II for the William Morris tearooms inside. There was no appreciation of groups to speak of (is this adequate now?) and all buildings had to be 'in unaltered original condition' which meant that hardly any of the humbler eighteenth century or earlier buildings qualified because virtually all of them will have had their windows changed. There were no career prospects at the time so very few of us, particularly those of independent means, took the job seriously, and on a monthly contract we were on a knife edge forever, constantly under threat of dismissal. One of us was actually sacked for not eating sandwiches for lunch, and taking a proper lunch break! The Department also adopted a device for stopping us claiming night subsistence and travel expenses by moving us to new detached duty stations as soon as one was working more than 45 miles from one's base. One had no car, no car was provided, and it was not a condition of employment to have one. How the work could be done under those circumstances is not something that I could ever really understand!

The standards for listing were very restrictive in those days and we were constantly being criticised for not going faster. The investigator who did a whole county without leaving his house was warmly regarded, another who spent half the month working, the other half in the saddle with the local hunt sending in hand written descriptions of buildings like 'nice barn' was thought highly of also. Garton was a terrible man to work for with a volcanic temper and no sense of order or priorities, only arriving in the office each day at midday, and when economy cuts came he was inclined to shed the slower and more worthy investigators rather than the slipshod and fast. It was a rotten job, badly paid and resulted in much intellectual cruelty. I was taken on as an investigator on January 1 1948 and was entrusted with checking the lists of others against photographs in the National Buildings Record and Wartime Salvage lists and in some cases visiting to see if the work was all right. It was rather difficult as one of my first jobs was being sent to Whitehaven in Cumberland, a place I knew nothing about and in an altogether different culture from more southerly counties. The work was so slipshod in some areas that whole surveys had to be redone. Many authorities were furious at the idea of lists at all and in one case, when the authority exploded with rage, I had to do the whole list all over again. They wanted it drastically cut down, but it was so poor I ended up by compiling a new list nearly twice as long! And that was the City of Worcester!

Garton was not just machiavellian and ignorant, he was a ruthless intriguer. Aware of the fact that if he sacked unworthy investigators he might well not be given replacements, when it came to some permanent posts being offered he passed me over for an outside applicant as this would increase his workforce of staff. The fact that this chosen staff member could hardly tell one building from another and lost the nation several valuable buildings was not felt to matter too much! I was entrusted with the completion of the list of irreplaceable monuments for the Brussels Treaty Powers, the list of Amenity Towns and Villages, the list of Outstanding Country Houses for the Gowers Committee in 1948, and several others I forget. In later times I did, much against the Advisory's Committee will, a list of all theatres known to me in England and Wales of architectural interest – by towns and architect's names, and (also in my spare time) the first ever list of historic parks and gardens. Also in my spare time and for myself, I compiled a list of historic houses with outstanding contents, and a supplementary list of houses still owned by historic families which I had not visited and were not open to the public, which might also be found to have fine contents.

The Advisory Committees could be quite unhelpful at times, and Sir John Summerson I found particularly obstructive and uninterested in preservation. He was quite bitterly opposed to the idea of theatres being listed and had once declared in one of his books that no auditoria of any London theatre rose above the merest mediocrity.

So now we come, years later, to the standards for listing cinemas, which in a sense, I also played a significant role in. I was quite convinced from my own inspections of the Astoria and the Imperial Theatres in Brighton that they should be listed as Grade II and from my inspection and photographs and English Heritage's photographs that the decorations were all still there almost completely unaltered and should be immediately listed with the Astoria. I could not go in the building and tear the hessian off the walls and the ceilings down without sanction from English Heritage and I could not see why I should be put to that trouble. After all, I have been involved with listing longer than any other living person and I feel that after half a century I know my stuff.

The original staff of nearly thirty-five investigators had in the meantime been whittled away by cuts to eighteen, and then down to a mere eight, crises of one kind or another being commonplace in the post-war years. This put paid to any idea that the work could be completed in the original estimated time of eighteen months. At one time the strength of the force for the whole of England and Wales was down to only four. Lists that had been completed in the field lingered on office shelves for as much as eleven years, and when they were brought down and work started on them it was obviously impossible to service them, because their identification of houses as being occupied by Mrs Crabtree, or shop premises, had long since ceased to be so occupied and the lists needed a great deal of new work. What was also wrong by now were the standards being adopted. An absurd insistence of individual, unaltered merit meant that virtually no cottages could be listed because few of them had original windows. The fact that they stood in groups, and had great merit as groups, was not sufficiently considered at the beginning. Victorian and Edwardian buildings and engineering structure had few champions before the destruction of the famous Euston Station arch, and our lists were woefully inadequate here too. There was no Victorian Society in 1945; everything Victorian was considered to be vile! Buildings in groups had had some attention after years of enforced loneliness, and some buildings, particularly cottages, were sometimes allowed statutory listing on group value grounds, but this was interpreted very oddly by some. The presence of an unlistable building in the middle of a group would destroy the chances of the group being considered.

The first positive steps towards the identification and listing of buildings of historical value were taken during the war in the 1940s. This arose from the idea that air-raid wardens, firemen and others ought to be provided with some kind of guide to buildings of importance that might suffer from war damage. It was obvious to those who thought about the matter at all that there were certain buildings which needed special care after bomb damage, particularly medieval parish churches, cathedrals and other architectural monuments of importance or historical value. The resulting lists were called 'salvage lists', and were hastily drawn up by local architects who produced the information as fast as they possibly could from available evidence and knowledge. They went alongside a scheme initiated by John Summerson and Walter Godfrey to take photographs of buildings of value during the war. before they could be damaged, and they set up an establishment in Oxford in one of the colleges. It was to be called the National Buildings Record.

Public feeling had been aroused by the destruction of historic places by Nazi bombers, and there was a general desire that our towns and cities should be rebuilt in the best possible way, with these architectural treasures preserved for the future. Parliament passed the Town and Country Planning Act and gave permission for the minister to compile lists of buildings of special architectural or historic interest, or approve lists compiled by others. Soon a team of investigators had been appointed and a photograph of these first anointed appears in

149

Preserving the Past, a book edited by Michael Hunter and published by Allan Sutton in 1996. It is, perhaps, worth listing the members of the group, for they were a varied crew of professionals and amateurs from all walks of life. They included Miss E.M. Gardner, a former civil servant and an expert on mills and milling, who lived in Ottery St Mary in Devon; Miss Mary Ward, the honorary secretary of the Petersfield Society; Mrs Margaret Tomlinson, an architectural photographer for the National Buildings Record, later for the *Victoria County History*, and a distinguished historian; Miss Mary Francis, a newly-qualified young architect from London; Miss Molly Blomfield, a National Buildings Record worker from Colchester; Mrs Webster, an architectural enthusiast from Grantham in Lincolnshire; Miss Mary Brockbank, another enthusiast from the City of York; William Oswald Collier from London; Peter Spokes, a historian from Oxford, who was eventually to become Lord Mayor of that city; Antony Dale, the biographer of James Wyatt, and local historian from Brighton; S.J. Garton – more of whom later; David Manning Sanders, a local architectural historian from Sennen in Cornwall; Edmond Holt, a photographer and architectural historian from Bristol; A.W. Bickersteth, an architectural historian and county gentleman from Kirkby Lonsdale in the Lake District; David Verey, an architect from Bibury in Gloucestershire, who later became High Sheriff of the county; Michael Gibb, an architect from Sevenoaks, who later left to do similar work in his fatherland of Scotland; T.E. Legg, an architect and photographer from Beccles in Suffolk; G.B. Martindale, an architect from Carlisle in Cumberland; Edward T. Long, an architectural writer from Norwich in Norfolk; Herbert Honeyman, from the Society of Antiquaries of Newcastle upon Tyne; J.C. Shepherd, an architect from Henley-on-Thames, who shared full-time duties with his wife, another architect who had been very closely involved with the building of the Shakespeare Memorial Theatre at Stratford-upon-Avon; Cyril Harrington, a very able architectural historian and photographer from Settle in Yorkshire; the very shadowy C. Francis from Taunton, who I never did get to know; Francis Kelly, from Towcester in Northamptonshire (who is not to be confused with the present admirable Francis Kelly of English Heritage), who had very restricted skills and was to die a terrible death while still on duty; Tudor

Edwards, an architectural writer and producer of guidebooks, from the Midlands; another architect, A.B. Chatwin from Birmingham; and Edward Roberts an old boy from Yeadon in Yorkshire, who had great enthusiasm for the stone-built buildings of his native countryside and rather curiously had no enthusiasm for the brick buildings of the same area, but he was very knowledgeable in his own way. Sitting proudly in the middle of the group was Garton himself. Missing from the photograph were Mrs Charlton Bradshaw, a classical archaelogist from the British School in Rome, and Humphrey Whitbread, a Georgian period enthusiast from Bedfordshire.

Garton, the appointed Chief Investigator of Historic Buildings, known as Sammy or Dick to his friends, was in full charge. John Harvey, the distinguished medieval architectural historian and writer, remembers him as 'a many-sided artist – a musician of professional standards on the violin and the French horn, a painter in oils and a considerable watercolourist, a distinguished connoisseur both of wine and beer'. However, I could detect nothing artistic or intellectual about him at all. He was brutish, rude, dirty, unpleasant in appearance and remarkably like the notorious hangman of Horncastle in Lincolnshire, William Marwood. He had a frightful old car with a stinking paraffin stove on the back seat, lived in a humble dwelling in Norwood with a bicycle in the shabby entrance hall and a hamster revolving in a cage on the dining room sideboard, had no books to speak of, nor was he an avid reader, nor was he greatly curious about architecture or historic buildings at all. He was also dismissive of other people's opinions, and liked peppering his conversation with little bits of Latin, like *ex cathedra* and *ad hoc*, so as to appear terribly cultured. He once said it wouldn't matter very much if all the country houses were demolished because they were all hidden away in parks and were not readily visible. When Winslow Hall – the only country house we can be certain was actually designed by Christopher Wren – came up for sale and was potentially under threat, he almost persuaded himself to let Sir Philip Magnus, our principal at the time, throw the building away. When Fawley Court in Buckinghamshire, one of the very few other houses also thought to be by Wren was similarly threatened, he visited it and gave it the thumbs down on the grounds that it had been refaced externally in red brick. On another occasion, a stranger phoned the office enquiring about buying a house in Norfolk for demolition and he told them to go ahead as no one would stop them. He rubber stamped grossly incompetent and prejudiced reports on several major houses, notably Gopsall Hall in Leicestershire, Huntroyde in Lancashire, Fairford Park in Gloucestershire and Coldbrook Park in Monmouthshire.

Garton enjoyed downgrading buildings that might be under threat, notably Mapledurham House in Oxfordshire, which he made of less importance than a barn in the same parish.

Looking back, the situation was vastly different then. There were few books. Industrial archaeology as a science was scarcely born. The work of the National Buildings Record (as it was then) was virtually in its infancy and the whole collection was housed in a very small series of red boxes in what had been the first-floor drawing room of No. 38 Onslow Gardens in South Kensington, the same building in which we had our meagre offices. Nothing existed in the way of a *Dictionary of Architects* (such as appeared later in 1954 written by Howard Colvin) and the only source I had of that kind were handwritten extracts from the Architectural Publication Society's *Dictionary of Architecture* which came out way back in 1852. Incidentally, when the Colvin *Dictionary* was published it was not made available to all members of the staff but one chained copy of it was bought for the chief investigator's own bookcase and remained unread. I suggested that every investigator should have one and was laughed at. The result was that the majority of the lists were produced in complete ignorance of the information contained in the *Dictionary*, and it was never considered to be anyone's job to check to see if any information of this kind had been missed. Another serious fault was the dictum that investigators should not waste time inspecting well-known mansions which had been illustrated in *Country Life*; it was enough merely to grade the building and give a reference to the *Country Life* entry. This might have been all right in the case of recent articles where the house *only* was of architectural interest, but it completely ignored the possibility of there being listable ancillary buildings nearby, such as stables, entrance lodges, obelisks and other park and garden features, many of which might have been of great architectural quality in their own right.

As far as Sir Nikolaus Pevsner's 'Buildings of England' series is concerned, the first volume, *Cornwall* was not published until 1951, and to a great extent these volumes were based on our own field work, the series only being completed many years later. Serious research in connection with our work was always frowned upon as a great waste of time and nothing more than a personal indulgence, but personally I always felt that I was doing the right thing in resisting this up to a point. As I mentioned earlier, perhaps the most important of the reasons why our lists needed total revision was the fact that the Advisory Committee in its original instructions laid down such restrictive rules about the listing of country cottages and farmhouses that it became virtually impossible, except in outstanding cases, to place medieval and later country cottages and farms on the statutory lists unless they were really *exceptionally* good in their own right. This meant that many of our best buildings of this kind in East Anglia, Kent, Sussex, the West Midlands and elsewhere were not listed. To require ancient structures to be in 'unaltered original condition' was to my mind, absolutely absurd.

Ridiculous professional decisions were invented for Georgian streets with one parapet level, all basically of one build. Those with sash windows without glazing bars were not listed even if they had fine interiors. Those with glazing bars, even if they were almost wholly modern within, would be listed. Seaside towns would have bits of squares and streets listed where common sense should in my view insist that the street and square must be considered as a whole and listed in total. Architectural details can always be restored if the main structural bones have survived.

Eventually, the first round of investigating ended in 1969, 25 years after the first legislation had been enacted, and we were left with a collection of lists which all needed doing again. The original surveys done by neophyte investigators were much worse than the original instructions had thought likely. People employed on a monthly agreement and told to do things as fast as they could or they would be dismissed, had rushed about, produced lists that picked up the most obvious buildings, and hoped that the fact that they had not been round the back streets or visited country houses or parks on the outskirts would not come to light. The chief investigators, political animals anxious to please their masters and be honoured, were part of the enterprise and went along with it. The staff, more likely than not to be dismissed, often did the most appalling work – no research was done and their visual judgement sometimes left much to be desired.

The reduction in staff numbers was crippling, but the pathetic corps struggled on. In 1978, according to articles in *The Architects Journal* and elsewhere, a Civil Service report actually suggested that all statutorily listed buildings in the main grade (Grade II) should be abandoned to the local authorities, a step which would lead, it was said, to the complete loss of most of our architectural heritage. There are few ministers who have had charge of listed buildings that I can remember very much about. Most seemed to be totally philistine. The only ones I know of who consciously and deliberately made important contributions to preservation were Hugh Dalton, Anthony Crossland, Anthony Greenwood, Lord Kennet, Richard Crossman, Duncan Sandys and Michael Heseltine. Of the many others, the least known the better. Of the political parties, far more Labour ministers actively supported preservation, but of all the ministers the one really great contribution came from Michael Heseltine. Duncan Sandys was useful because he invented the idea of Conservation Areas in the Act of 1967 and founded the Civic Trust. But the Conservation Area concept had to be given legislative teeth in 1972 and 1974 for it to be really worth much at all. It was Michael Heseltine who ordered that means must be found to produce a comprehensive list of buildings of special interest, and he who pioneered the foundation of English Heritage as an organisation of experts standing outside the normal Civil Service.

The Royal Commission on Historical Monuments was inadequate and by present standards very unscholarly. They simply had no idea how to date plain medieval wooden roofs. When recording Westminster Abbey they actually forgot to include them at all in the completed text. All of these original medieval roofs were destroyed during the recent works to 'Save Westminster Abbey' at a cost of £6 million. No one knew how to date early roofs until we were all taught by Essex County Council's expert, Cecil Hewitt, in his book *English Historic Carpentry* published in 1980. Similar fog existed over chimneys and smoke extraction until recently, people having strange ideas about the universality of louvres, of wood or pottery over great hall rooftops and not really understand that fireplaces commonly had plastered timber chimneys or smoke hoods and that the gables in the ends of hipped medieval roofs were once open for smoke expulsion.

I remember that it was considered splendid that the whole of the County of Norfolk was covered by one investigator (without a car) in one year. Before we even started doing Norfolk afresh we could see that hundreds, nay even thousands, of historic buildings listable by the standards of 1946 had been totally ignored and had thus gone unprotected. Similarly highly unsatisfactory lists existed for many other counties. The hard truth of the matter was that the great majority of medieval, Tudor, Stuart, Georgian and Victorian houses and other buildings in the unrevised areas were unprotected by statutory listing.

It worries me a lot that so many buildings that I have seen are no more, or that some of them have been wrecked by alterations or fire and no visual record survives at all. I remember seeing photographs of the fine old ceilings incorporated by Salvin in the rebuilding of the now destroyed Campsea Ash High House in Suffolk, but where are the pictures now? Why were painted panels by Laguerre removed from Fetcham Park in Surrey and sold at Christies? Where is there an adequate record of Theobalds Palace in Hertfordshire? Not all of it survived obviously, but there was half of one side of one courtyard still there in 1967 because I went all over it. Antony Dale agreed with Andrew Saunders, then the Chief Inspector of Ancient Monuments, that it could be unpicked to see what it was; whereas it could and should have been kept in its entirety as I had said. I protested pointlessly, and unfortunately it was destroyed by fire instead. Deepdene in Surrey was pulled down, without the National Monuments Record recording it; lovely mahogany brass inlaid doors, coloured lacquered doors and fitted bookcases were all packed onto lorries and carted away. At a much earlier sale at the Deepdene, Crowthers of Sion Lodge had bought a pair of torchères then painted Southern Railway green, and at Crowthers they stayed until Peter Hone discovered them and restored them to their original burnished gold and black exquisiteness. Now identified as by Thomas Hope. They are now in Lord Faringdon's collection at Buscot Park, but they might have been lost too. (On a later occasion I was pleased to identify for Peter Hone two panels from the great Gibbons/Quellin altarpiece in Whitehall Palace which he had found in a shop in Camden Passage and these are now in the Victoria and Albert Museum.) I saw a group of lovely early eighteenth-century houses in Sheen Road, Richmond before they went, and the original Maids of Honour Cake Shop again in Richmond before it was destroyed to make way for a clothes shop. Similarly the wonderful old Banbury Cake shop in Banbury, a gem of its kind and irreplaceable. In the main part of the great medieval City of Salisbury original buildings were destroyed because the developers insisted on 18 foot frontages for every shop. Salisbury and Shrewsbury have suffered a great deal of unnecessary destruction, as has York, but then they had such a very great heritage to destroy. The bomb-damaged ancient cathedral cities like Canterbury and Exeter were redeveloped after the War with little taste.

Destruction was going on everywhere. On one occasion Garton drove me in his stinking car down to the village of Billingshurst in Sussex where a good range of old houses and cottages were likely to be demolished to make way for a petrol station. I made my protest but they were allowed to go and the petrol station took their place. In 1998 the petrol station has itself now been pulled down. How much better it would have been if the spoiling of the village had been stopped all those years ago!

Local authorities have often been described as the worst possible people to own historic buildings because they seem indolent, unimaginative and unwilling to move without being embarrassed into action. Certainly the number of major historic houses in parks they allowed to rot and be pulled down is shocking and disgraceful, but they seem not to have changed very much over the years. Always ready to accept gifts of estates, they prove, all too often, unworthy custodians of historic buildings. The most destructive of all local authorities was Derby City Council, who have managed to destroy two important Georgian country houses, Markeaton Hall and Darley Abbey. Not content with that, the magnificent James Paine Assembly Rooms followed by reparable fire damage and a fine old house in the market-place with enriched plaster ceilings were also destroyed. Other local authority losses were The Oaks at Carshalton in Surrey, formerly a seat of the Earls of Derby and probably largely by Robert Adam; Alkincoats Hall at Colne, the Jacobean dower house of the Parkers of Browsholme; Workington Hall in Cumberland, the seat of the Curwens, with splendid Carr of York interiors, standing on the remains of a house associated with Mary Queen of Scots which were suffered to remain.

How infinitely better was the local authority that owned Tredegar Park near Monmouth! They did a wonderful job with that marvellous Stuart house. At Rufford Abbey in Nottinghamshire, the early remains were kept but the later additions were removed; the archaeologists made sure of this. They did not care about later buildings, however good, in those days.

Buildings effectively lost because of inaccurate and misleading reports by listing investigators include Fairford Park, Gloucestershire, Cheshunt Great House, Hertfordshire, and Hadlow Castle, Kent (actually reported on by the revered Inspector of Ancient Monuments, G.H. Chettle). Chettle made his reputation with the restoration of the Queen's House at Greenwich, work now much questioned; Chettle said that the tower at Hadlow Castle was packed like a toothpaste tube with dry rot! Stand Old Hall, Lancashire (one of the finest medieval timber framed halls in existence anywhere, which I inspected and graded as Grade I, and which Garton, who had not seen it, downgraded to Grade II, is another example, as are the magnificent Gopsall Hall, Leicestershire; Honingham Hall in Norfolk; Tickencote Hall, Rutland (an Inspector of Ancient Monuments denied its Queen Anne date and importance); Scriven Hall, Yorkshire; and Coldbrook Park in Monmouthshire.

Another house lost when the Government of the day refused the local authority funds to acquire and preserve it was Kirkleatham Hall in Yorkshire (1954). And it was said that it was the Labour politician Peter Shore who was also largely responsible for abandoning Mentmore to the auctioneers while it was the Tory, Harold Macmillan, who threw away the Euston Station Arch.

What was always so mistaken was that the Advisory Committee seldom stuck to the question it was asked – namely, whether the building was of sufficient architectural or industrial interest for the minister to hold a public inquiry into the proposals under consideration (usually, total demolition). They held their own discussions at the table and decided the fate of the building then. I was not surprised that they were less and less often consulted for their views and towards the end I found myself being asked to give that advice. The whole legislation had been devised by an ultra right-wing society called The Georgian Group

157

and it was introduced to the House by Sir Edward Keeling, MP for Twickenham. It was so framed (but not deliberately) that it actually encouraged destruction rather than preservation. One could safely buy any stately home that was on the market and if refused consent for demolition, claim compensation for the loss of the value of the lead on the roof. Marble chimney pieces were at the beginning not highly valued and such things as fine plaster ceilings and staircases were always destroyed because they had no commercial value whatever at that time.

The work was incredibly demanding, it really being expected of us that we would examine every building within each local authority area on foot. Someone in my first few weeks asked the then Minister how many lists had been completed under the Act, and he stood up and said, mistakenly, that there had been eleven or twenty, or whatever. This was not true at all, so in order to make amends before anyone found out, a pack of provisional lists was hurriedly dispatched! Unfortunately, these included the draft list for Hastings in Sussex, with a foreword which had the most alarming results! It had been the practice that investigators should write short forewords to the lists describing generally the area and its buildings, building materials, geography, or anything else that could be jotted down in a few minutes. They were not often carefully read or scrutinised. In this case the investigator had made a ridiculous comment about the place saying how harmful the union of Hastings with St Leonards had been, and that the whole place had, as a result, been turned into 'a howling wilderness of mean and ugly villas!' Hastings ignited completely and threatened to take an immediate deputation to the Minister to protest! Needless to say, grovelling apologies were made and the practice of sending forewords out was completely forbidden for many years.

Listing was never an easy ride for us, and in the beginning the more philistine local authorities were furious about the whole idea. Many were the areas where authorities rushed to destroy buildings that were going to be listed because draft surveys were sent to them before they were statutory. In Nottingham the Council destroyed the Queen Anne period Abel Collins Almshouses (the only quadrangle of almshouses of that date in existence) over a weekend, while in Worcester the Council wrote and said that they disapproved of the whole list. I was actually dispatched to Worcester to see them, with the list in hand, and knowing the limitations of the particular investigator, agreed that I would do the entire list all over again, looking at every single building and noting carefully their detailed criticisms of individual items. They had already destroyed a whole medieval street called Lich Street, with the lych gate opening into the Cathedral Close. I did my work very thoroughly, called to see the Matley Moores at Greyfriars in Friar Street (actually the only street where the council asked for more listings), and noted the Council's view that Britannia Square, a delightful layout of very rare Regency villas, was past its prime and that the properties were now of no practical use or purpose! I did my work very carefully because I knew that it was not a thorough job and ended up making the list nearly twice as long! It had indeed been poorly done in the first place but the ultra-philistine Council proceeded to devastate much of the city until a photograph appeared in the *Daily Telegraph* and Keith Joseph, the then minister, asked for an explanation from his staff. The peacetime planners had effectively bombed Worcester. And still they went on.

There was similar trouble in many places. Conservatives were against listing if developers stood to make money from new buildings, socialists were against listing if this meant that 'insanitary' housing was likely to be preserved. It was a no-win situation; redevelopment was enthusiastically encouraged by architects, engineers and planners, and by politicians on all sides.

In places like Reading, Exeter, Plymouth, Gloucester, Bristol and many others, lines were drawn on maps without any regard to historic streets or historic buildings. Old streets had broken-off ends, made inaccessible to nearby roads – Plymouth suffered in this way particularly badly: they actually constructed a roundabout encircling the seventeenth-century Charles Church, leaving it sunk in a deep hole like a deflated gasometer while the best surviving old street in the city had its end blocked off completely. Exeter was also very roughly treated, even after terrible bombing. The plans for widening the High Street, if not stopped would eventually even have destroyed the ancient Guildhall. With the War's destruction of much of Southernhay, the whole of Barnfleld Crescent and Dix's Field this was much too much by far.

In Whitby, extraordinary houses approached outside by wooden steps and galleries (eighteenth-century flats of a unique kind) were destroyed. Whitby is and was a place full of interest with a great many important houses dating from around the time of the birth of Captain Cook. In addition to the houses of Georgian sailors there were a considerable number of Georgian mansions, both in the streets and standing alone in small parks or gardens. These big houses had extraordinary windows to the staircases, in one strip from the ground floor up through all two or three floors of the house. The staircases were often superb and one house I remember, since destroyed, had a complete room of eighteenth-century blue ground Chinese wall paper. At another house I called at, the owner, Lady Harrowing, sent for the police and had me tracked down in the street. Shrewsbury was also sacked by the planners and a substantial number of medieval and sixteenth-century timber framed houses were lost.

In Poole, Dorset, incredible damage was done and really fine Georgian houses were destroyed, but Dorset is a funny county generally, a throwback to feudal times. Dorset County Council went to desperate lengths to try to destroy Kingston Maurward Old Manor House, which they would not sell until forced. Graded I, it was eventually bought and saved. In Bristol, many houses in Guinea Street were destroyed – lovely early eighteenth-century ones with interesting plasterwork inside. The Bath House at Arno's Castle was lost to Portmeirion, and the Theatre Royal, an Arts Council property dating from 1766, which was a scheduled ancient monument and not subject to listing building control, had all its old stage machinery destroyed, its 1913 frontage replaced by a modernistic frontage in black brick and the lovely Georgian Cooper's Hall adjoining the theatre had an alien staircase installed into its main hall as an entrance to the theatre.

In Gloucester, that most hideous of all cathedral cities, with skyscraping lampposts over great roads, medieval houses were destroyed in St Mary's Square and much damage was done elsewhere to a place that had so little to spare. I remember telling one Historic Building Council meeting that Tescos were the most destructive of all major developers at that time and I remember what harm they had done in Cirencester, Gloucestershire and to the Castle Hotel at Dudley in the Midlands. In Devizes, such an important old town, a Tesco shop was built to a different scale than that shown on the plans, and this

160

enormous structure wrecked the scale of the intimate street in which it stands. I was surprised afterwards to discover that Stewart Young, who was on the Historic Buildings Council and who I was addressing, was actually a director of Tescos!

In Dover, Kent, the preservation problem was serious because the handsome Georgian houses on the seafront had been damaged by shellfire and regrettably they were all lost. In Hove, Sussex, there was a mad idea that the Regency Brunswick Square and terraces should be redeveloped. Queen Mary and Queen Elizabeth (the Queen Mother) were in Brighton in 1951 to open the Regency Festival in the Royal Pavilion and Queen Mary is reported to have sent for the Mayor of Hove and given him a dressing down! She did not approve of vandalism at all. These squares were saved and the Regency Society of Brighton and Hove came into being. In spite of this, practically everything in Brighton was lost from here on, a disaster more or less set in motion by a previous MP Sir John Carden, who had advocated not just redevelopment of the whole of Brighton seafront but the demolition of the Royal Pavilion itself. He was knighted for his services to Brighton which were otherwise quite considerable. Since 1945 Brighton has suffered many acute losses, and is now one of the most despoiled towns in England. An outbreak of freemasonry between developers, planners and councillors probably added fuel to the flames.

Maidstone in Kent has also been diminished and the loss of the medieval All Saints Vicarage which had been the home of one of the Washingtons seems to me quite inexcusable. Vinters Park, a very interesting house formerly belonging to the Whatman family of paper-makers, and well documented, also went. In Faversham, the town was blighted for years by an absurd scheme for a new road cutting across a marvellous medieval street called Abbey Street. One must be thankful that the scheme was quashed and the street has become a wonderful example of conservation care and repair. It is now perhaps the finest example in England of the major rescue of an ancient and historic town.

Coventry faced enormous difficulties after the war because it had been practically destroyed by bombing, but here and there were reminders of what had been one of the great cathedral cities of medieval England. Not the bombed St Michael's, which was just a large parish church, but a cathedral which had been lost centuries ago and had originally been a Benedictine priory. Coventry had been immensely rich in medieval times with a great many fine churches and other buildings. The bombing left just fragments here and there: a medieval timber-framed house stranded on a bombed site or among modern buildings. Years after the war consideration was given to making Spon Street, the best surviving ancient street, into a museum street and to the possibility that the other medieval timber-framed houses in the city might be taken down and carefully reconstructed. In part these plans bore fruit.

Terrible things happened in Bath with dozens of decent Georgian houses being destroyed. In fact it was so bad that the Minister of the day intervened and arranged for one of his own architect planners, Roy Worksett to take over and at the same time become Professor of Architecture at Bath University. The Bath Preservation Trust had for a while before this been rendered effectively impotent by the infiltration of vandals, Freemasons and developers into their ranks.

At Basingstoke in Hampshire, the new development plan provided for the demolition of practically all listed buildings save for the old almshouses and the church, and the place became a paradise for road planners. In fact, the whole of Hampshire is infested with gyratory road schemes in its towns.

Surrey County Council prided itself on its 'County List of Antiquities' which was published, and people were entitled to place bronze plaques on their houses to say they were included. But this did not mean a great deal because it was not a comprehensive survey, but a one-man thing largely organised by a man called Fred Strange. Surrey is a very rich county architecturally, with a wonderful variety of building materials in the Guildford and Godalming districts which were much beloved by Edwin Lutyens and Gertrude Jekyll. Guildford suffered badly, even in its splendid High Street, losing the Lion Hotel for a Woolworth's store, and nearly losing the medieval Bull's Head Inn in favour of a shoe shop, in spite of it having been a tavern for 400 years. Most unusually, if not uniquely, the Council refused consent for change of use to a shop and even more remarkably, having been closed for some time, it was reopened as an inn. There were apparently already eleven outlets for shoes in the street at that time!

162

Fires were plentiful too, some no doubt caused by arsonists, and they claimed many hotels as well as country houses and other buildings: Coleshill and Sunninghill Park in Berkshire; Syndale Park in Kent; Dunsland and Lindridge, both in Devon; Weald Hall in Essex; Cheshunt Great House in Hertfordshire; Foots Cray Place in Kent; Assington Hall in Suffolk; Seagry House in Wiltshire; Studley Royal in Yorkshire; Thornes House near Wakefield, also in Yorkshire; Cuddesdon Palace in Oxfordshire; the Gloucester Hotel at Cowes; and in Brighton the highly important Bedford Hotel just at the very moment that the then minister was about to intervene to secure its protection from a demolition proposal. Members of staff at the Bedford were burnt to death in the fire.

The uphill battle of the appointed first investigators was made worse by the political attitudes of the press and certain members of the public, who wanted to be free from wartime restrictions and regulations. The Englishman's home was once again to be his castle, and I remember on one occasion in 1948, when visiting a house near the Crystal Palace as part of my survey of Croydon, being greeted by a white-haired old harridan who practically dragged me into her house: 'I have been waiting for one of you for years!' she shouted at me, 'Now will you sit down and hear what I have to say about the government and its taxes and the way it wastes people's time and money and resources and ties us all up in regulations and red tape, and you will sit there and hear me out!' And so I did, and so she did, and I wasted a good hour of tax payers' money sitting there listening to her diatribe. It cost the nation all of half a crown. I had other memorable encounters at this time; when I was seized in the seat of my trousers by Lord Halifax's dog at his house, and so never got inside it. At another place, where a large country house stood in a derelict park and the house looked to be similarly derelict, a window opened upstairs after I knocked on the door and an elderly hag with a greatly bloodstained bandage on her head stared out and shouted that I could not come in. Still feeling obliged to look around outside if I possibly could, I repeated my request and asked that 'If I can't visit the inside, might I look around the outside, Please?' 'No, go away,' she said. And at that point there was activity behind the front door, with a pulling of bolts and freeing of locks and there stood a rather grand looking man I assumed to be the owner, who from his brown-stained fingers, nostrils, chin and teeth, was clearly an incurable chain smoker and perhaps something else too. The 'squire' said he thought my visit most interesting and invited me inside immediately, but the bloodstained old hag arrived immediately and countermanded his permission. But I did see a little of the inside, a thoroughly damp one, with lots of green mould growing on Victorian carved black-oak furniture. Released to the open air I had a good look at the outside and was then invited by the 'squire' to see his music room in the park, a building of no interest other than to himself, for it contained his grand piano and piles upon piles of music scores. I thanked him and went on my way, wondering what all this meant. Later, somewhat shaken by it all, I speculated that the bloodstained old hag was his housekeeper and protector and that the 'squire' was both mad and actually dangerous! Sadly, I cannot recall the name of the house; I suppose fear must have expelled everything from my mind!

Other unpleasant situations were the times when I was inspecting buildings in a decayed condition. I once had to (pointlessly, as I had protested) mount a ladder up the front of the Theatre Royal in Portsmouth, over the teeming High Street. I was no engineer or expert on cast-iron structures! On a holiday visit I remember trespassing in the grounds of Shireoaks Hall in Nottinghamshire which I knew had extremely extensive water gardens, probably created there about 1700 by its owner, the government surveyor Sir Thomas Hewitt. It was once the most astonishing historic water gardens in the kingdom, consisting of lakes, ponds, cascades and other features on a grand scale. The house itself was derelict and had not been occupied for a very long time, but it was clearly a fragment of a big Elizabethan house, perhaps by Robert Smythson, greatly cut down and fiddled with. But it was the garden layout I wanted to see, and I poked around and then saw an extraordinary sight: a largish tree with fire in its upper branches! I could only imagine that someone had set fire to a wasps' nest up there, and so I walked beneath it to get a better look and – crack! – the whole branch fell to the ground immediately behind me! A second earlier and I would have been dead! One should never trespass on other people's property, I felt, after that.

Admin civil servants always regarded themselves as little gods. Not that they were gods; but they shut themselves away in their rooms and had no social or any other contact with professional officers if they could avoid it. If anything received publicity and it was good, the administrators took the credit. If blame could be apportioned at all it was to the investigators, whether justified or not. It helped the admin lot if they were in a completely separate building within reach of ministers. The advantage of grass roots contact with the investigators would never have to be explained to them in their remote buildings. They dictated policy to ministers; to a professional mindful of his career they were a source of promotion and honours, and he might tend towards being a toadie.

The Lloyd Warburton years were long and immensely troublesome. How long and how troublesome I no longer wish to remember. Remote in his office on the other side of Savile Row, he seldom appeared. I think he must have had a manic dislike of his job as far as preservation was concerned. I remember well a staff meeting called in connection with a press release in October 1977 by Lady Birk, the most disastrous minister we ever had. What was proposed was the slowing down of the resurvey of England to meet staff cuts. The aim was to cut eleven professional and administrative posts and concentrate on the work of grant-aiding historic churches and town schemes. By then we had only four investigators in the field in England and it was a little difficult to see how these posts were relevant to the economy of the country. Four investigators would not fill a London taxi. Lady Birk addressed the meeting with us and was quite conciliatory, but the staff were seething with rage and she called on Lloyd Warburton to bring the meeting to order. 'Cool it Lloyd,' she said in a loud stage whisper. She also brought forward the old chestnut that the department should try and organise voluntary help to do the work for us. Organisations invited to a launch meeting were the SPAB, the Georgian Group, the Victorian Society, the Ancient Monuments Society, the Council for British Archaeology, the Civic Trust, the Council for Rural England and Save Britain's Heritage, but if any of them seriously thought for one minute that volunteers could possibly be found to do this exhausting detailed work they were all disappointed and nothing came of it. Lloyd was also behind various moves to limit my involvement in professional work, making it clear that I was not to have anything to do with the draft list of historic parks and gardens under a small committee set up by the chairman of the Historic Buildings Council, Jennifer Jenkins. Also disturbing was a message I had from Eleanor Murray, Secretary of the Georgian Group who expressed astonishment that I was still at my desk having heard that I was to be dismissed. Lloyd also tried to have me removed from all the Historic Buildings Council committees. Somehow I formed the opinion that he did not like me.

I really knew Lloyd Warburton hardly at all and so I was very surprised one day that he was seeking early retirement at very short notice. The cause of the problem was a threat to the preservation of the century-old fish market at Billingsgate; handsome and very classical buildings designed by the city surveyor J.P. Bunning in 1854/5. Brian Anthony had recently been appointed to succeed Antony Dale on his retirement and had practically no experience in listed buildings. He visited Billingsgate to inspect and report on it. In the meantime there had been a general election and the minister responsible, Lady Birk, had been replaced by the Tory, Michael Heseltine. I never saw Brian Anthony's report but I suppose he recommended listing. Lloyd Warburton must have exploded with rage because it was rumoured that he had spoken to the Town Clerk in the City and had said something to the effect that Heseltine must be a bloody fool to list it. Unfortunately, the telephone conversation was recorded. Heseltine got to hear of it and Lloyd was suddenly relinquishing his job! Lloyd had made so much trouble for me over the years, and now he was in deepest trouble himself. Heseltine remembered the incident briefly in his recent autobiography *Life in the Jungle*.

Finally, there was the incident of the threat to the Shaftesbury (formerly Princes) Theatre in London. There had been a scare at the theatre when it was reported some plaster had fallen from the auditorium ceiling and there was fear in certain quarters that the building might be unsafe. The owners then declared it unsafe and closed it and there was an immediate fear of demolition. I inspected it in a great hurry one lunchtime. I found photographs of it when it was first built, which showed that it had been very little altered, and I recommended it for listing. Lloyd Warburton recommended that the Advisory Committee be consulted first and, as I suspected, they came to a contrary conclusion. All hell then broke out and the Greater

166

London Council had to save the situation by enlarging their adjacent Conservation Area to embrace the site of the theatre and thus stop any demolition without consent. Whether the scare about the plasterwork was justified or a demolition ploy I know not, but eventually the minister himself intervened and asked the Advisory Committee to visit the theatre for themselves and provide their comments. They had never, ever, stood up for the preservation of any theatres before and had rubber stamped the demolition of the early theatre at Newbury, the Theatre Royal, Leicester and the St James' Theatre, London, but felt compelled to change their minds over the Shaftesbury and recommend listing. I thought you might like to know this if you do not know already. The Shafesbury Theatre was built in 1911 to the designs of the eminent theatre architect Bertie Crewe and is remarkable for its magnificent plasterwork inside.

Also threatened for a time was the Lyceum Theatre in Talbot Street, Sheffield built to the designs of another eminent architect WGR Sprague in 1897. It has a very fine auditorium with superb plasterwork of Rococo design. The Lyceum closed as a theatre in the mid 1960s and became a bingo hall, only for its owners to make an application to demolish the building in 1972. Its future had been jeopardised by the construction of a new small theatre called the Crucible. The formation of the Lyceum Theatre Trust was successful in its campaign to keep the building and it has been beautifully restored and reopened; one of the few success stories in the theatre world today.

My family background was not in any way theatrical except that my great uncle Charlie had developed a passion for the theatre in the latter half of the nineteenth century. Following two visits to a panto at Drury Lane Theatre in 1868 when he had been completely overawed by a procession of great giants across the stage, he began a collection of theatrical memorabilia which became so large and important that it was given on his death to the British Library. As a child, I was taken to the Streatham Hill Theatre on occasions where I particularly remember a 'real' steam train on the stage in the production of *Cavalcade* and there were trips to London occasionally, particularly to an enchanting show called *Where the Rainbow Ends* where a knight in floodlit shining armour filled the centre stage, and to *Peter Pan*, with Jean Forbes Robertson and with Kirby's Flying Ballet at the Winter Garden

Theatre, transporting the fairies on strong wires across the stage. Both shows were considered to be morally improving.

After 1940, my visits to the theatre were increased and there were several to the Palace Theatre in Reading. Out of all the shows there that I particularly remember are a production of the Aldwych Theatre farce, *Rookery Nook*, with Ralph Lynn starring in it and a production of Patrick Hamilton's *Gaslight*. The others are all forgotten now.

The war ending in 1945, there was suddenly a fuss in *The Times* about the possible fate of what was claimed as England's oldest theatre. The Theatre Royal dated from 1766 and was in King Street, Bristol. I had never heard of it before and sprang into action by writing to the SPAB and rushing about doing theatre research generally. This has been a part of my life ever since and inspired me to compile a list of theatres of interest throughout England. The great old London theatres were obvious individual candidates but there were many like the disused one at Newbury in Berkshire, which still had Georgian fabric and there are one or two others like that at Margate, that Regency one, the Theatre Royal at Leicester (now lost) and most important of all, the theatre at Richmond in Yorkshire, which dated from 1788.

In the years following the war there was suddenly a great demand for theatre performances and many buildings not built as such were pressed into service to satisfy the demand. The Young Vic Theatre Company, for instance, toured small theatre venues and I came across them when in Whitehaven in Cumberland doing a production of Thomas Dekker's *Shoemakers Holiday* in a hall. I also remember another touring theatre production of Menotti's chamber opera *The Telephone* in a hall in Whitby in Yorkshire. However, this enthusiasm and the resulting demand was not to survive long after the introduction of television. The theatrical venues which had opened closed even faster than they opened and even cinemas found themselves no longer required. Hundreds of theatres and cinemas were to be demolished in the ensuing years and nobody did anything about it. They were regarded as being unworthy of being listed for architectural reasons. Even such major structures as the Grand Theatre in Leeds and, in a slightly different category, The Tower at Blackpool with its splendid ballroom, were also regarded as unlistable, whereas now Blackpool has been listed and graded I. The only reason why the Shaftesbury Avenue and Charing Cross Road theatres survived the onslaught of commercial development was because the freeholds were the property of the Greater London Council, for not one of them had been listed. They might all have gone otherwise.

11

The Destructive Fifties

Although work probably dominated the year 1950, my memories centre entirely round the move from Streatham to Bedfont, a task involving many vans because so much was stored up in the loft over the house. Much had to be done at Bedfont, electric light, a bathroom and a better kitchen had to be installed before we could go, but fortunately some of our furniture was already there, housed in a disused room – all the stuff from Grandpa Sherborn's house in Wyatt Park Road, Streatham, together with things from Aunt Ada's and Uncle Charlie's. Quite an amount.

The garden at Fawns Manor was just lovely: beautiful lawns, flower-packed beds, closely-clipped laurel, privet and yew hedges, upstanding poplars, ancient apple and pear trees, towering ashes, a big round yew on a mound on the lawn, perfect gravelled drives and blossom-heavy pink rhododendrons. There was pampas grass, with its saw-edged leaves and acanthus with its architectural ones, nodding lilacs, green-speckled laurel, purple buddleia and rows of modern roses rising above the tennis and croquet lawn. The orchard was stuffed full of pears, apples, cherries, nuts, Victoria plums and peripherally with gooseberries, red- and blackcurrants, raspberries and blackberries. Our spaniel dog loved the soft fruit and would pick it straight off the bushes with his mouth.

To the north-east of the house lay stables with accommodation for twenty horses, with a hayloft above and two coach-houses, all disused since a stud farm had been run by the artist Cecil Wilson, a conscientious objector, who was a tenant in the First World War. The orchard ran all round the east and south of the walled garden, with its walls plugged for trained fruit. Here we were, in February 1950, proudly reinstalled as squires after a gap of thirty-eight years, yet we had replaced a family whose treasured home it was, whose garden was really entirely their creation, whose son had spent the war years in appalling prison conditions in a Japanese prison of war camp and whose only dream during that time was to return to his beloved home. We were in possession of our ancestral home but the Vindens and their sacred dreams had gone. I fear that we were guilty of an emotional crime.

In 1950 my parents were 57; I just 26. It was a great challenge to recreate the family home; to return to the village, which had become a suburb, and in which to all but the very old or to the religious who saw our monuments in the church, we were totally unknown. The inhabitants of the council estate to the south and east may have wondered why they had roads named both after the family and the house. Church-going, which we tried, was a bore; obviously we could no longer claim our seats in the chancel, and the Vicar merely preached against the sins of those who only occasionally attended church rather than every Sunday. We allowed a party to be held each year in the garden by the Townswomen's Guild, mother, as President, presenting the prizes to curtseying guests.

It took ages to get the house straight and not until three years later was the last packing case opened, its contents dispersed, and the long room at the east end of the house made into a bedroom.

That year an increasing number of country houses were lost. We had regained our family seat as others were losing theirs. Tabley Old Hall, a marvellous medieval relic in the middle of a lake in Cheshire, finally gave way to subsidence and decay; Rood Ashton in Wiltshire, a Tudor Gothic early nineteenth-century house by Jeffrey Wyatt and Thomas Hopper, was ruinated. Rufford Abbey, basically a medieval building with the twelfth-century undercroft of a Cistercian abbey had been the subject of a row between the owner Henry Talbot de Vere Clifton and the County Council, the owner wanting to demolish and the Council placing a preservation order on it. Clifton retaliated by serving a purchase notice on the Council which they resisted, and the Minister of Town and Country Planning (who was then Hugh Dalton) gave consent for demolition. Most of this vast house was of late seventeenth century date, but the early parts of the house survive. Ockham Park, in Surrey, the seat of the King family and partly by Nicholas Hawksmoor; Weald Hall in Essex, the seat of the Tower family, a lovely early eighteenth-century fronted Jacobean house with fine interiors including a splendid one by Robert Adam; and Bury Hill in Surrey were all damaged by fire and demolished. Part of Hawksmoor's Ockham was saved and restored. Etwall Hall, in Derbyshire, an interesting house of about 1700 built of stone from Tutbury Castle which had contained portraits of its owners the Cottons, together with the clothes they had worn in which they were painted, was pulled down by Derbyshire County Council to provide a site for a school; and Papillon Hall in Leicestershire was one of the few works by Edwin Lutyens that went.

I do not know the precise date Cuffnels in Hampshire was demolished but it had been a gorgeous late Georgian house created for the Rose family, I suspect to the designs of Samuel Wyatt, but with a south front lengthened as a copy of the existing work by Sir John Soane. It had an especially elegant and rare painted drawing room with a ceiling with curved sides, and a staircase on a grand scale. Another utterly deplorable loss was High Sunderland, near Halifax in Yorkshire, which was the setting of Wuthering Heights in Emily Bronte's novel of that name published in 1847. High Sunderland was basically a fifteenth-century timber framed house, the home of the Sunderland family way back to 1274 and at one time it boasted panels of armorial glass in the hall windows. A mullioned-windowed and battlemented stone pile with an impressive Jacobean doorway crowned by statues of naked boys, it was a really marvellous old house. Regrettably it fell into poor repair on its remote hillside setting and was pulled down. Halifax had not cared enough.

Kilnwick Hall, in the East Riding of Yorkshire near Great Driffield, the seat of the Grimstons, was one of those rare houses where all of the building's history was recorded, and it had fine details of many different periods. The Justice Room was completely lined with fine quality early sixteenth-century linenfold panelling, and there was much plasterwork of mid-eighteenth-century date by Thomas Perritt. The dining room had a marble chimneypiece by Sir Henry Cheere, and the house was much changed to the designs of John Carr of York in the 1770s. It was a sad loss but the Justice Room panelling went to Burton Agnes, and other features to Goodmanham, Sewerby and Raighton.

This period also saw the loss, again in Yorkshire and south-east of Leeds, of Methley Hall, the seat of the Saviles, Earls of Mexborough, a complicated house of many different sixteenth- and seventeenth-century dates with an impressive great hall with a lofty carved screen across one end. What was quite interesting was the way Antony Salvin had restored the house in 1830, recovering its sixteenth- and seventeenth-century character. Not lived in after about 1920, but kept in good order, it was occupied as a school during the war and this would have continued if the park had not been requisitioned for coal mining. The school would not renew its lease. The great hall screen was salvaged.

The little known but extremely talented architect Samuel Saxon, a pupil of Sir William Chambers, designed Buckminster Hall in Leicestershire for Sir William Manners between 1795–8. Modest in external scale, it had a two-storey pedimented frontage onto a courtyard with facing two-storey pedimented blocks. If the house had been only one room thick and they had been in line with the house the place would have seemed absolutely colossal. The main feature of the house was its hall with its massive flying staircase, unique in English architecture. The park was laid out by Humphrey Repton in 1791 and lies not far from Grantham.

A very sad loss in 1950 was the characterful Spixworth Hall, just outside Norwich in Norfolk, a Jacobean brick-gabled winged house of 1609 built by William Peck. Basically an E-shaped house, it had been changed by its owners, the Longe family, in Queen Anne times when the part between the gabled projecting wings was filled with a two-storey flat-roofed extension with a rich wooden cornice surmounted by a wrought-iron balcony railing right across the building. The gables were Flemish curls with pineapple ornaments while the centre had a columned porch and an armorial pediment at roof level. Inside there was an ornate plaster decorated ceiling and a chimneypiece with the arms of James I. Its treasures were sold up in 1911 and the house lingered on with wartime use in 1914–18, then again as a private house and then as a furniture repository until the end eventually came.

Gibside, County Durham, a seat of the Earls of Strathmore, was ruinated about this time, and I remember one of Lord Strathmore's cousins, Rupert Gunnis, showing me some plasterwork in his car that he had picked up in the ruins as the house was demolished. The park had been clearfelled in the years up to the last war. James Paine's splendid Mausoleum Chapel now belongs to the National Trust, and there were other buildings by Paine in the former park but most had become ruinous. The park was once of very great importance indeed. Efforts to restore and replant the park and to restore the buildings it contains have been made in recent years, and the Banqueting House has been acquired by the Landmark Trust and saved.

The Festival of Britain took place in 1951, a national celebration of the centenary of the Great Exhibition a century before. It seemed to rain incessantly prior to the opening, but the idea was to prove that Britain was still alive and war was really over. Visits to Hull, Hereford, Worcester, Ludlow and Berkhamstead; a Grand Tour of Italy from Turin to Florence, Rome, Perugia, Naples, Capri, Pompeii, Sorrento, Sienna, Venice, Pisa and Milan; a hunt ball at Bury St Edmunds, November fireworks at Oxted and a weekend at the Vereys at Barnsley in Gloucestershire were the highlights of the year for me.

There were many country house demolitions in 1951, with three going in Lincolnshire alone: Haverholme Priory, Algarkirk Hall and Bishop Burton Hall, plus Tyberton Court in Herefordshire, a house now thought to be by John Wood of Bath. Other casualties were Clervaux Castle in Yorkshire, a great Gothic pile for Sir William Chaytor designed by Ignatious Bonomi in 1839; Snelston Hall Derbyshire, another Gothic pile, this time designed by Lewis Nockalls Cottingham, a careful architect also known for his pattern-book designs for ironwork; Langton House, Dorset; Liston Hall at Foxearth in Essex; Llangibby Castle in Monmouth, a classical house of later seventeenth-century date with an unusual, almost French, arrangement of subsidiary wings and a freezing cold situation; Bramley Park in Surrey; and Bolton Hall in Cumberland. I had never seen any of them and now never will.

Whitley Beaumont, the seat of the Beaumont family, with stunning classical stone elevations, possibly designed by Thomas Mann of York in 1680 (though works under William Thornton were in progress in the 1720s), and with a magnificent great hall or saloon added by James Paine in the 1750s also went. How many of the Whitley Beaumont interiors had survived I do not know, because the Beaumonts gave up the house in 1917 and a sale of the panelling and chimneypieces had taken place in May that year.

The year's most spectacular loss was the interior of Alton Towers in Staffordshire, a great palace in the Gothic style, designed in stages by seven early nineteenth-century architects, ending with Augustus Welby Pugin. This enormous house with great halls and galleries filled with pictures and other works of art had been created by the Catholic Earls of Shrewsbury but had not been occupied other than by soldiers in the last war, since a great sale of the contents in 1924. Only a photographic record, some wallpaper in the Victoria and Albert Museum and the ruinated shell remain. The spectacular grounds and garden buildings are still magnificent.

A very regrettable loss was Fornham Hall near Bury St Edmunds in Suffolk, a large house extensively altered for Sir Charles Kent to the design of James Wyatt in the 1780s and with quite attractive mid-nineteenth-century interiors in the French style. The park by Capability Brown has been completely destroyed by gravel workings.

One of the really bad losses in 1951 was Rolls Park at Chigwell in Essex, a house built about 1600 by the father of William Harvey, the discoverer of the circulation of the blood. The house was largely rebuilt, probably about 1660 on the restoration of Charles II to the throne, and it had a very splendid carved oak staircase with wooden flower-encrusted urns on its newels (it was taken to Hinchingbrooke near Huntingdon), and extraordinary two-tier chimneypieces of so-called 'artisan mannerist' type. The best room was the plaster decorated, lofty ceilinged, mid-eighteenth-century saloon, which had had family portraits inset in plaster ovals in the walls. I saw it during demolition. Rupert Gunnis told me how he could have had the house on the death of Sir Francis Lloyd as a bequest.

The worst loss was Gopsall Hall in Leicestershire, the great palace of the Earls Howe, which had been created by Charles Jennens – a rich Birmingham merchant and great friend of Handel, the composer. Jennens himself actually wrote the words for Handel for his *Saul*, his *Belshazzar* as well as the *Messiah*. The house was mainly the work of John Westley of Leicester, and was finished by 1749. It had a frontage of 180 feet (55m) and the interior was magnificently decorated with woodwork and plasterwork of great richness. Other architects like

James Paine and David Hiorns were involved and it is difficult now to assign the various rooms to the correct architects. The chapel with its carved red cedarwood fittings was splendid and the whole house was of magnificent quality. It was completely flattened.

One of the most romantic houses to go that year was Guys Cliffe in Warwickshire. The legendary Guy of Warwick's chapel, rebuilt by Richard Beauchamp, Earl of Warwick in 1422–3, yet remained, but the mid-eighteenth-century Palladian mansion built by a rich slave and landowner in the West Indies, Samuel Greathead, after he bought the property in 1751, was just the beginning of an enormous Gothic complex which rose from the banks of the river. Parts of the interior had painted decorations carried out by Bertie Greathead II, who died at the early age of 23 in 1804. The original entrance hall of the house had luscious plasterwork and sculpture. Only the shell of the house now remains. Belhus, near Aveley in Essex, was a remarkable large, early Tudor red-brick house with very important and interesting mid-eighteenth-century Gothic interiors, designed by Sanderson Miller, much admired by Horace Walpole. This also departed in that year.

The very worst year for the destruction of country houses was 1952. It is difficult to know where to begin! Coleshill House, the masterpiece of the mid-seventeenth-century architect Roger Pratt, among the most important buildings in Europe of its date and destined for the National Trust, was very badly damaged by fire and demolished by the owners' agent. Hoppyland Hall, the semi-ruinous seventeenth-century and romantic eighteenth-century Gothic house, rotted away beyond use or restoration. Other casualties were Great Nelmes at Hornchurch in Essex, a mid-seventeenth-century pavilion-type house of rusticated brick, with a stunning staircase; Langford Grove near Maldon in Essex, one of the masterpieces of John Johnson of Chelmsford, dating from the late eighteenth century and with a splendid staircase surrounded by monolithic alabaster columns; Harewood Park in Herefordshire, the rather plain Georgian seat of the Wren Hoskyns family, Calehill Park in Kent, a handsome Georgian composition with attendant wings, with the house for some reason then devoid of a main staircase; Hadlow Castle in Kent, a striking landmark with its great tower which could be seen from miles away, a fantasy in the Gothic style on a vast scale. The tower is almost the only part still surviving. And Halstead Place in Kent, a workmanlike Georgian brick structure which could easily have been adapted for other uses. Surrenden Dering in Kent, a house dating from 1630, was ravaged by fire. Llanwern Park in Monmouth, a very large, severe and rather boring house, probably by Francis Smith of Warwick and dating from the 1740s, later the home of the Liberal Viscountess Rhondda, was lost. Also, Glanusk Park in Breconshire, designed by Robert Lugar in Elizabethan style in 1825–35; Acton Park, a plain Georgian house near Wrexham; Newnham Paddox in Warwickshire, the seat of the Earls of Denbigh and a complex structure of various eighteenth- and nineteenth-century dates with much work by Capability Brown; The Lawn, or Swindon House, at Swindon, the eighteenth-century home of the Goddards, Lords of the Manor of Swindon; Kirby Mallory Hall, the seat of a family of baronets called Noel, now extinct; Bylaugh Hall, Old Buckenham Hall and Weeting Hall, all in Norfolk; Sulby Hall in Northamptonshire, a Soane house largely redone in the 1830s; Pendeford Hall in Staffordshire, a seventeenth-century house with a splendid oak staircase and a great stone chimneypiece; Scriven Hall in Yorkshire, the seat of the Slingsbys, a lovely stone-fronted house in splendid classical taste designed in the 1720s possibly by William Etty and William Wakefield, had been damaged by fire, but the walls should certainly have been preserved and not demolished. The stables of 1682 by Richard Thompson of Knaresborough still survive as a house now itself called Scriven Hall. Badger Hall in Shropshire, went in November. This was a large square house of 1730–50, built by Isaac Hawkins Browne and practically rebuilt by his son of the same name to the designs of James Wyatt between 1779 and 1783. It had a particularly beautiful dining room and drawing room, and an especially fine staircase. But what was lost at Badger was not just a fine Wyatt interior but one of the most important collections of Italian Renaissance works of art in England, collected by its Victorian owner Edward Cheney. Eighty-nine pictures had been sold in 1905, and all the Tiepolo ceilings in the 1930s. The rest went in a three-day sale at the house in 1945. A marble chimneypiece by Westmacott from Buckingham Palace also disappeared.

Halnaby Hall in Yorkshire, was one of the greatest losses in England.

A very remarkable Cromwellian house it was altered very lavishly in the mid-eighteenth century, and was the home of Anna Milbanke, the unfortunate wife of the poet Lord Byron. For sale for about £4,000 it was ultimately auctioned for demolition, the splendid plaster decoration of the saloon being taken with some of the structure to the Bridge Inn, Walshford Bridge and two chimneypieces were bought for installation in Kensington Palace.

The loss of Henham Hall in Suffolk, the home of the Rous family, Earls of Stradbroke, was regrettable also. Largely late eighteenth century by James Wyatt, it had been Victorianised inside and out but had good features of both dates. Drinkstone Hall, a rather plain and severe Georgian house and Sudbourne Hall, a plain Georgian house altered for Sir Richard Wallace, the founder of the Wallace Collection, were both lost that year, as was Ravensworth Castle in County Durham, a magnificent pile largely by John Nash, with enormous apartments in the Gothic style and containing a reasonable collection of pictures. The contents were all sold in 1930 and the house used as a school. Then all of it went except for two medieval towers of the original castle, but even they became ruinous.

Vinters Park near Maidstone in Kent, an early house, was modernised by the Whatman family of paper-makers in the late eighteenth century. The sale of the fittings took place in March 1952 and included numerous Georgian chimneypieces, a Jacobean panelled room and a beautiful two-tier Chippendale period chimneypiece. During demolition much of the Tudor structure was revealed including an extremely splendid open fireplace.

Finally we come to Brymbo, on the road between Minora and Ruthin, a house of 1624, and said to have been designed by Inigo Jones. Whatever the case for or against the attribution, the great stone doorcase was derived from Plate 158 in the fourth book of Sebastiano Serlios' *Tutte L'Opera D'Architettura*, published in Venice in 1594, and the main elevation could have been inspired by part of a design for a Palazzo forming Plate 155 in the same book. The house had later been the home of the famous Georgian ironmaster John Wilkinson, and its loss was a major one to Wales. Nothing survives at all. Even its site is scarcely discernible.

* * *

The year 1953 saw the Queen's Coronation, the procession for which I viewed from a stand in Green Park. It was also the year when Cyril Plant invited me to visit him in Repton, and I took with me, for two nights, Rupert Gunnis, who wanted to visit various places in the neighbourhood. I wrote to Charles Jenney at Calke Abbey for permission to see the house and we accordingly arrived there, driving down the two-mile long drive with its series of fastened gates to the house itself.

Charles Jenney (later to change his name to Harpur Crewe) was unfortunately away, but his brother Henry welcomed us and took us around. We were probably the first outsiders to see the place for a hundred years. The house amazed us – it had been totally untouched for all that time and there was not even electric light or a telephone. Like Erthig in Wales, the house was not only unmodernised and unchanged, Calke had never been written about or described since 1854. Even villagers on the estate had never seen it. The rooms were mostly shuttered up and unused, the furniture in some seemingly stacked to the ceiling. Could we see Queen Caroline of Anspach's state bed, we asked? We knew it was there from Burke's description in 1854 where it said it had never been put up; alas no! It was packed in boxes and had never been seen by anyone for years.

Where 1952 had been a high point of the destruction of country houses, the annual figure now fell slightly because there were now fewer to destroy! Certainly there were no added sanctions. In Hampshire, Cadlands, the seat of the Drummonds, bankers, was to go, a large eighteenth-century house largely by Capability Brown, Henry Holland and Jeffrey Wyattville, destroyed for the Fawley Oil Refinery. Also to go were the long semi-ruinous house, the immense Kippax Park in Yorkshire, plus Willesley Hall in Leicestershire, which had a fascinating frontage which I can imagine might well have been designed by a Leicestershire man and associate of Wren, Sir William Wilson. Also lost was the rather lumpish, substantial stucco house in Surrey called Denbies, built for himself in about 1830 by the architect and builder Thomas Cubitt, and belonging to his descendant, Lord Ashcombe.

A house that went in two stages was Teddesley Park in Staffordshire, a seat of the Lords Hatherton, a really big square lump of a house.

179

Seemingly designed by Charles Trubshaw for Sir Edward Littleton in the mid-eighteenth century, it had contained an important series of works by Michael Rysbrack. Its attendant wings, which looked as if they were sited the wrong way round, were to follow in 1961.

Coxhoe Hall, County Durham, was also lost. This was a rather delightful house built by John Burdon about 1750 with battlemented parapets and eighteenth-century alterations by James Paine. It was the birthplace of Elizabeth Barrett Browning and had some very attractive interior features, but the National Coal Board had let it fall into complete ruin after occupation by prisoners of war.

Streatlam Castle, also in County Durham, the seat like Gibside and Glamis of the Bowes Lyon family, finally disappeared from view that year, being blown up by the army as an exercise. The contents had been sold in 1922, the panelling and other decorative features in the meantime had been sold off, and the shell was left as a ruin. Only the entrance lodges, the bridge and a derelict orangery now remain. The architect of this extremely grand early eighteenth-century house was a very obscure man, Thomas Shirley.

Lee Priory at Ickham near Canterbury had passed through various hands until it was inherited by Thomas Barrett, who called in James Wyatt to rebuild it. This house, in the Gothic style, was highly praised by Horace Walpole, who called it 'a child of Strawberry'. Wyatt's work was largely swamped by alterations in 1860 by the new owner, Francis Phillips, who called in Sir Gilbert Scott to change the house. One of the Wyatt rooms is now in the Victoria and Albert Museum.

Pendarves, near Cambourne, in Cornwall, the seat of the family of that name, also went with the exception of a handsome range of Georgian stabling. A very large Georgian house, the chief feature of the property had been the beautiful grotto, embellished with brilliant crystals and gems which had been created in 1747.

There were even fewer losses in 1954, but Wales suffered with the loss of Llawrenny Castle, an immense Gothic pile in Pembrokeshire, and badly with Coldbrook House, a romantic house of medieval origin with four square towers and interesting Georgian features in the Palladian style. There was much of interest internally, with features of medieval date, a fine Jacobean oak chimneypiece that had come from Raglan Castle and lovely Georgian details, notably plaster reliefs over the internal doors of the entrance hall representing farming scenes. Two of these reliefs were taken to Clytha Park, one to Walnut Tree Farm at Llanthany Vach and one to Bryngwyn Manor near Raglan, but everything else was lost including the staircase with its toplit domed ceiling and halved mahogany doors with their original locks and handles. Coldbrook had been the home of the immensely rich and gay Sir Charles Hanbury Williams, who Dr Johnson disliked so much. Williams shot himself at the house on 12 November 1759, and the house descended through the Herbert family until the contents were sold up on the death of Lady Herbert in 1952. Another Welsh house to go in 1954 was the National Trust owned Dolaucothi, which had descended from the Lloyd Johnes family from Hafod and had been designed by John Nash.

Watnall Hall in Nottinghamshire was a Queen Anne house, formerly the seat of the Rollestons, with fine old stained-glass panels in the windows and wrought iron entrance gates by Huntingdon Shaw. It had been recommended for purchase by the nation by the Historic Buildings Council, but was instead allowed to be destroyed. Tong Castle, the ruins of a romantic eighteenth-century Gothic castle, probably from the designs of Thomas Farnolls Pritchard, the eccentric Shrewsbury architect, had been grafted onto an ancient ruin for the Durants and had been the birthplace of the famous Mrs Fitzherbert. Birch Hall in Essex was a fine but severe stone-built classical house designed by Thomas Hopper for the Round family, and Fremnells, in the same county, was a seventeenth-century house drowned for a water reservoir. In Cheshire, Marple Hall, a substantial seventeenth-century gabled and mullioned-windowed house, the home of the Bradshaw family, had been in parlous condition for years. In Herefordshire, Eywood was a rather mangled Georgian house that had been the home of the Harleys and had a Capability Brown park.

Kirkleatham Hall in Yorkshire was lost because the government of the day refused Redcar Council permission to purchase it for their use, and it was sold by auction for demolition in September. A large house, most of which was by John Carr of York, it was basically of seventeenth-century date, remodelled and completely changed internally. The ancestral seat of the Turner family, it had been lived in by them until 1948 by a direct descendant. Kirkleatham village was one of the most important and splendid complexes of eighteenth-century buildings in England, with a contemporary church (with a mausoleum added by James Gibbs), a hospital with a splendid chapel, the Old Hall, formerly the Free School of 1709, stables, gateway and cottages. Its loss was avoidable and a disgrace. Kirkleatham and its buildings were of national importance.

Apley Castle in Shropshire (so called because it occupied part of the site of a castle for which a licence to crenellate was granted in 1327), was a standard brick house with a pedimented Ionic portico built to the design of John Hiram Haycock of Shrewsbury in 1790. The owner then was St John Charlton, and the house was doubled in size in 1859 and turned back to front another loss.

Nearer London were two major losses. First Panshanger near Hertford, the seat of the Cowpers Lords Desborough, a Gothic style house designed by Humphrey and George Adey Repton and with a splendid gallery by John Nash. Panshanger was of some historical interest because of its political associations. The picture gallery had held one of the finest collections in Europe. Barn Elms at Roehampton, standing in a park and long used by the Ranelagh Club, also bit the dust. It had very pleasing elevations, quite a grand staircase and was historically interesting as the home of Jacob Tonson of the Kit Kat Club, who owned the portraits of the Kit Kat Club by Kneller, now in the National Portrait Gallery.

A shocking loss because it was an integral part of the unique village of mansions at Heath in Yorkshire, was the Elizabethan Heath Old Hall, a wonderful old house which had been slipping into ruin for many years. Its best feature was the great Tudor Jezebel chimneypiece, taken to Hazlewood Castle.

1954 also saw the last of Albyns at Stapleford Abbots in Essex, the former seat of the Abdy family. This big Jacobean house, basically a remodelling of an Elizabethan one, had been greatly despoiled by the sale of its fittings and panelling in 1926. A mere fragment, but occupied as a house, it survived its war damage until its ruins were cleared away.

Calehill at Little Chart in Kent was a great square George II house built for the owner Phillip Darell, with flanking wings each crowned by

Lost - The Grotto, Oatlands Park, Surrey

Lost - Lowther Castle, Cumberland

Lost - Hafod, Wales

Lost - Willingham Hall, Lincolnshire

Lost - Pit Place, Epsom, Surrey

© Surrey County Council

Lost - Hadlow Castle, Kent   © English Heritage N.M.R.

Lost - Garth , Welshpool, Wales   © D. MacCarthy, English Heritage N.M.R.

Lost - East Cowes Castle, Isle of Wight

Lost - Eaton Hall, Cheshire

Lost - Onslow, Shropshire

Lost - Euston Station,
The Great Gateway

Saved - The Shaftesbury theatre

© English Heritage N.M.R.

Saved - The Lyceum Theatre, Sheffield
© Peter Johnson, PMC Communications

Lost - Imperial Theatre, North Street, Brighton, East Sussex

clock towers. The interior had been done over on a number of occasions and for some reason stood without any main staircase. Only the Catholic chapel was retained.

Gogmagog Hills House in Cambridgeshire, closely associated with the history of horse racing and the family seat of the Earls of Godolphin went about now. It was the dwelling and burial place of the celebrated Godolphin Arabian. Only the handsome Georgian stables survive. The property was given by its last private owner, Terence Gray, to the Cambridge Preservation Trust and they pulled the house down!

Roundway Park, or New Park, in Wiltshire was also pulled down. A charming house largely by James Wyatt, it stood in a park by Humphrey Repton. Its site was wanted for a school by the local authority.

In 1955 I visited York and Wakefield but more importantly, I travelled with Cyril on the Aarlberg Express to Vienna, a city still occupied by Russian troops. We visited the Hofburg and Belvedere Places; the Kaisergruft (the burying place of the Hapsburg Kings); St Stephen's Cathedral, with its curious roof slates in coloured patterns; the Karlskirche, whose elaborate baroque façade included two 'Trajan' style columns; a performance of the *Count of Luxembourg* in the only available theatre, the Volks Oper, the opera house still being in ruins; and Sachers Hotel for supper and to taste the original Sacher torte in its proper setting – it is the finest of all chocolate gateaux.

From there we went to Villach to stay on the edge of the Wortersee for a few days and then on to Venice, Padua, the Palladian Villas and then home. It was at this time that Bedfont Lodge, Bedfont village's most important listed house, was left unoccupied. It was inspired by Asgill House at Richmond and was built for himself to his own design by the Prince Regent's miniature painter George Engleheart. Left empty and abandoned, it was ravaged by thieves and local boys, and demolished.

In 1955 the floodgates of country house destruction opened yet again, Wales suffering with the destruction of Harpton Court, Rhiwlas and Stackpole Court. Stackpole, in Pembrokeshire, was an immense house, the home of the Scottish Earls Cawdor and at one time a treasure house of pictures. Shropshire also suffered very badly with Alderley Hall and

183

Leaton Knolls going. Ousden Hall in Suffolk, Garboldisham Hall in Norfolk and Conington Castle in Huntingdon – the puzzling but I suspect largely Georgian seat of the Cottons, said to incorporate parts of Fotheringay Castle – all went. The Midlands was to lose several houses including Guilsborough Hall in Northamptonshire, and Egginton Hall in Derbyshire. This was a house by Samuel Wyatt (1792–93), William Baker and Benjamin Wyatt of about 1760 and the former seat of the Every family, baronets who had given up the house following the bankruptcy of Sir Oswald Every for £1,000,000 before the war. The house had since been damaged by wartime occupation and dry rot. It was a good house with a lovely bowed and domed entranced front but an utter wreck after wartime use.

Why did new town authorities have to think that their job was to create a new town and scrap everything else there? Fineshade Abbey was pulled down following a demolition sale in November. This was a very large house, named because it stood on the site of a priory of Black Canons, which in turn stood on the site of a castle pulled down in the reign of King John. For nearly two centuries it was the home of the Kirkham family. It changed hands in 1750 and was rebuilt by John Monckton, half brother of General Monckton, Wolfe's second in command at Quebec. It is tempting to think that the splendid dining room with its rich stucco and carved wood decorations could have been designed by James Paine, as he had worked for Monkton's brother at Serlby Hall. Only the handsome stables survived.

Another piece of local authority demolition was the destruction of Childwall Hall, Liverpool, a house built for Bamber Gascoyne to the designs of John Nash in the first decade of the nineteenth century. It had been given to Liverpool by the Marquess of Salisbury and was swept away to provide a site for a county college.

The greatest loss of that year was Bowood House, a magnificent mansion and home of the Marquess of Lansdowne. It was a splendid building by Henry Keene, with excellent alterations by Robert Adam of 1761. The demolition sale was in July 1955 and the decoration of the dining room was bought by the Corporation of Lloyds of London for their boardroom. Adam's Diocletian Wing survives and now serves as the main house, but this is no compensation for the loss of the 'Big House'. Its demolition, in spite of its great architectural interest, was never opposed by the Georgian Group at all and led to a very angry letter from James Lees-Milne to *The Times* in protest.

Sundorne Castle, near Shrewsbury was the seat of the Corbets, who built the house in the 1740s and who remodelled it in Gothic style in the early nineteenth century. It was an attractive house, and large, but had been given up as home by the Corbets as long ago as 1914. Requisitioned in the war, its end came that year.

Wiganthorpe Hall, which lay between York and Malton, was designed by John Carr of York for William Garforth, soon after he brought the estate in 1778. Rather simple externally, the house contained many fine and attractively decorated rooms with splendid mahogany doors, marble chimneypieces, decorative ceilings and a quite magnificent double staircase hall. The property of Mrs Emily Withers, who died in 1951, the contents were sold in 1953 and the house was available for purchase for about £2,000. There were no takers and the house was completely demolished.

Onslow (never apparently called Onslow Hall) in Shropshire was the seat of the Wingfield family. A complicated house of fifty odd rooms it seemed externally to be a great Greek revival house of the 1820s with a large and impressive pedimented Greek Doric portico, being the central feature of the remodelling of the house by Edward Haycock. But it also incorporated a very fine Adamesque dining room, surviving from alterations by George Steuart of Shrewsbury in the 1780s and there was a splendid sixteenth-century oak ceiling in the kitchen. Haycock's great staircase hall was particularly impressive.

Among other houses to go were Blake Hall in Yorkshire, Stella Hall, County Durham, Owlpen Park in Gloucestershire, Broxwood Court in Hampshire and Saltmarshe Castle in Herefordshire – the Gothic revival home of the Barneby family, which had its own specially built picture gallery.

Kenyon Peel Hall in Lancashire, the ancient seat of the Kenyons, was a gabled black and white, timber-framed E-shaped house which the family were prepared to give away, and which was nearly accepted by the Salvation Army. A report from Rentokil then discovered woodboring beetles with Latin names in the house, and this ended all hope.

Widey Court in Plymouth, in what Winston Churchill once told Lady

Astor was 'her blasted city' (which indeed it was), had been the headquarters of Charles I during the Civil War and from here he had demanded the surrender of the city. Still retaining Charles I's rooms, it had many features of Georgian date. A housing estate covers the site now. Poor old Plymouth.

Grizedale Hall, and Claughton Hall, both in Lancashire, also went, as did Fornham Hall just northwest of Bury St Edmunds in Suffolk. Built about 1760 for Sir Charles Egleton Kent, it was greatly remodelled in the 1770–80 period for Charles Kent to the designs of James Wyatt, and promptly sold to the then Duke of Norfolk in 1789. It changed hands on many occasions. The Wyatt part showed him at his most finicky, but it had a later overlay of 1860's Louise Seize decoration. A very large house indeed with much character, it was a considerable loss. The park later devastated was by Capability Brown.

Paultons Park in Hampshire was destroyed by its own family that year, it having been run unsuccessfully as a hotel for about nine years. There is now a zoo and pleasure park there. It was an extremely attractive early nineteenth-century house by John Kent of Southampton with fine furnishings.

In 1956, Fairford Park in Gloucestershire was destroyed, for which I could see no justification. This was a square, upstanding seventeenth-century house, variously said to have been built about 1650 or 1691 and heightened by an extra storey in 1730s. It was built originally by the Tracey family, who also built Fairford Church, famous for its stained-glass windows ... Fairford Park eventually became the centrepiece of marvellous ornamental gardens, designed and recorded for ever by Thomas Robbins. It had a good Doric-columned temple which went to Barnsley House, and a fine orangery with Coade stone details which was taken by the National Trust. The Soane-designed marble chimneypiece and some 1730s flock wallpaper were saved by me for the Victoria and Albert Museum, and Soane's staircase went to Corsham Court in Wiltshire.

Aramstone in Herefordshire was a striking looking house of about 1730, reminiscent of the architecture of Francis Smith of Warwick. It was demolished by its hereditary owners and a new house built. It was a perfectly lovely house of the period.

186

The precise date of the building of Cowick Hall is not certainly known to me but it was the seat of the Dawnay family since the Middle Ages. It seems to me that its architectural development was closely allied to the social advancement of the family from 1660 onwards with the Restoration of Charles II, and the advancement of Sir John Downe to the Viscountcy of Downe in 1681 and his two marriages in 1662 and secondly in 1663. It is not a typical Yorkshire house at all and is far more like one of those early classical houses in Kent with their giant orders of classical pilasters embracing each of the four elevations. It seems to me to be typical of the Charles II period, only slightly altered since then externally by James Paine in the 1760s and 70s. Cowick was threatened with demolition but was fortunately bought by a paint company for use as its headquarters and looks very fine set in its park.

Stoke Edith, the seat of the Foleys, was also pulled down in 1956, but it was just the unfinished reconstructed shell of the great house which had been burnt out in an enormous fire at Christmas 1927. The splendid Thornhill wall paintings all went in the fire and most of the contents but the walls were stabilised, rewindowed and reroofed, but it was never completed inside. Costs had escalated out of all reason.

Scrivelsby Court, near Horncastle in Lincolnshire was a very large and picturesque medieval timber-framed house and the home of the Dymoke family, Hereditary King's Champions and Standard Bearers of England. The house was pulled down after many years of dereliction, a new home being made in the medieval brick gatehouse. Fire destroyed the interior of the magnificent Highhead Castle in Cumberland. This was a grand Gibbs-style house built in the late 1730s by the amateur John Brougham for his nephew Henry. Built on the site of a medieval castle dating from 1342 of which only a little survived. The Georgian outside walls still remain.

Bure Homage in Hampshire was sufficiently curious as to make H.S. Goodhart Rendel describe it as 'bizarre'. It was built for a French noblewoman, the Baroness de Feuchères, in 1836 to the designs of John Davies and William John Donthorne. Warneford Park, also in Hampshire, had a number of curious follies and other buildings in its grounds and ceased to be in that year, along with Sarnesfield in Herefordshire, Culverden Castle in Kent and Gresford Lodge in Wales. Alkincoats Hall near Colne in Lancashire was an inexcusable council-inspired loss of a valuable and useable seventeenth-century house which had been passed to the council by the Parker family on condition that it be used as a museum. In fact it was used for refugees during the War and was totally neglected. It fell into poor, but remediable, repair. Sheepy Magna Hall was a good, simple house of about 1700 in the architecturally starved county of Leicestershire. Perdiswell Hall in the City of Worcester was a thoroughly decent eighteenth-century house which was ravaged by fire and then demolished. Also to go was Woodborough House near Radstock in Somerset, a large but rather muddly building with extensive Victorian alterations.

In 1957 I was placed on detached duty at Repton in Derbyshire, an ingenious Civil Service device for avoiding paying hotel and travelling expenses. One was simply expected to exist out of one's salary. One's job is very like that of a commercial traveller in that one has to use a car and stay overnight in the place where one is working. However, I cannot imagine that one would get many commercial travellers today to buy their own cars, travel between their homes and their places of work 125 miles or more away in their own time at their own expense, and pay their own hotel bills! Of course once one was working more than 45 miles from one's base and thus claiming hotel expenses, one was then moved on to, in my case, Barnard Castle, two hundred and fifty miles from home, on the same basis! But this was later and Repton was the place for the time being – looking back on it now I really ought to have resigned. I was just being exploited. This first year found me doing large chunks of Leicestershire, but I made private visits to Herriard Park, the home of the Jervoises and a large Queen Anne house designed by John James, where I lunched with my friend John Harris, and followed that with a tea-time visit to the Duke of Wellington at Stratfield Saye. Herriard has since been pulled down and Stratfield Saye has since long been open to the public. Other visits were to that marvellous, recently near ruinous Carr of York house, Basildon Park in Berkshire, so splendidly restored by Lord and Lady Iliffe, and to an evening party at St James's Palace graced by the Queen Mother to celebrate the eightieth birthday of the SPAB (Society for the Protection of Ancient Buildings).

One of the most serious losses during 1957 was Tendring Hall in

Suffolk, built by that very rare architect Sir John Soane for Sir Joshua Rowley between 1784 and 1786. It was rather plain externally but inside was a splendid staircase. Humphrey Repton, who visited it in 1791, hurried to record in his 'Red Book' of proposals for the park that 'neither its situation nor the outside of the building were suggested by me, on the contrary, had I been previously consulted the house would neither have been as lofty in its construction, nor so much exposed in situation'. So there! Tendring was demolished by the Rowley family. Assington Hall, also in Suffolk was destroyed by fire in August that year. It was a typical Tudor brick manor house.

Also to go was the immense Gothic-style seat of the Lowthers, Earls of Lonsdale, in Westmorland. Called Lowther Castle, it was built to the designs of Robert Smirke – his very first job at the age of 25 in 1804. The frontage was, and is for it stands now as a ruin, 450 feet long. It had had a whole series of Gothic state apartments, a very very grand Gothic staircase, a fine picture collection and a park of 600 acres laid out for the earlier house by Capability Brown.

In the County of Derby, the fire-damaged early eighteenth-century red brick house called Hopwell Hall (the seat formerly of the Pares family) went, and in Nottinghamshire the late eighteenth-century Oxton Hall, former seat of the Sherbrooke family, was demolished.

Forest Hall in Walthamstow, built for the Goring family (who also built the original house on the site of Buckingham Palace), had an extremely fine staircase of around 1690 and a room with a corner fireplace resembling those at Hampton Court – thus indicating a designer from the circle of Sir Christopher Wren and John Talman – was also lost.

Garnons in Herefordshire, one of many Nash castle-style houses was largely demolished leaving a still substantial part, while in Surrey there were two unforgivable losses, The Oaks at Woodmansterne near Carshalton, a house very largely by Robert Adam in his castle style but with a slightly earlier grand drawing room which had been attributed to Robert Taylor, and the enchanting Pitt Place at Epsom with lovely rooms, bits said to be from Oatlands Palace, and a pedimented conservatory made with cast-iron Greek Doric columns from Nash's Regent Street. It was a marvellous old house. Also reprehensible in the highest degree was the destruction of the Georgian house, Belvedere, at

Erith, designed by the Athenian Stuart in the 1770s for Sir Sampson Gideon, Lord Eardley, and retaining a magnificent gilded saloon of an earlier house by Isaac Ware. The house could so obviously have been converted into flats without any significant loss of architectural merit. It was destroyed by a charity, the Royal Alfred Institution.

One of the saddest losses, after an auction sale in September 1957 organised by the Oxford University Chest, was that of The Hoo at Kimpton in Hertfordshire, formerly a seat of the Brand family. This was a square house of the 1660s with a splendid staircase, the newels of which were crowned with pots of carved wood flowers. There were remarkable carved wood dado rails, skirtings and other features in all rooms as well as classical marble chimneypieces all of the same early date, with several more features added by Sir William Chambers a century later. The outside, however, one has to admit, had been spoiled in Victorian times by cement rendering and it looked rather like a very bad French town hall.

In June 1958 The Georgian Group went to Ramsbury Manor in Wiltshire, a lovely 1660s classical house now known to be by Robert Hooke. It had ceased to be the property of the Burdetts and had been restored by the Earl of Wilton and had just been sold to Lord Rootes, the motor manufacturer. Hawnes, or Haynes, in Bedfordshire was also visited, plus Wrest Park and Flitton church, with its tombs of the De Grey family, Dukes of Kent.

My holiday that year was a tour from Inverness, with my cousin Jeanne. Aberdeenshire was visited and then it was up to John O'Groats and across to the Orkneys from Scrabster by boat. The great surprise for me in the Orkneys was the splendid Norman cathedral at Kirkwall. Back at Scrabster we drove all along the north coast to Cape Wrath, and all down the west coast. The hell, among all this unspoiled beauty, was finding anywhere to stay at all, the area being almost totally unpopulated, with only small cottages scattered about. In one cottage we stayed in, the marmalade was full of dead bees! From there we went over to Skye, staying at Portree and visiting Dunvegan Castle. From Skye we went to Carlisle and thence to Blackpool, a marked, and invigorating, contrast to all the wonderful and desolate scenery of the previous weeks. We danced in the Tower Ballroom, the most splendid room of its kind in Britain, a *fin de siècle* masterpiece by the theatre architect Frank Matcham.

In May I was given the special job of reinvestigating the most important Cornish villages and fishing ports, changing an absurd situation of pedantic and individual listing into a meaningful exercise, redsigned to protect whole areas as groups. Unfortunately, the totally unspoiled harbour frontage at Mevagissey, then the only one which retained all its old buildings in Cornwall, has since been harmed by some rebuilding. I sneaked in a visit to Blisland church, so admired by Betjeman, at this time.

The work in Derbyshire and Leicestershire continued into the following year, many of Leicestershire's most beautiful villages coming my way there. In May the Georgian Group organised a marvellous week in Dublin during which time we visited both universities, the Mansion House, many individual houses, plus Powerscourt, a most marvellous house since destroyed by fire, with breathtaking gardens; Malahide Castle, since sold up; Birr Castle, the home of the Rosses, where we were all given lunch; and Phoenix Park in Dublin where we were all received by the President of Ireland.

In September I was back at work in Nottinghamshire, seeing some marvellous but little-known country houses: Bunny Hall, an extraordinary brick early eighteenth-century house built for the half-mad wrestling baronet, Sir Thomas Parkyns; Papplewick Hall, attributed to Robert Adam, but probably by a contemporary; Newstead Abbey, the medieval and later monastic establishment made into a house by the Lords Byron and with a very, very important Georgian park layout; Linby Hall; and Thrumpton Hall, with its splendid staircase of solid Carolean scrolled balustrading, which I only later discovered Woodborough Hall also had. Late seventeenth-century Annesley Hall, with is extraordinary mid-seventeenth-century iron railed staircase with brass ball finials, and panelling, and garden terraces was also particularly rewarding. Annesley was later burnt.

Later in the year there was a Georgian Group weekend to Liverpool where we saw the outsides only of Croxteth Park and other buildings, but also had a wonderful reception in the magnificent James Wyatt interior of the Town Hall, a building containing some of the finest Regency furniture and chandeliers in England. An extra trip, organised for a small, privileged few, was a visit to Ince Blundell Hall, with its wonderful picture collection and furnishings, and the Pantheon, with its unique collection of classical and neo-classical statuary, still just as it was in the eighteenth century. Lamentably, this important house was to have its collection dispersed, the Blundell family having bequeathed the estate to the Catholic Church, and all its contents have now gone.

Bulwell Hall in Nottinghamshire was lost, along with the romantic Hafod, way out in the country by Aberystwyth in Wales. What a house this was! It is described in *Wild Wales* by George Borrow: 'A truly fairy place, beautiful but fantastic, in the building of which three styles of architecture seemed to have been employed. At the southern end was a Gothic tower; at the northern end an Indian pagoda; the middle part of which had much the appearance of a Grecian villa. The walls were of resplendent whiteness, and the windows which were numerous shone with beautiful gilding.' Borrow's visit there must have been in the mid-nineteenth century. Hafod was an extremely pretty Gothic villa, the early work of Thomas Baldwin of Bath begun in 1786. It was altered by John Nash, who added an octagonal library in 1796. In 1807 it was burnt out and reconstructed to the designs of Baldwin, with several magnificent chimneypieces, doors and other fine items from Alderman Beckford's wonderful Fonthill Splendens in Wiltshire, then being pulled down for replacement by Fonthill Abbey. It was added to, to the designs of Antony Salvin, in the 1840s, when an enormous Belvedere tower and, most astonishingly for the date, a wing with an indoor circular swimming pool 20 feet in diameter were added. Hafod was a creation of the collector and bibliophile Thomas Johnes who died in straitened circumstances in 1833. The house, in its gorgeous setting, was then bought by the Fourth Duke of Newcastle who was in fear of his life from marauding mobs who had attacked and burnt his property, Nottingham Castle, and had marched on his country home at Clumber Park. Hafod was largely ruined in 1949–51, and the ruins were finally blown up by the Forestry Commission in August 1958.

Stubbers, a modest brick-built eighteenth-century seat in Essex, still retaining portraits of its owners let into the panelling in the entrance hall was also to go.

Burwell Park in Lincolnshire, a substantial red-brick pedimented country house, probably of mid-eighteenth-century date with lavish plasterwork inside, had had a chequered history and was latterly used for storing crops. It was demolished that year. Even the great staircase was completely destroyed, as was normal in demolition cases at the time.

Ashburnham Place in Sussex, which had been the home of the somewhat retiring family of Ashburnham, was an incredible house. Clearly resenting strangers, they had even refused Dr Waagen, director of the Gallery in Berlin, permission to visit, and Murray in his *Handbook* to Sussex written in 1877 remarked that it was impossible to get inside. In terms of contents and interest it was easily one of the great treasure houses of England. Everything about it was absolutely superb, in perfect condition and breathtaking in quality. I visited it twice: those lovely rooms with their panelled or painted walls with delightful eighteenth- and nineteenth-century wallpapers, the curtains, pictures, draped beds and dressing tables, Chinese armorial porcelain, Chelsea candlesticks, ormolu mounted commodes, carpets, lighting fittings, were all out of this world. It was inherited by the bigoted Protestant Rev. John Bickersteth from the Catholic Lady Catharine Ashburnham in 1953, who scattered its contents and pulled the house down in 1958, building a Christian centre there. He even refused to attend her funeral.

On the 8 September 1959 my parents went to an auction sale at the neighbouring Stanwell Place, where the assassinated King Feisal of Iraq had been living. He had bought the house while at school at Harrow. Stanwell Place still had marvellous stone gatepiers designed by James Gibbs in the 1750s for Governor Phillips, but the house was mostly dull Regency. It went later.

This year, found me back in Derbyshire and Nottinghamshire. I visited Carnfield Hall; the now demolished Alfreton Hall, a Francis Smith of Warwick house; Radburne Hall, a fine house by William Smith of Warwick; the then abandoned Winkburn Hall (since restored); and Ossington Hall, a hitherto unrecognised house by James Gibbs of 1729, but afterwards demolished. Ossington Hall was a handsome mansion, formerly the seat of a branch of the Cartwright family who built it in 1729. William Denison, a woollen merchant of Leeds, bought it and died in 1782 leaving a fortune of £700,000, a large part of which he had gained by one ship's cargo which had arrived at Lisbon immediately after that city had been destroyed by an earthquake. The church situated near the Hall is a lovely structure and was designed by John Carr of York and largely paid for by the Denisons. John Evelyn Denison was Speaker of the House of Commons and was raised to the peerage as Viscount Ossington by Queen Victoria. Lady Ossington, a great temperance reformer, built the Ossington Coffee Tavern in Newark, a remarkable building, to the designs of Sir Ernest George and Peto in 1882.

The architect of Ossington was James Gibbs and it was built in 1729 for George Cartwright, a subscriber to the first edition of *Gibbs Book of Architecture*. It is an unknown work by Gibbs but the house is a virtual copy of the exterior of Kelmarsh Hall in Northamptonshire which was built at the same time. There was a drawing, unsigned, but probably by him for one of the side elevations. The drawing room fireplace was reproduced as one of his designs in his *Book of Architecture* published in the year the house was built. Gibbs' building consisted of a pedimented main block joined by quadrants to matching hipped roofed wings but in 1784 John Carr of York was called in to add a drawing room (later, in about 1830, converted to a dining room) and to rebuild the church. In about 1838 a new drawing room on a grander scale and in the Louis XV style was added, the highly ornamental gilded ceiling being made from moulds previously used by Lord De Grey when rebuilding Wrest Park in Bedfordshire. In the 1830s a splendid set of red velvet curtains was provided for the great Carr drawing room on its conversion to a dining room and these I bought at the auction of the contents in 1960 and passed them on to the National Trust for their house called Spring Hill in Northern Ireland. In the sale among the lots sold were the family costumes, consisting of men's suits, many of very fine quality, of late eighteenth century date. Coats, breeches, waistcoats in paduasoy and taffeta, worsted, chenille, velvet, satin and brocade, besides hunting and military coats and boots were part of the collections. I bought many of these lots and they are now in Birmingham Museum. I also bought a wax portrait relief of Edward Denison the Bishop of Salisbury by Richard Cockle Lucas and after many years this is now in the collection of Tim Knox at his home.

194

The adjoining church, perhaps Carr's finest, contains two very good full length statues of William and Robert Denison by Nollekens.

Ossington Hall was completely demolished in 1962. I tried to get hold of the Gibbs chimneypiece illustrated in the *Book of Architecture* but was informed that it had been stolen from the house before the sale, and so I suppose it is irrevocably lost. Muskham Grange, also in Nottingham and again now demolished, had some very pretty late eighteenth-century interior features.

I spent a weekend in Norwich in September with the Georgian Group visiting Houghton Hall, Kimberley Hall, Cavick House at Wymondham, the Assembly Rooms in Norwich and various other places. In September and October I was back in Cornwall for the office, finishing off St Ives, Mevagissey, Kingsand, Cawsand, Charlestown, Cremyll, Gunnislake, Padstow, Mousehole, Polperro, St Germans, Quethiock, Sheviock, and other places. I finished off the year in Ault Hucknall, Tibshelf and Blackwell, Ollerton and Southwell in Nottinghamshire.

After 1958 there was not much left to destroy! However, Garnstone Castle, or Garnstone House, in Herefordshire, was very regrettable, being one of John Nash's castle-style mansions built for Samuel Peploe in the early 1800s; Paxton Hall in Huntingdonshire was a rather plain Georgian house; May Place in Kent was a Tudor House which had been the home of the ill-fated Admiral of the Fleet Sir Cloudesley Shovell, who lost both his ships and his life off the Isles of Scilly in 1707; Branches Park in Suffolk was a rather overblown and altered Georgian house; and Oteley Hall in Shropshire, that county that is so loaded with great houses, all went.

Brome Hall in Suffolk was also to go – anciently the seat of the Cornwallis family, it had originally been a large house built round three sides of a courtyard with a great hall, but was reduced in size when bought by the Kerrison family. Brome was the home of the celebrated, but defeated, general commanding the British forces in the American War of Independence. The house was requisitioned by the army in 1939 and never lived in again. The whole house including an alleged Tompion clock over the porch went.

The great house at Kippax Park in Yorkshire also went about now when the ruins were sold by the Bland Davidson family. With a frontage 600 feet long it was an eighteenth-century building of several different dates, largely by Daniel Garrett. The house had deteriorated steadily over the years since the sale of the contents way back in 1929.

Ragdale Old Hall in Leicestershire, the Dower House of the Shirleys to Staunton Harold, was basically a medieval timber-framed house of importance, and it had magnificent early seventeenth-century additions including great bay windows and a massive and lofty porch displaying the arms of the Shirleys with no fewer than fifty quarterings on it. Easily one of the most outstanding buildings in Leicestershire it was destroyed that year.

By 1959 most of Byram Park in Yorkshire had either been demolished or had collapsed. Much of it had been designed by John Carr of York for Sir John Ramsden, but Robert Adam had designed a library complete with carpet for it, a drawing room, breakfast room, and even a lamp and pedestal in 1780. There is still a charming Georgian orangery converted into a house, a Regency iron bridge over the lake, some quite interesting seventeenth-century gatepiers decorated with cartouches, and the Capability Brown park with its great lake. The great Adam marble chimneypiece from here is now at Muncaster Castle.

Shavington Hall near Market Drayton in Shropshire was pulled down that year by the Heywood Lonsdale family. It was a huge house, red brick and really rather plain, built for the then Earl of Kilmorey in 1685, the architect or builder being unknown. It had been bought from the Kilmoreys by the Heywood Lonsdales in the 1880s and they commissioned Norman Shaw to do a massive restoration, and the whole house bore the character more of Norman Shaw than anyone else, save for the original massive oak staircase. I attended the auction sale of the contents there.

12

Interlude: Visits to Erthig

In an account that must by necessity concentrate on the destruction and ruination of so many wonderful houses, it is nice to pause for a moment to consider a success story. It is the story of the mouldering house at Erthig near Wrexham in North Wales, which must be familiar to many people by now. Erthig was not an unknown house; it was written about and illustrated in *Country Life* many years ago. Its stunning early eighteenth-century furniture had been noted in many books. But now it was known to be in parlous condition, verging on dereliction caused by structural faults derived from coal mining operations beneath the house. The structure had split and cracked in many directions, rain was known to be coming through the roof, windows were broken and the gardens and grounds were completely abandoned and overgrown. I very much wanted to see it.

But it was July 1973 that was the memorable month. I went on a great tour with Gilbert Bradley to North Wales, and having been generously invited by Lord Anglesey to visit Plas Newydd we decided to stay in Beaumaris. His great house stands virtually on the shore of the Menai Straits and had been the home of the Pagets for a great many years. Now that their great Tudor house in Staffordshire, Beaudesert, had been given up and demolished, all the chief family treasures now remaining were gathered in the one house. Not then open to the public and seldom seen by anyone, it was marvellous to be given a personal tour. In the Museum I was allowed to touch two very special items – one, the wooden artificial leg made for Lord Uxbridge when he had his real leg shot off at Waterloo, and the actual trouser of his leg, still bloodstained and with the mud of Waterloo still on it. The Rex Whistler painted room is undoubtedly the finest room in this interesting house

197

and its collections are particularly noteworthy. Lord Anglesey then asked if there was any other house in Wales I might like to see? 'Oh! Erthig, of course,' I replied. And before anything else was done a phone call was put through by Henry Anglesey on his private switchboard, straight through to Philip Yorke at Erthig. We were on our way.

Lord Anglesey had told us that there were 35 gardeners and that they were allowed in the house – but he also explained that they were all sheep!

One knew of Erthig from old *Country Life* articles and from visits by various friends at various times. Stories of this extraordinary house, split in half by mining operations, its ceilings and roof falling in, the great treasures in its rooms and the totally untouched historical character of the interior were known well in artistic circles, as was the eccentricity and retiring nature of its occupants. Finding the house right on the edge of Wrexham, was in those days rather a problem, because one had to find one's way through a rather complicated pattern of humble Victorian housing to a road which ended in a thicket and a pile of rusted wrought iron, representing what had been the original main gates and driveway. The drive itself, potholed and practically derelict too, with fallen trees and branches, eventually led up to James Wyatt's rather boring ashlar faced main elevation. Entry was not through the front door but into the old servants' hall, then used as a kitchen as well, and where Philip Yorke and his fellow former actor and present friend, called variously Mr Heyhoe or Mr Houha, lived most of their time. We were welcomed a little warily – they clearly were nervous of strangers – but after a while conversation warmed up and refreshment – whisky at teatime – was offered. We were then taken on a tour through the ground floor rooms, in one of which, the saloon, I seem to remember telephone engineers were working and had part of the floor up. Perhaps we would like to stay for supper, or spend the night there? Both ideas filled me with foreboding if not actual fear, and craven soul that I am, I said that we very much wanted to explore Wrexham and see its great parish church, one of the marvels of Wales. But my friend Gilbert Bradley put a stop to my refusing a bed for the night and our immediate plans were settled.

Into Wrexham we went, saw the church, had a wretched meal and then arrived back at the house. Our hosts were still awaiting supper, a kipper each boiled in water on a Calor gas cooker in the servants' hall. As darkness fell and time sped by, we were given blackened eighteenth-century silver candlesticks with lighted candles in them, taken upstairs and shown our rooms. I was given the single sized Chippendale four poster in the Red Room, the bed curtains in ribbons, no carpet and with no bedding – a camper's sleeping bag being placed on it for me. That was for me – I was shown where the lavatory was along the corridor. Gilbert Bradley was given a great four poster bed placed then in what is now the West Room which has since been laid out as a children's nursery. My room had oak panelled walls, his had earlier panelling painted white and his bed was huge and with a great mound of feather-mattressing on it (it is now in another room). The burglar alarm system was considered quite sound, a lightweight table being placed in the corridor loaded with empty tins; any burglar entering the house would walk into the table upsetting all the tins and thus awakening the household. How I ever slept, I cannot imagine because I am a worried, restless, sleeper, and the candlelit room ought to have been peopled by ghosts. I slept like a log!

The following morning we were given breakfast and allowed to wander all over the house and grounds as we pleased. The state bed was not there – it had gone to the Victoria and Albert Museum for conservation and repair, and the Chinese wallpaper had fallen from the walls onto the floor. In the best rooms was stunning early eighteenth-century furniture, the whole contents untouched by loss or sale over the years. The kitchen quarters were not approachable, as the ceiling of the main kitchen had fallen in, and all the outbuildings, still with their contents, were in a near ruinous state. Of the gardens, only structural features like the long canal and Blashfields terracotta pots were intact, along with the more substantial trees. Everything else was overgrown or in ruins. We bade goodbye to Phillip Yorke, who was off to the National Coal Board offices in Wrexham on his motor bike, to argue his case about compensation for damage to the house.

I have been back to Erthig three times since the National Trust took over and it is just wonderful what has been achieved. Not only has all the structure been put in order, but all the furnishings as well. The restoration of the kitchen has been an eye-opener, but what is really totally unexpected is the restoration of the gardens. What was a desolate wilderness inhabited only by sheep has now been conserved and replanted, and one can now see the pleached lime hedges as never seen before in recent times. Even the garage, with its old cars and the old carriage houses and workshops for the estate craftsmen have been restored. The 1992 guidebook still gives one little notion of what it was like. I saw Phillip Yorke only once more, in 1978. He was in the garden, and dropped dead in Marchweil church the following day!

In 1992, when I was browsing among a whole pile of books for sale in Brighton, I found a copy of *Bradley on Gardening* published in 1732 and carrying the Georgian period Erthig bookplate. It was vastly over-expensive for me but I bought it at once and before I could look at it properly had sent it to Martin Drury at the Trust for return to the house. If it had not been for the bookplate one would not have known where it had come from; indeed I do not think that there was any record of it ever being there. But such is the case.

Oh! Beloved Erthig!

13

The Sixties

January 1960 found me in North Derbyshire investigating Barlborough, Whitwell, Ault Hucknall, Glapwell, and places nearby, but I went to spend a night with David Verey at the Cairn Hydro Hotel in Harrogate in Yorkshire. To my great surprise I was elected a Fellow of the Society of Antiquaries of London that very day. I had no warning at all.

I visited Somerly Park in Hampshire with the Georgian Group on 21 May – what a stunning collection of pictures Somerly has, and what a very grand house it is! In May I also installed a swimming pool in the old stable yard at the home in Bedfont, felling seven full-grown trees, erecting fencing all round, thoroughly repairing the stables themselves and having the ground resurfaced with gravel and stone paving. It looked very good indeed and was to provide great pleasure for the next twenty odd years. The Whitsun weekend was spent exploring Hastings and Rye, and I even managed to drive all the way up to Aylesbury from Hastings to see Nether Winchendon House.

September saw me on holiday in Devon, later returning to work in northern Derbyshire and Nottinghamshire. As December was reached I was moved up to Barnard Castle to start on Reeth, Grinton, Marrick, Arkengarthdale and nearby places. Barnard Castle was 250 miles from Bedfont and the whole journey had to be made in my own time and entirely at my own expense including hotels. There were no motorways then, and each journey took me two days. It seems it was a punishment.

Of houses, Huntroyde in Lancashire, the seat of the Starkie family at Whalley, was a very elegant late eighteenth-century house somewhat reminiscent of the work of Carr of York with elegant Adam-style features including an extremely handsome staircase, fine chimneypiece and mahogany doors. The Georgian house, and a Victorian wing were pulled down.

It was a bad year for houses and there were several losses. Walmsgate Hall in Lincolnshire went. The most remarkable feature of this largely Edwardian house was the chapel, and significant parts of it have been re-erected at Langworth, not terribly far away. Wiseton Hall, a plain workmanlike Georgian house and the seat of the Layock family, was replaced by an inferior Georgian-styled house for the same family. Other casualties were Aspenden Hall in Hertfordshire, a Georgian-style house whose drive was haunted by a fully occupied ancient Rolls-Royce; Alfreton Hall in Derbyshire, the seat of the Morewoods and designed by Francis Smith of Warwick in 1724–5, made unsafe by coal mining but with one of the most incredibly fine collections of silver in any country house I have ever seen; Brockenhurst Park, the seat of the Morants in Hampshire, with fine Georgian rooms and wonderful contents, particularly furniture; Stratton Park, near Biggleswade in Bedfordshire, a wreck of a house of various dates, spoiled outside and full of chickens, but with a fragment still of one of those scroll-panelled Stuart staircases; West Grinstead Park, another of those unappreciated but stunning castle houses by John Nash; and worst of all, John Nash's own home, East Cowes Castle on the Isle of Wight. It had been in hopeless condition for many years and a housing estate now covers the site. The list continues with Maiden Erlegh, an early eighteenth-century house, latterly the home of Woolfe Barnato, the diamond king; Tusmore Park in Oxfordshire, a very handsome Georgian house by Robert Mylne, built in the 1770s; Cuddesdon Palace, the mid-seventeenth-century home of the Bishops of Oxford (very possibly designed by Thomas Wood, the designer of the Old Ashmolean in Oxford) and dating from 1679 – having been empty for years it was conveniently damaged by fire and then pulled down; Horton Old Hall at Bradford in Yorkshire, one of those amazing substantial stone-built, gabled and mullioned windowed houses so typical of the seventeenth century in the north of England; and Elmley Castle in Worcestershire, an earlier house enriched by seventeenth- and eighteenth-century plasterwork which had been the seat of the Savage family. In Suffolk the magnificent Redgrave Hall, designed by Lancelot 'Capability Brown' for Rowland Holt, circa 1770, had been demolished in 1947, but the sixteenth century great hall of Sir Nicholas Bacon's huge house there had been preserved only to be bulldozed that year without any warning. The splendid park survives with its great lake, designed by Brown at the same time as the house.

Panton Hall in Lincolnshire originally built in the early eighteenth century to the designs of Nicholas Hawksmoor for Joseph Gace, and practically rebuilt to the design of John Carr of York for Edmond Turner in 1775, was also lost that year. However, many of the fine internal features, such as chimneypieces and doors had already been taken to another Carr house, Basildon Park in Berkshire for incorporation there.

By 1961 there was a very great easing off of destruction, but Harrold Hall in Bedfordshire, a rather chewed-up Tudor and Jacobean house with an extremely fine Elizabethan staircase was lost, although the staircase itself was taken to Bedford and erected in St John's House near the church of that name. Westbury Court in Gloucestershire a house of little interest went, but it stood, derelict, in immensely important late seventeenth-century water gardens, and these were threatened by an existing planning permission to build a new house within the gardens, which lasted for seven years until the permission expired. The National Trust eventually took over the gardens and restored them superbly. Rushbrooke Hall in Suffolk, an extremely attractive moated Elizabethan house with Georgian interiors was destroyed by the scientist, Third Lord Rothschild; Burleigh Hall in Leicestershire, a very romantic seventeenth- and eighteenth-century house with lovely features, fine staircase and attendant buildings, was destroyed by the future Loughborough University. Eaton Hall in Cheshire was the seat of the Duke of Westminster and still retained its late seventeenth-century core. It was largely the work of William Porden, in 1804–12, but was almost completely remodelled by Alfred Waterhouse in 1870 in magnificent style. I remember visiting it with the Victorian Society when it was being demolished, and a storm came on and the thunder roared and lightning flashed, and the rain fell in torrents through Porden's plaster vaulted ceilings. It was incredibly dramatic. It was a pity that the Duke of Wesminster could not keep the house, which was replaced by a concrete Modern Movement house, and has since been remodelled yet again. Syndale Park in Kent was an unrecognised very important house dating from the mid-seventeenth century and built in the classical style following Inigo Jones. It was damaged by fire and lost. The design was copied from Andrea Palladio. The Ministry's investigator had completely failed to recognise its date or its original design, in Palladio's *Quattro libre del archittura* of 1561. The interior had a little original panelling and an early eighteenth-century staircase.

Barnard Castle in Durham was 250 miles from home. Heavenly-looking in fine weather, it was famous for the severity of its winters and while Darlington, sixteen miles away, could be humid and wet, Barnard Castle could be submerged in deep snow with many of its roads impassable for cars. I started there in January 1961, staying at the Kings Head Hotel in the main street, and was the only person resident. In February I went up to Edinburgh for a week's research on my own, but in the meantime there was to be four months' further work in the Durham countryside, mostly remote hillsides, but sometimes places with resonant names like Scargill, Bowes (with the original Dotheboys Hall from Dickens' *Nicholas Nickleby*), Lartneton, Rokeby and Crackpot.

At Easter I took extra leave to help some friends and the curator at Dyrham Park, the former seat of the Blathwayts in Gloucestershire. This was a splendid seventeenth-century country house which had recently been taken over by the National Trust with government-purchased contents. The idea was to finish off the arrangement of porcelain, small pictures and other items, polish time-neglected furniture, blacklead and burnish grates, and generally prepare the house for opening on Good Friday. I particularly remember doing the large iron grate in the central hall, a Chippendale period cabriole gate-legged dining table, and helping to arrange some attractive Chinese porcelain vases which we collected from the kind Petos at Iford. Opening day was astonishing! Gilbert Bradley, Donald Smart, John Kenworthy-Brown, Nevill Coghill (later to become famous for his musical version of the *Canterbury Tales*), and I all placed ourselves on duty as guides, and when the doors opened something like 800 people came through in the first afternoon! Guided tours proved impossible and we stationed ourselves at strategic points, explaining the rooms we were in at the top of our voices, and in the drawing room we were compelled to take the ropes back and push the furniture away from the possibility of accidental damage. Easter Monday was the same. It was a rewarding and marvellous experience and taught me quite a few things that might be useful in the future. That year I went twice to Edinburgh to do research into Gibbs in the Earl of Mar's papers, and spent three weekends in Brighton.

On 27 May I went to see Clarence House, the home of the Queen Mother, with the Georgian Group.

The Georgian Group took us later that year to see Fort Belvedere, then the home of Gerald Lascelles and most famous as the home of the Prince of Wales as prince and as king up to the abdication in 1936. It is a 1740s mock castle, altered in the 1820s and much tarted up by the Prince. We also went to Hall Barn, the home of Lord Burnham, a strange classical house of 1651 greatly extended and beautified during the nineteenth century, principally (I would guess) to the designs of Charles Barry, about 1830. Since our visit it has been totally reconstructed, with all the nineteenth-century additions and all the splendid interiors destroyed and the contents sold. The garden still remains fine, with its canal and temples, but the approach through the park has been much damaged by the road cut through it.

In August my holiday was spent in Holland with Cyril, staying in Amsterdam and The Hague and visiting Delft, Haarlem and Schveningen. The preservation of historic buildings in Holland was clearly very very far in advance of anything we were achieving in England. One of the most beautiful buildings in Amsterdam, and one of the most moving emotionally I thought, was the Great Synagogue, a splendidly preserved building of about 1700, complete with all its furnishings and a superb collection of great Dutch brass chandeliers. The truly awful story of the annihilation of the Jews in Holland by the Nazis, and the killing of the entire congregation of this building is one I could never forget.

At the end of the month I visited Linton Park near Maidstone to view the sale of the contents of the great house there, the property of Olaf Hambro, and then went back to the winter slog in Durham.

January 1962 found me transferred to the City of York which was much better, with work involved in investigating parts of the East Riding. Escrick Park was visited, which had a grand mid-eighteenth-century staircase crowned by the remaining half of a splendid ornamental ceiling. I also went to Naburn Hall, the seat of the Palmes family since about 1200, Bell Hall in the same parish, a remarkably unspoilt house of about 1680, and the Georgian village of Heslington.

Weekend visits included one with the Georgian Group to Donnington Grove, a Georgian Gothic fantasy designed in 1763 by Horace Walpole's great friend John Chute and lived in by the interesting Mrs Daisy Fellowes. The house contained extraordinary things, including much Victorian embroidery decorated with parrots and macaws which excited one elderly Georgian lady exceedingly, each time declaring the bird to be a macaw until she actually found one that was. I remember Ian Grant, the honorary secretary of the Victorian Society being in absolute hysterics over the incident. Lord Tollemache's Helmingham Hall was where I remember one of the ladies' hats was blown into the moat. The best weekend ever was one with the Victorian Society based on Chester, where we saw many churches and houses designed by the Victorian Chester architect Douglas, who was responsible for so much of the imitation Tudor and Jacobean timber-framed building in the city.

Scores of Yorkshire villages were visited, along with Everingham Park; then a hotel and before its restoration by Francis Johnson so that Lady Herries could occupy it, the since rebuilt Garrowby Hall where Lord Halifax's dog attacked me and buried his teeth in the seat of my trousers before I could ring the doorbell, the Hall at Holme on Spalding Moor with its very interesting documented early eighteenth-century interior; Saltmarshe Hall, still lived in by the very last of the ancient Saltmarshe family, but in a pathetic state of privation; Hotham, the home of the Clitherows, who used to own Boston House at Brentford, which was a grand unknown house (since sold); and Londesborough where the famous architect Lord Burlington had lived, and where the house had long since gone but I found an orangery and a walled garden with ball-topped gatepiers surmounted by iron flags which had the appearance of having survived from Robert Hooke's garden works in the 1660s.

Casualties that year included Wilton Park, a secret services establishment during the war, and quite a handsome Georgian house; Darley Abbey in Derby, a good Georgian house owned by a philistine council; Mainsforth Hall in County Durham, the property of the Surtees family. Arley Castle in Worcestershire, designed by the little-known architect Richard Varden in 1843–4 for the Earl of Mountmorris, an immensely impressive 'castle' incorporating two seventeenth-century staircases from the earlier house; and Park House at Elmley Castle, the sixteenth-century home of the Savage family, whose great tombs are in the nearby church. The house had been the subject of considerable expenditure in the early eighteenth century and had very fine interior features of that era.

Early in February 1963 I was ill and away from work. In May, the Georgian Group went to David Style's repurchased and wonderfully furnished ancestral home, Wateringbury Place, a house of 1701 and situated in Kent. It was sold some years later by Christies, for over £4 million, at that time their biggest house sale ever. Work was still going on in Yorkshire: Howden, Wressle (with its castle); Cawood, with remains of an archiepiscopal palace; Camblesforth, with its fine and almost unknown Wren period hall, and Hatfield, with its astonishing Norman and later Royal manor house. In September, my detached duty ended, and I went to the Army and Navy Club in Pall Mall to view the contents, as practically all the original furnishings were being dispersed prior to demolition. I bought several lots there.

House losses that year included the fascinating seventeenth-century artisan mannerist-style house, Bloxholm Hall in Lincolnshire built for Septimus Cyprian Thornton. During occupation by the Manners family in Georgian times, it had added to it a giant coat of arms, motto and crest of the family, the crest itself being a giant peacock. It was one of the finest of Mrs Coade's greatest works in artificial stone.

Beaupre Hall lay at a point on the map where the boundaries of five countries are apt to become confused in one's mind. It was actually at Outwell near Wisbech in Cambridgeshire, but in the county of Norfolk! It was perhaps the last of the great mediaeval courtyard manor houses in the locality. The house remained much as it had been finished early in the sixteenth century, but it declined rapidly in status in the eighteenth and nineteenth centuries and fell into ruin. When pulled down an army of bungalows was already marching towards it.

Fire caused the loss of Lindridge in Devon. Evidently built for the merchant Sir Peter Lear in 1672, it had some stunning interiors including a great hall of that date. Completely burnt out, the exterior of 1916 was of no interest or merit.

Atherstone Hall in Warwickshire was the seat of the Bracebridge Holts, who were descended from the Holts of Aston Hall. It was a plainish Georgian stuccoed house but with two splendid rooms in it with extremely fine marble chimneypieces. That year saw its demise, as well as that of Blankney Hall in Lincolnshire, the ruins of which had survived from a great fire caused by the WRAF during the war. A very large stone-built house of about 1660 with a few Tudor bits, it had been greatly enlarged in Victorian times. It was the seat of the Chaplin family and had a very handsome pedimented stone entrance doorway of about 1660.

January 1964 found me back in the London office and there were to be fewer visits away. In May the Georgian Group visited Southill Park in Bedfordshire, with its magnificent furnishings, the home of the Whitbread family, and a few days later I went to a view of the auction of the contents of Patshull Hall near Wolverhampton, the seat of the Earls of Dartmouth, after they gave up living at Sandwell Park near West Bromwich because of the deterioration of the neighbourhood. Many fine pictures and items of furniture were to be dispersed. Patshull had for many years been partly occupied as a hospital.

The event of the year for me was the rearrangement of the inside of our house, Fawns Manor, including a dining room of my own, decorated with a red wallpaper copied from a Tudor box lining in the Victoria and Albert Museum. It had been produced by Coles to celebrate Shakespeare's quatercentenary. One of the sad visits of the year was to Manydown Park in Hampshire, a house of early origin completely remodelled in Georgian times with a particularly attractive and complete Adam-style ballroom with its original mirrors and console tables, danced in by Jane Austen who enjoyed a very brief period of engagement with a son of the house, Harrison Bigg Wither. The house had structural faults but it was a great pity that it was totally demolished. Being on the doorstep of the expanding town of Basingstoke its loss was quite unnecessary. The Ministry of Works gave it a damning report.

That year produced a field crop of architectural martyrs, including Markeaton Hall in Derby, a Georgian house and formerly the set of the Miller Mundys; Jordans at Ashill in Somerset, the home of John Hanning Speke the discoverer of the source of the Nile, pulled down by his family; Cothelstone House, a handsome classical building designed by C. Harcourt Masters for the Esdaile family in 1816–20 and also in Somerset, with a lovely landscape setting and a fine collection of old masters.

Elford Hall in Staffordshire, with a 600-acre estate was presented to the City of Birmingham in 1936 for the relaxation and enjoyment of the people by Mr F. Howard Paget. The house, a fine one built to the designs of Francis Smith of Warwick for the ninth Earl of Suffolk in 1733 had been neglected for years and this gave Birmingham an excuse to destroy it.

Garendon Hall, or Abbey, in Leicestershire was essentially a splendid early Georgian classical house grafted onto the remains of a Cistercian abbey founded in 1133. The architect was the talented amateur owner, Ambrose Phillips, who inherited the estate at the age of twenty-three and embellished it with a series of buildings of great originality, architectural importance and significance, chief of which were a triumphal arch based on the Arch of Titus in Rome, a round temple based on the Temple of Vesta in Rome and a lofty obelisk. He achieved all this before his early death at the age of thirty in 1737. What he did inside the house is not known, but it was certainly greatly altered about this time and a classical front added with a pedimented portico, but work was being carried out here to the designs of Joseph Sanderson as late as 1745. The house was flanked by quadrants of wrought-iron railings each having a copy of the celebrated pedimented gateway by Inigo Jones from Beaufort House in Chelsea. It was one of my most interesting finds ever. Curiously the Victorians had opened up the whole of the Georgian front block and made it into one colossal room and then added a mansard roof over the top, so a new house for the present day could very easily have been built inside the outer walls. Instead, it was destroyed and I hear the surviving parts of the monastic buildings went as well. An act of great vandalism. I could never bring myself to visit the place again.

In April 1965 there was a view of the sale of the contents of Herriard Park in Hampshire, where I had only comparatively recently had lunch. This was followed by the demolition of the John James of Greenwich house. Much of the furniture bought new for the house when it was built about 1700 had remained there and was sold.

In May Cyril and I flew to New York with the National Art Collections Fund visiting the Metropolitan Museum, the Pierpont Morgan Collection, the Grolier Club, The New York Museum, the Brooklyn Museum, the Guggenheim Collection, the City Hall, various churches, Philadelphia with the Society Hill Rehabilitation Quarter (on which I was to write an article for *Country Life*), the houses in Fairmont Park, Winterhur, Washington with the National Gallery, the Senate and House of Representatives on Capitol Hill, the White House, Georgetown with its old houses, Baltimore Museum and Art Gallery, Williamsburg, Richmond with its museum and art gallery, the Civil War Museum and other places. Looking back on it I think this visit to America was the most exciting and permanently rewarding thing I have ever done. The quality of the museums and galleries and their contents is unbelievable; of their painstaking restoration of old buildings there can only be the very highest praise. How I would love to go back to Williamsburg! And to think of my surprise that the church there, called Bruton Parish Church, was founded by the Page family of Bedfont, that some of them are buried there and others returned to Bedfont and lie in its churchyard under matching gravestones. The Sherborns and Pages had been close friends and neighbours for years!

In Lancashire the much decayed Rawtenstall Hall was to go. This was a seventeenth-century stone-built house now close to the bus station. After a fire, the romantic and important Cheshunt Great House in Hertfordshire, a medieval building with a great hall, an early eighteenth-century staircase and other features was needlessly swept away. Duntish Court (formerly called Castle Hill) in Dorset, built to the designs of Sir William Chambers about 1760 for the curiously-named Fitz Foy, who was buried in the adjacent church, had fine interiors but was lost in that year.

Not demolished but actually blown up was Bayons Manor at Tealby in Lincolnshire, built for the Tennyson D'Eyncourt family to the designs of an obscure Lincoln architect, William Addams Nicholson with some help from Antony Salvin. A huge mock medieval castellated manor house of great character, it was given up as a residence after the last war and had fallen into ruin.

Deepdene, near Dorking in Surrey, the home of the great collector Thomas Hope, went soon after the British Railways Board gave up the buildings as an office. An immense pile with a great tower, the estate had been bought in 1807 by Thomas Hope and was the subject of enormous expenditure from then on. It was here and in his house in Duchess Street that he formed his great collection of statuary and antiquities. Thomas Hope was Thorwaldsen's greatest patron, and his collection of ancient Greek vases was said to have numbered as many as a thousand! After Hope's death the house was further altered by his son, H.T. Hope, and the great stair hall and main entrance were entirely by him. The house had beautiful doors of blue lacquer and mahogany, inlaid with brass and stair balusters of solid bronze. Lord Francis Hope sold the contents in 1917, after the house had been lived in for twenty-one years by Lilian Price of New York, later the Duchess of Marlborough. One of the Hope treasures was the Hope Diamond, so dark in colour it resembled a sapphire, and weighing 444 carats. Lily Marlborough had a fierce dislike of many of the classical statues in the house and had a considerable number of the male nudes removed to the icehouse or to the furthest reaches of the park, refusing even distinguished scholars like Fürtwangler permission to visit and see the collections. After the Hope ownership ended in 1920, the house became for a while a hotel run by the notorious purveyor of peerages for Lloyd George, Maundy Gregory. No adequate photographic record of the interior of the house exists anywhere that I can discover.

My friendship and admiration for Rupert Gunnis lasted for the whole of his life, which sadly ended on 31 July 1965 while staying with his old friend, the Duke of Wellington, at Stratfieldsaye in Hampshire. He had not been very well for some time but it was a shock to discover that he had passed away. Memories of all those country house and church tours came flooding back. Never again would one have the thrill of making important artistic discoveries in the arts world in the company of such an expert on so many subjects. I would remember for ever the strange experience of climbing inside the dismantled organ case in a church in Devizes to check on the temporarily exposed monument behind it which was now revealed for the first time in a century!

Other Gunnis inspired trips down the years included visits to Stonyhurst in Lancashire to stay and to go through their papers and similar visits to Shugborough Hall in Staffordshire and Stoneleigh Abbey in Warwickshire. I was disappointed that I had not been remembered in Rupert's will but nothing could take away from me fond remembrances of all those interesting and exciting occasions during his lifetime. The funeral took place on 5 August 1965 at Chiddingstone Church in the shadow of his birthplace, Chiddingstone Castle.

The great event of October 1966 was the Council of Europe Conference held at Bath under the chairmanship of Anthony Greenwood, the Minister of Housing and Local Government, based on the City with its important Roman remains and magnificent Georgian squares and terraces. The meeting included visits to the magnificent eighteenth century landscape garden at Stourhead in Wiltshire and also the National Trust owned Lacock Abbey with its adjacent village where we were shown, among other things, the effect of the removal of overhead wires and cables from the village scene. Crowning the occasion socially was the banquet hosted by Anthony Greenwood in the Assembly Rooms in Bath, on Friday 7 October.

The year 1966 saw the loss of Wolseley Hall in Staffordshire, the home of the Wolseleys, a family almost as old as God himself. It was a pretty, Georgian Gothic house inherited by the baronet with the title when only ten years of age in 1954. It had been abandoned as a residence the very same year. It was chiefly notable for a magnificent late seventeenth-century staircase, made by the great carver Edward Pierce, which curiously had been removed from the earlier house there and stored in the stables until 1854. The limited remains of the staircase were bought by a Mr Reeves and taken to Tiverton in Devon, but very little survives. The panelling of the great drawing room, also by Pierce, was taken to Gawsworth Hall in Cheshire, but it was cut down and rearranged for re-erection and is no longer completely intact.

Very, very much regretted by me was the loss of Honingham Hall near Norwich, a splendid house built in 1605 by Sir Turner Richardson, Chief Justice to Charles I. It was a typical plastered Norfolk manor house of the date, built on an E-plan with mullioned windows and crowstepped gables. It became the property of the Townsends later and in 1737 Townsend called in William Kent to enlarge and alter the house and lay out the park. Townsend unfortunately died the following year and only the library was remodelled to Kent's design.

Osmaston Manor in Derbyshire, a vast nineteenth-century house, also went, the staircase being taken to the hitherto unspoilt and exquisite Wootton Lodge in Staffordshire, where the eighteenth-century staircase was destroyed to make room for it.

Silhill Hall, the ancient timber-framed manor house of Solihull in Warwickshire, already old at the time of the Battle of Crecy in 1346, was destroyed by Malcolm Ross, its owner, in March. Ross had bought the house as the site of a petrol station and claimed it had been blown down in a gale. Ross was fined the maximum sum of £100 with £84 costs. He must have laughed all the way to the bank. The law was almost immediately changed as a result. The house had been bought for £15,000 and the cleared site was worth four times that amount. The new Act, in 1968, repealed the two-tier system of listed building notices and building preservation orders and in effect applied building preservation orders to all listed buildings. Fines for contraventions would be calculated in connection with the supposed financial gain achieved in future. It made a very great difference indeed.

Sadness was a great feature of 1967, with the death of my great friend Cyril Plant in March so soon after our trip and the death of Rupert Gunnis. Visits to historic buildings included one to Elvaston Castle in Derbyshire where the local authority buyers wished to demolish the buildings. I like to think that my visit prevented this. It was later to form the setting of the film of D.H. Lawrence's *Women in Love* and has survived to become a valuable amenity for the area. There was also a visit to an old-fashioned grocers' shop called Mason's Stores at Dorking, which had lovely seventeenth-century brickwork, an extremely fine double-bowed Georgian shopfront and the remains of interesting Tudor or Jacobean wall paintings. The rebuilding scheme, necessary for this dilapidated structure, had been quite carefully designed to retain all the important architectural features.

In May I visited Bulford Manor in Wiltshire, a lovely old chequerboard gabled stone and flint house which the army thought that they would demolish. I gather that it was saved.

On 12 June, I went up to Edinburgh, having been chosen by Sir Mortimer Wheeler as the guide for Swanns Hellenic Tours trip around Scotland's historic houses and castles. I rushed around to meet the National Trust and tour representatives and to find tourist leaflets, clan and tartan leaflets, leaflets about Mary Queen of Scots, information about the imaginary boundaries between the Lowlands and Highlands and a crate of champagne and glasses. I gathered my flock of Americans and others in the hotel, made a welcoming speech, filled them up with champagne and was then floored by an American who asked me how Scotland got its name! I had not thought of that one and hoped that the questions in the next ten days would be confined to the architecture, history and contents of the buildings we were to see. Things I knew about. It was a marvellous trip, touching Edinburgh only briefly, but taking us to Mellerstain, Hopetoun, Abbotsford, over to the Isle of Bute to see the marvellous Mount Stewart, to Brodick Castle on the Isle of Arran, and to Inverary Castle (since very badly damaged by fire).

On 18 November a great fire broke out at Dunsland House in Devon, which completely burned the place out, leading to demolition of the walls. A lovely old house, formerly the seat of the Arscotts, it had been acquired for preservation by the architect Philip Tilden, who bought it from the timber merchant who had acquired the estate after the war. A basically medieval house, with a classical William and Mary block, it had hardly been altered at all. It was rich in panelling, fine plasterwork and other features and had been beautifully restored and furnished by its new owners, the National Trust. Rumours in Plymouth suggested that the fire was caused by burglars because a piece of the Chinese tobacco leaf service borrowed from Saltram and taken to Dunsland, had been seen for sale, but the mystery has never been solved. Indeed a very sad loss.

The supply of houses for destruction was now truly drying up, but the immensely important betowered Italianate Mount Felix (formerly

214

Walton House) at Walton on Thames, built to the designs of Charles Barry for the Fifth Earl of Tankerville, went following a fire. Its riverside setting had already been wrecked by new buildings right in front of it. Tyneham in Dorset, a medieval and Tudor house, was wrecked by being in a battle practice zone, and Swinburne Castle in Northumberland, a splendid Georgian Classical house probably designed by William Newton of Newcastle in the late eighteenth century, also went.

Willingham House, or Willingham Hall, or North Willingham Hall, to give it three names, in Lincolnshire, had been built in 1790 after the marriage the previous year of Ayscoghe Boucherett with Emily Crockatt, the heiress daughter of the owner of Luxborough Hall in Essex. The house has been attributed to the little known but able Robert Mitchell and with its grand portico was very impressive indeed. The Boucheretts were French and great patrons of Sir Thomas Lawrence, who stayed there many times. The interior was elegant and very much in the Wyatt style. The main staircase, of mid-eighteenth-century date, which had come from their previous house at Stallingborough, went from there to a house near Glasgow. The demolition sale was in May.

By far the worst loss of the year 1967 was the great propylaeum archway entrance to Euston Station, designed by Philip Hardwick and built in 1846. Easily one of the greatest examples of Greek revival architecture in these islands, its classical columns of the Greek Doric style were the tallest of any building in London at the time. The site of the archway was threatened by a scheme for the redevelopment of the underground station nearby. The Pynford Construction Company offered to move the archway bodily on wheels for a short distance that would permit the development to go ahead for £13,000, while the demolition contractor, Mr Valori, so much disliked destroying the portico that he offered to number the stones and re-erect them at his own expense on a site chosen by British Railways. The offer was refused and so Mr Valori had a solid silver model made of the arch and presented it to the Victorian Society.

The protests of the Royal Fine Art Commission and the Greater London Council were to no avail. Harold Macmillan who was then Minister saw to that. The fractured stones were then thrown into a derelict canal.

In 1968, fire almost completely destroyed the barrack-like eighteenth century Shortgrove in Essex, only the stables, which were far more handsome being saved. Pentillie Castle, a Gothic fantasy by William Wilkins, built for J.T. Coryton in about 1810 was pulled down except for one side of the quadrangle which was of an earlier date. The stucco rendering had proved to be a disaster, but the contents were still fine.

In Kent, following the sale of the contents of Sutton Place at Sutton, which I had viewed, the house was demolished. Quite a large house, it had been made a lot grander by Sir John Lethieullier when he bought the estate in 1699. It had a very grand staircase of original date.

In 1969, Hall Barn and Charborough Park were visited for the office and there were June and July holidays in the West Country for me. An annoying incident was in July when someone got into the swimming pool courtyard at home and threw all the furniture – cast-iron seats, lampposts, deckchairs, tables, sun umbrella, stoneware barrels, marble busts and heavy iron rollers – into the pool itself. It was an extraordinary sight to see.

The curiously named Hall Barn, the former home of the Waller family set in magnificent eighteenth-century parkland, was a substantial and rare mid-seventeenth-century house of unknown but stylish authorship. It was then owned by Lord Burnham, the proprietor of the *Daily Telegraph*, and he reduced the house by half and in the process the state rooms and main staircase, all I guess designed by Charles Barry, it was in Barry's style and the owner was a leading member of the Traveller's Club. The contents, which were very fine indeed, also went.

Hill Hall in Essex, a very important Elizabethan courtyard house in brick with classical details, built by Sir Thomas Smythe Secretary of State to Edward VI and Queen Elizabeth, was largely burned out in 1969. It contained what was for England a very remarkable series of wall paintings. In use as a women's prison, it caught fire on 19 April and was almost destroyed except for the brick outer walls which were all saved.

Marbury Hall in Cheshire also disappeared in 1969. Formerly the seat of the Smith Barry family, the house was almost certainly the

'Aston Park' recorded as having been the work of the architect James Gibbs, and it had internal features and plasterwork reminiscent of his style and period. However, it was greatly altered to the designs of Antony Salvin in the 1870s 'somewhat in the character of Fontainbleau'. The house was the property of Imperial Chemical Industries who locked it up and abandoned it to its fate. There was no alternative to demolition as it had fallen into such a dreadful state.

The most alarming threat to a historic place in 1960s concerned the medieval abbey town of Tewkesbury in Gloucestershire. Before the War a range of houses backing onto the Norman Abbey had been bought by an organisation calling itself The Abbey Lawn Trust with the idea of clearing away a collection of almost derelict and slummy property in order to expose views of the Abbey from Church Street itself. Nothing had been done and by 1965 a formal application was actually made to demolish the buildings. Very few people suspected that they were fifteenth century houses of a very rare character incorporating shops and workshops which had probably been built under the auspices of the Abbey itself. Clearly this scheme could not possibly be allowed and eventually, through opposition, the proposals were turned right around and the buildings repaired and saved. Personally I would not have taken the restoration quite as far as it has been and I would certainly have wished to retain some at least of the Georgian external panelled window shutters with their windows. But the houses do make a most valuable contribution to the street scene in this beautiful ancient town and are now safe.

14

The Seventies

Goldingtonbury in Bedfordshire was to go during 1970, along with Turville Park in Buckinghamshire, but there were also two major losses.

One was Old Palace House, in Theobalds Park, Hertfordshire, which was half of one side of the double-courtyarded Theobalds Palace. Sir John Summerson had already demonstrated that the existing house occupied the site, but he had never penetrated the interior. Sure, all the original decoration had gone but there were the floors, walls and roof of the original palace of James I, and here James had died in 1625. The property of Cheshunt Urban District Council, it was quite neglected but could easily have been sold to a sympathetic buyer. My report on the house was ignored and an agreement was made between Antony Dale and Andrew Saunders of the Ancient Monuments Inspectorate that it could be picked to pieces to see what was there. But tragedy overtook foolishness and house was torched by vandals in July. It need never have gone.

The other was Highcliffe Castle, a magical house near Christchurch in the Gothic style and designed by J.B. Donthorne for the first Lord Stuart de Rothesay between 1833 and 1834. It incorporated genuine medieval features from the Grand Maison des Andelys, in France, but was left derelict, burnt, and left again as a ruin. Preserved with its superb contents it was a stunning place with its magnificent rooms. Work has now been done to restore the ruins, hardly a full answer to a problem which should never have been.

In 1970 my father had collapsed and remained gravely ill throughout that year. By 1971 he had made little progress, and died on 9 January. It was a sad occasion but my mother bore it well and there were quite a few of our relatives and friends still alive who could come to the funeral.

In Plymouth that year I had a nasty accident carrying a suitcase and was taken to hospital, having slipped discs and torn ligaments in my back. I was not back at the office until 20 September in spite of constant criticism and abuse from the head of my office, now Antony Dale. I had known Antony Dale since 1948 and we were both original members of the staff. He had succeeded S. J. Garton on his retirement and had been Chief Investigator for some time. He was in full charge of the Conference in Bath in 1966. In December I visited Clarendon Park in Wiltshire where there was a proposal to demolish the handsome early eighteenth-century house there, the stables having been converted into a new house.

The Rocks at Marshfield in Gloucestershire, an amazing Gothic-style house looking more like a castle and incorporating medieval parts, was very largely ruined and just abandoned, although I understand that parts have since been saved. Woodbastwick Hall in Norfolk, the overblown and largely Victorian and Edwardian seat of the Cators, went, and fire destroyed Easthorpe Hall in Yorkshire.

In 1972 there was a miner's strike throughout February, and three-hour power cuts were frequent, but it all ended on 2 March. Mother was very nervous all the time.

In August, an old friend brought an old acquaintance of his, Bob Henry, to Fawns to meet me. Bob was staying as his guest in the house he rented in Dorset Square, Marylebone. But Bob was in fact a great villain, returning to Fawns in the early hours of 27 August and stealing a friend's car from the drive. He then drove to Chertsey and entered another friend's home with the keys found inside the car. He was back later that night, smashing open the door of our kitchen and three days later, with an accomplice, he attacked me with a three-foot iron bar in the garage, intending to do me in, open the door of the house and presumably then beat up my mother, who by then was seventy-nine. Fortunately I was able to grab the iron bar and drive both men off. The police, if they did anything about the incident at Bedfont, never told me anything about it and I think actually they did nothing at all. I knew the man; he had been brought to the house. He had not, as he said, been at sea for eleven years, but in various prisons.

In September, my mother was being cared for by a visiting sister, and I went on a great holiday tour of Lincolnshire, Nottinghamshire, Yorkshire, Durham, Northumberland, Lancashire and Warwickshire, looking at country houses and churches, and in December did another tour around Ross-on-Wye with Peter Reid as my guest. The year was to end with a Christmas carol service at Feltham Borstal.

The Grange, or Grange Park, in Hampshire was also to suffer from major demolition that year. It had passed through various families, but had been mainly built in the years following 1662 for Sir Robert Henley, to the designs of William Samwell, a contemporary of Wren's and a designer of considerable originality. Internally the domed upper corridors were fine but the house was chiefly notable for its early nineteenth-century Greek Revival exterior by Wilkins and C.R. Cockerell. The house had a most tempestuous history of ownership, passing to the Drummond family, then to the Barings, and was eventually bought by W.L.C. Wallach with the express intention of furnishing it with treasures and giving it to the nation, and he enlisted the help of the late Queen Mary. He died at the age of 93 in 1964 and I had actually visited him at the house. Nothing came of his gift – all the contents were sold and the estate was bought back by the Barings, who proceeded to start demolition work, though the shell was saved as an ancient monument – hardly an adequate alternative to an exceptionally important house fully furnished with art treasures.

Witley Court was taken into guardianship that year. This was a marvellous ruin of a great classical house, built over the site of a medieval and Jacobean one. The ruins of the great nineteenth-century building included spectacular gardens with great fountains. The adjacent church has a wonderful baroque design by James Gibbs with features brought in from the great house of the Duke of Chandos, Canons at Edgware.

Dingley Hall in Northamptonshire was ruined at about that time. This was an extraordinary house, with parts dating from about 1550, with a great range added to the designs of Hugh May in the 1670s and 1680s. The work of the 1550s is an amazing architectural

220

feast. The house, derelict for so many years, has since then been restored as flats by the architect Kit Martin.

Welton Place, also in Northamptonshire, which might have received some attention from James Gibbs, as the Clarke family were subscribers to his *Book of Architecture*, was also to go, as was Whittlebury Lodge in the same county, an immense pile built in 1865 for the then Lord Southampton to the designs of William Burn.

Blyth Hall in Nottinghamshire was a four-square towered building built in 1684–5, possibly to the designs of William Talman, and greatly altered by John Carr of York in the 1770s. It possessed a fine staircase ceiling almost certainly by Edward Gouge and once had a garden laid out by George London. It had been greatly despoiled by the sale of its fine internal features in 1930.

Hints Hall in Staffordshire was a house of seventeenth-century date, burnt out with loss of life in the 1790s and redone in late Adam style: It was also demolished in that year, and was probably the original home of the Derbyshire alabaster columned chimneypiece which now lives in the drawing room of my Brighton home.

Of the losses in 1973 the most serious was the destruction of Workington Hall in Cumberland, save for its medieval parts. The seat of the Christian Curwen family, it was chiefly famous as the refuge of Mary Queen of Scots after the disastrous events of 1568. She arrived there in a rowing boat, destitute of money with only the clothes she was wearing. She remained until she was taken to Carlisle Castle with dwindling chances of freedom, and thence to Fotheringhay in Northamptonshire where she was beheaded, nineteen years later. A fair amount of this house survived but the chief parts of the house with its grand apartments was designed by John Carr of York in 1793. Occupied by soldiers in the War, thieves then stole the lead from the roof and the family gave it to Workington Council for use as a town hall. They did nothing at all to maintain it, and it ended up being largely pulled down except for the earlier parts.

On 23 February 1974 I received a visit from Christopher Wall, who said nothing, and Bobby Gore, who said too much. Both were from the National Trust. I had written to the Trust some months before, and had been entertained to lunch by Robin Fedden at the St James's Club. I was offering them the entire contents of Fawns, and if they wished they could have the house as well. The visit was to inspect the house, and Bobby Gore's opening remark was that if I was to leave the Trust anything in my will, they would sell everything. The room in which this remark was made contained pictures by Gainsborough, Lawrence, Wright of Derby, Lely, Romney, Brooking, Towne, Daniel Gardner and Hans Eworth; furniture of Chippendale period onwards; and fine ormolu candelabra and a chandelier. There was no curiosity to see the remainder of the house, but I dragged them round it and at the end said to them, 'Are you turning down a bequest of about a million pounds then?' To which the reply was yes (as if it was the cleverest thing anyone had ever said). I slammed the door behind them as they left. It was quite clear to me that the Trust's advisers in those days must have been turning down properties and treasures for years in a similar way, and one could probably blame them for many of the losses of historic houses or their contents, just through being tactless and thoughtless. Of course, a letter of apology was sent to me but I thought the incident a howling disgrace.

In April I had a short holiday in the West Country, visiting Yatton Keynell Manor, Draycot Park (where the demolished seat of the Cowleys used to be) Bristol, Sudeley Castle (which I liked outside but thought the interior rather disappointing), and Clearwell Castle in the Forest of Dean. Here, a hard-working local family had rescued an extraordinary Gothic house which subsequently turned out to have been designed by Roger Morris in 1728 and was thus the earliest Gothic Revival castle in England. People had failed to see its great importance.

I also visited Crowcombe Court, owned by a property speculator called Gassy Harris, a wonderful house of 1734 designed by Nathaniel Ireson, the Wincanton potter, architect and builder. It had the most gorgeous rooms and decoration, but had been fire damaged and the splendid heraldic plaster ceiling over the stairs had gone. It seemed to be full of gas cookers and refrigerators stored for subsequent use in flats in Minehead, but was otherwise almost wholly empty. The unique painted dining-room floor was covered with cookers and the smoke from the fire had blackened the eighteenth-century flock paper in a closet upstairs, but the secret staircase enabling the master to visit a servant's room above was still there, and the essential features of all the main rooms were well preserved. The house had been the home of the Trollope-Bellew family, who still lived locally. From there we went and had tea with the Starkie-le Gendres at Gaulden Manor, with its marvellous Elizabethan plasterwork. Also visited was Dunster Castle, a remarkable late seventeenth century house splendidly sited in a park, and Hatch Court, a 1755 house with corner towers, designed by Thomas Prowse, whose only surviving original internal feature was a very remarkable china closet; otherwise the house inside is early nineteenth century and later. I have a portrait by Gainsborough of its architect Thomas Prowse in my collection. The site of Jordans the home of John Hanning Speke, the discoverer, in 1862, of the source of the Nile, was not far off; Plymouth much further. Here I saw the ruins of Boringdon House, the cradle of the Parker family before they became very grand and moved to Saltram and which after various disasters is now a hotel. Chambercombe Manor, which I rather forget, was also seen.

In May I went to see Burderop Park near Swindon, an early eighteenth-century house, containing a marvellous painted decorated Elizabethan oak four-poster bed, which after the contents had all been sold up was found to belong with the elaborately painted walls discovered when building workers began to make the place into offices. From Raglan and Clytha Castles – one medieval and the other a Georgian folly of high quality – to Hay, with its array of antiquarian bookshops, and then on to stay in beautiful Tenby, one of the most enchanting of all British seaside resorts. The siting and the architecture quite lovely.

The site of Stackpole Court, the great palace-home in Wales of the Scots Cawdors, was next, then Angle with its curious castle and church with a detached memorial chapel or mausoleum with an effigy of a medieval Sherborn who had lived in the Castle. The site of the Victorian Lawrenny Castle then recently demolished, Abermarlais and the dangerously ruinous Aberglasney followed.

On 31 March 1974 I went to Steeple Aston Manor, Milton Manor near Abingdon (for the umpteenth time), Studley Priory (a hotel for lunch),

Greys Court and Rotherfield Greys Church. On 5 April the London Appreciation Society visited Fawns and in May I was off again looking at country houses. This time the base was the Three Crowns at Chagford, and the places seen were Knightshayes, Castle Drogo, Fardol Manor, Cullompton church, Kingsteignton church and the Regency cottage orné built for Dr Thomas Whipham in 1816 by John Rendel and called Vicar's Hill. I also saw lovely Trewithen, a charming Georgian house in a charming setting, St Neot Church with its splendid medieval glass, Pencarrow, the home of the Molesworth-St Aubyns, with a lovely park and Ipplepen church with its splendid carved screen. I made a flying visit to the Scillies. On 17 May I was interviewed by Barry Norman on BBC Television for the Ministry in a programme called *Going Places*.

In June I went to lunch with the Munthes at their Wimbledon home, Southside House. Their house was stuffed full of amazing treasures, largely inherited from Lord Wharton. In July I went to a great party given by Geoffrey Villis and Colin Rock at 40 Belgrave Square, lent to them by the Galliers Pratts, the owners of that wonderful Shropshire house, Mawley Hall, which is so beautiful inside, with its gorgeous plasterwork and woodwork. (Incidentally it had been bought by a Conservative MP, John Talbot, for demolition.) How could *anyone* have thought of destroying it?

Other places I saw that year were the site of Kilnwick; the outside of Brantinghamthorpe, bought from the Sykes's by Sir John Sherburn; the site of Willingham Hall; Walpole St Peter Church; West Walton Church; Felbrigg Hall; Shernborne church, where the Norfolk Shernbornes are buried; Holkham Hall, William Kent's wonderful house for the Cokes, Earls of Leicester; Castle Rising Castle and priory; and Oxburgh Hall, a rather sombre but important medieval, moated brick house and the home of the Bedingfields.

I also made time to visit Hunstanton Hall, the home of the Le Stranges; Castle Acre; Framlingham Church with its tombs; Glemham Hall; the marvellously untouched and unspoiled church at Dennington, where I found that one John Sherborne had been rector in 1599; Somerleyton, a rather overrated Victorian house built by the Crossleys, the carpet manufacturers; Sotterley Hall near Beccles at the kind invitation of the owner; Honingham Hall, where the owner had destroyed the handsome and interesting William Kent and Jacobean house on the promise that he would restore the more important stables as a house, but had not done so; the site of Boyland Hall; Morningthorpe Church where the Irbys were buried; Southwold Church; Christchurch Park at Ipswich; Bungay; Beccles; the Tattingstone Wonder, a block of Georgian cottages disguised on the side visible from Tattingstone Place as a complete church with a battlemented tower as a feature of the view; and Flatford Mill.

On 6 December a car crashed through the boundary fence to the garden in Bedfont Road, and six days later another car crashed into the garden wall further down the road and demolished that. Was this an omen of some kind?

The previous year having gone out with two bangs, 1976 started with me buying a large quantity of fruit trees and flowers from the Syon House garden centre. On Good Friday I visited Blenheim and Chicheley and, on Easter Monday, Lullingstone Castle, sadly depleted of many of its best things, and Leeds Castle, which looks marvellous in its moated setting, but the interior, which was like a 1930s Hollywood film set, seemed to me almost horrible.

In May I went to Weston Park in Staffordshire, Brewood (with its extraordinary Georgian Gothic Speedwell Castle), Heaton Park, Tatton Park (with its splendid contents and interiors), the early Ordsall Hall, Wythenshawe Hall (a greatly restored and rebuilt early timbered house), Lotherton Hall near Leeds, Temple Newsam, Chatsworth and Holme Pierrepont Hall, a curious very early red-brick house with a very elaborate carved and scrolled balustraded Stuart staircase.

In June I went to Greece and Crete taking with me Peter Hone, visiting all the expected archaeological sites, staying in wretched hotels and 'enjoying' horrid beaches. The one thing I did not really expect to see were stone memorial slabs of seventeenth-century date with scrolled cartouches and angels' faces, just like the gravestones we get in Cotswold churchyards. These were in the museum at Heraklion in Crete. I loved the temples and monuments and scenery, of course, and the gorgeous vases and statues to be found in the museums.

In August another trip took me to Lacock with its village and Abbey, Dorchester; Kingston Maurward Old Manor House, now restored from dereliction in the face of fierce unhelpfulness from Dorset County Council; Wolveton House near Dorchester, Dorset with its weird stone staircase; Forde Abbey; Shute Barton and Shute House, Cadhay; Combe House at Gittisham; Godolphin again; Trelowarren, now almost bare of contents; Youlston Park, locked up and abandoned but advertised as open to the public daily; Portledge, a hotel but still containing Pine-Coffin family items including a remarkable collection of eighteenth-century tiles; Dunster Castle again; and Crowcombe church.

1976 was a year for promotions and retirements and a general shake-up in office affairs. Antony Dale retired and I was promoted to Principal Investigator of Historic Buildings. On 13 December we had burglars in the middle of the night. Would they never leave us alone?

On 2 January 1977 the West Bromwich Civic Pride Association came to see the house. It was a long way for them to come, and in particularly severe weather, but it worked out well. It was quite a dramatic year with a car crash for me in February, and a number of deaths, including my father's brother, Uncle Leslie, who died in May at the age of eighty-two, after years as a widower on his own and in failing health.

My mother's health had been deteriorating for years, and early signs of senile dementia had been replaced for some time now by a permanent and serious condition. Fears that a fire or explosion could be started by her at any time, or that when alone when I was at the office she might be the object of an attack by an intruder, were with me all the time, and whenever I was out in the evening, or needed to go away on holiday or on duty, arrangements had to be made for someone to be there with her or to call in to see how she was. No local nursing was organised, other than sporadically, and requests that she be taken into a nursing home run by the National Health Service fell on deaf ears. However, it was essential that action be taken, and eventually her doctor had her certified insane and transferred in August to St Bernard's Hospital at Hanwell on a permanent basis. In the meantime, in order to get over the risk of overturned fires, central heating was installed and all electric fires removed.

In June I went on holiday, leaving mother cared for in the house, and visited Chavenage in Gloucestershire and Nailsea Court in Somerset,

226

where I stayed as the guest of the owner, an old friend called Hugh Whitefield. Nailsea was an important but much restored manor house containing lovely things and the pride and joy of its owner, a solicitor in Bristol. From there I went to visit Kitley, near Plymouth, the seat of the Bastards; then down to Penzance and back to Gloucestershire to stay at Stow-on-the-Wold, visiting the Roman villa in Chedworth and Bedfont House at Chipping Campden, to lunch with my newly-discovered cousins, the Griffiths family who lived at Bedfont House then.

July sped past. On 25 August my mother was taken into hospital. A lodger, Timothy Mear, recommended to me by a friend, was to move in five days later, after mother's dining room had been redecorated, rearranged and furnished as a sitting room. Very comfortable it was too. All this arranged I went on holiday to a friend's cottage at Branscombe in Devon, with a final night in a hotel in Plymouth on 20 September. I telephoned home that evening only to be told that there had been a big burglary that afternoon and that all my clocks had gone. No sign of any entry had been found; how then had it occurred? I drove home the following day to deal with the police and insurance. In October and November burglar alarms were installed, which made the insurers feel rather more secure.

On 3 January, 1978 I gave a big party at the office to mark the thirtieth anniversary of my joining the Ministry of Town and Country Planning. It was a lunchtime affair with plenty to drink and eat and the majority of my office friends were there.

In March my other Uncle Leslie died, and I went to the funeral at Dengie in Essex but could not manage to get to the memorial service at St Brides, Fleet Street, in April. He had been my godfather – a rather meaningless office, I find, in this day and age.

A few days later I spent the weekend at the Old Ship Hotel in Brighton, visiting Dungeness with its lighthouse; Battle Abbey; Cuckfield Park; Sheffield Park; Ditchling; Sompting Church with its amazing Saxon tower and spire; Arundel Castle; the Roman Catholic cathedral at Arundel; the parish church, Uppark for the umpteenth time; and Petworth.

On 2 May I was promoted to Principal Inspector of Historic Buildings; I was not to rise any further, this was the peak of my career.

In June I was able to visit Buckingham Palace with the National Art Collections Fund. It was by that time the only royal residence, apart from Balmoral, that I had not been inside. There was nothing to surprise me because I had already seen photographs of the interior, but it was interesting to actually be in those famous rooms and to be free to sit in them as one liked. In the same month I embarked on another country house tour, this time encompassing the site of Carden Hall in Flint, burnt down years before; Erthig; and Bodrhyddan Hall, where we were entertained and shown the house by Lord Langford, who told us an amusing story of how he once feared that the house had deathwatch beetle in it. What was he to do? Tap, tap, tap, it went, so he telephoned the Bishop of Bangor. The bishop must have deathwatch beetle in his church – he would know at once. The bishop offered certain advice but before anything was embarked upon, the real cause was discovered; it was merely the toggle on a window blind tapping out its false message on a window pane!

We also stayed at Plas Uchaf, Glan Conway, visited Bodnant with its lovely gardens and old Pin Mill building, and Portmeirion, the extraordinary creation of its owner/architect Sir Clough Williams-Ellis, whose dying wish was to have his ashes placed in a canister and fired from a cannon out to sea to the sound of a band. This had been done, but the container had not been pierced, and Sir Clough's mortal remains, bobbing about on the ocean wave, had had to be sunk by shotguns from the shore! Penrhyn Castle, the great Norman-style bogus fortress was next, and I liked it little internally; one cannot enjoy everything. The next stop was the huge and ruinous Samuel Wyatt house called Baron Hill in Anglesey, which had always been the seat of the Bulkeleys. From there we went to Henllys and Beaumaris, and then to Gwydir Castle, a house which once had an exciting interior; however it had all been burnt out and replaced quite differently, and was no longer greatly interesting. Another fire damaged house, the vast and impressive Kinmel Hall, built to the designs of W.E. Nesfield in the 1870s, was still standing, just as the fairly recent fire had left it. It was still more or less complete and very fine externally, but the fire damage on the top floor and at the rear was extensive. Fortunately, the interior was not very exciting – vast plain apartments, making it look more like a school (its latest use) than the country mansion of Henry Robert

Hughes, its *nouveau-riche* builder, whose initials appeared on all the rainwater heads. Other houses visited were Dorfold Hall, the fine Jacobean house of the Roundells; Gawsworth Hall, a fragmentary house with a puzzling original terraced garden layout; Peover Hall, which astonished us with its amazing magpie-pattern timbered kitchen ceiling and its stable block suitable for princes; Muncaster Castle in the Lake District; Belle Isle on Windermere; Storrs Hall; Holker Hall; Hutton in the Forest; the burnt out Highhead Castle; Dalemain; Leighton Hall, with its Gillow furniture and live eagles; and Abbot Hall at Kendal.

On 14 July there was yet another burglary at home. It happened in the afternoon and the police had been and found no sign of entry. I returned at approaching midnight, I suppose, only to find the alarm bells ringing. What had happened was that a burglar had climbed up the wrought-iron entrance porch during the afternoon and with a spade from the garage had settled in a valley on the roof and chopped a hole through the tiles and the lath and plaster ceiling. He then dropped down onto the landing, his objective being the china cabinet in the side hall, which he could see through a window onto the garden. He knew there was a burglar alarm system, and by cutting a way through the roof, he would bypass all the alarm wiring – a clever scheme which did not work. He got to the china cabinet without trouble but he was not to know that the cabinet itself was alarmed, and the opened doors triggered it. The police arrived on the scene quite quickly, surrounded the house, found no sign of any entry, concluded that it was a false alarm and went away – leaving the burglar crouching on the floor inside. He took a number of things from the cabinet, dropping and smashing several in the process, and returned through the hole in the roof back to the garden. Why he did not leave by a door, seeing that the alarm bells had been triggered and were still ringing, has never been clear to me. The police caught him loitering in Staines a long time later, but who he was, and whether he was ever charged with the burglary, I was never told. The local police were very strange like that, seldom informing me as a victim about anything.

On 26 July I visited Welford Park in Berkshire, then an unknown house. It was the seat of the Puxleys, successors to the Archer Houblons, and a good seventeenth-century classical house with considerable atmosphere, where I identified eleven pictures for them. In August it was Cornwall again; many houses previously visited were visited again. On 13 August the first meeting of the Historic Buildings Council Gardens Committee was held, which later was to be almost completely run by me.

In October I was to visit Wisbech and Ashbourne for the office. November started off with a strange Ford Transit van being found in the drive; two further vehicles were spotted at Christmas. What was behind these incidents, I wondered?

In 1979 I visited Romsey for the office in February, and in March there was a sale of the contents of Dengie Manor following the death of my uncle. In April I visited Shrewsbury and Faversham, in Kent where there was a problem concerning the restoration of a house in Court Street. In May I went to Potton in Bedfordshire, and in June to Odiham in Hampshire.

On 24 June I gave a garden and house party to seventy people – drinks in the garden and a buffet supper prepared by myself, all to honour the seventh centenary of the mention of Fawns in archives – the actual date being 24 June 1279. It was to take about fifty years from then before my family were recorded in the locality. The occasion was a lovely evening; warm, sunny and happy.

In July I set off on holiday for Burnsall in Yorkshire as a base for visiting a number of historic places. Most pressing was the site of Kirby Hall at Ouseburn, one of my great friends Peter Reid's greatest discoveries. This magnificent Palladian house was begun in September 1747 to the designs of Richard Earl of Burlington and Roger Morris and was completed by John Carr of York. The client was Stephen Thompson, an ancestor of the Meysey Thompson family, and it descended with them to Henry, first and last Lord Knaresborough; the last owner at its demolition in 1920.

The building of the house is well documented in correspondence from Stephen Thompson. There was an exquisite interior and the whole house was finished by 1756. There had been a series of copies of the Raphael Cartoons by Sir James Thornhill which had previously been at the Duke of Chandos's house at Cannons in Middlesex, then just demolished, and it was also Thornhill who painted the ceiling of the dining room. Every detail of the house was magnificent. Still surviving are the stable block with its octagonal clock turret and the Ionic Temple, while the entrance lodges are by Robert Lugar. The park itself was laid out by Papworth in 1833 at the same time as he built a conservatory here. In 1864 a stone bridge by the cascade was added.

The fabric of the house was sold by auction in lots on 15 October 1920, Lord Knaresborough's son and heir having been killed in the War. The catalogue is a tragic record of the house.

I have a feeling that the huge classical picture in a Georgian frame at Newburgh Priory must have come from Kirby but I am only guessing. The laundry wing, entrance lodges and family mausoleum all still remain. It was one of the finest houses of its date in the whole of England.

I also visited Ripley Castle; Little Mitton Hall; Burnsall Church; Broughton Hall, the seat of the Tempests; Stockeld Park; Ribston Park; Jervaulx Abbey; Nun Monkton Hall; Sutton Park; Constable Burton; Swinton Park; Prince and Princess Christian's little shooting box at Moorcote at Ellingham; Norton Conyers; Studley Royal; Fountains Hall and Abbey; Skipton Castle; Stonyhurst College (which had been the home of the Lancashire Sherborns); Whixley Hall; Beningborough Hall; Newburgh Priory; Shandy Hall at Coxwold; Bolton Abbey; The Folly at Settle; Hagley Hall in Worcestershire; Harvington likewise; Nunnington Hall, the site of Thirkleby Park, the Wyatt house formerly the seat of the Franklands; Goldsborough Hall; Allerton Park; and Bewerley Grange and chapel – quite a trip.

On 23 July Auntie Elsie died. The funeral was at Dengie.

In August I visited Romsey again for the office, and during a trip with friends Ian Grant and Paul Taylor to see Mapledurham and Basildon Park with a picnic lunch, the driver, Timothy Mear smashed the car up in Reading, just by Eldon Square. The wreckage was carted away; the picnic being devoured in the Square garden.

A September holiday took me to Lytes Cary and Glastonbury; Hatch Court, Dunster Castle and Crowcombe Court; Athelhampton and Wolfeton; and to Bettiscombe, with its screaming skull, where we were entertained to tea.

On 11 September I went to Reading by train from Dorset to collect my repaired car, and the following day went off to Penzance. I had been staying in Lyme Regis with friends, and wanted to go down to Penzance to see a great friend of mine, Commander England, who I was worrying about. Alas! My unspoken fears about his hidden health problems proved only too true, and he lived only a few more weeks.

Home again I was able to entertain the John Smiths from Shottesbrooke. I had met John Smith at an office seminar a few months before and played host to him at luncheon before he was due to make his speech to us all. They were delighted by Fawns and its contents and promised a return invitation before very long.

In September another country house trip took me to the remains of Uffington House near Stamford, burnt before the First World War. I had tea at The George, then went to the site of the Hood's family house, Nettleham Priory, and then to Barton on Humber to cross the estuary by ferry. Alas! The boat had gone and we were marooned with the choice of an eighty-mile journey by road from Barton to Hull, where we were expected at the Station Hotel, or searching for supper south of the river. Everywhere seemed absolutely dead, with not a hotel, café or restaurant to be seen, and then suddenly we noticed a small Georgian pub on a street corner in Barrow. It was very small, with only a small bar and no one about; however in we went and indeed they did do food, but the staff had gone home as it was late. However, the land-lord was willing to do something for us himself and served us with delicious wild duck in the two-table dining room. Eventually it was time for the ferry crossing at 9.30 and we arrived at the Station Hotel in Hull only to find that the restaurant facilities were closed at weekends. We were told there was only a buttery bar, and if we wanted anything else we would have to go out! (The hotel has since been destroyed by fire, I think.)

Based in Hull, visits were paid to the Ferens Art Gallery; Wilberforce House; Maister's House with its splendid staircase; the Whaling Museum; the superb thirteenth-century church at Patrington; Burton Constable, the magnificent seat of the Constables of which some absurd government at one time accepted the total destruction; Spurn Head; Burton Agnes, one of the most beautiful houses in England with marvellous woodwork and plasterwork and, if you like that sort of thing, a splendid collection of very modern pictures; and Sledmere, the Adam period house near Bridlington belonging to Sir

Tatton Sykes, with very grand interiors and contents.

On 9 December I went to lunch with the John Smiths at Shottesbrooke, where I heard about all the inner workings of that remarkable organisation, the Landmark Trust.

15

The Eighties

In January 1980 I paid one of several visits to Pallant House at Chichester, a lovely early eighteenth-century house built by a Portugal merchant – or one who imported port wine into England – and there discovered that the great vaulted basement had been where all his stock of port had been stored. Not so much a case of living above the shop but of actually living above the warehouse, in a house of rare dignity and quality! I was to go there more than once because the Very Reverend Walter Hussey, Dean of Chichester, whom I knew, had given his collection of important modern pictures to be hung in the restored house. The inside had been much mutilated apart from the main stair, and needed careful handling and repair.

On 14 February I had a shattered windscreen on my way to visit Ston Easton near Bath, a lovely eighteenth-century house with several fascinating features. On 3 March I visited Dogmersfield Park, the early eighteenth-century former seat of the St John Mildmays, which I found contained one of the finest suites of early- to mid-eighteenth-century state rooms in England, all with perfectly gorgeous plasterwork, woodwork and chimney piece. Alas, the rooms were all soon destroyed by fire and they are completely unrecorded so far as I can discover.

On April 3 1980 I went to see Menabilly, the seat of the Rashleighs, a fine old house scarcely touched in recent years. Daphne Du Maurier had rented it for a time and it may well have been the house upon which she based Manderlay. I later went to Oxfordshire, to see Rousham Park, Swerford Park and Farnborough Hall; also to Chesterfield, to Beauforest and Chislehampton. In June I visited Carhampton in Somerset from which the Luttrells took an earldom for a time, to see a brass wall monument made by my ancestor Charles Sherborn, for two members of the Escott family in the mid-eighteen century. During part of that holiday I went to a house auction in Tiverton and bought a silver-mounted black ebony peppermill and various oddments. I also went to Topsham and to Ugbrooke, the great house belonging to the Cliffords. This had been rescued from disuse and temporary usage as a grain store and had had its furniture and pictures restored to it. Nettlecombe Court, an Elizabethan and Georgian house in North Somerset, formerly one of the many seats of the Trevelyans, and its church and tombs was also on the programme and I collected an ogee brass canopy from Lawrences at Crewkerne which I thought would make a most attractive valance for the open fireplace in the sitting room at Fawns.

On 28 June I visited Wrotham Park near Barnet, a great mid-eighteenth-century house by Isaac Ware, and the home of the Byngs. The house was open for charity and had never been opened before, or illustrated internally in any magazine. It was an exciting visit because, following a fire in 1883, the whole building had been burnt and one simply had no idea what might be there. It was a delight to find that the house was extremely rich in fine contents and that the fire had not destroyed them.

Burglars struck again on the 11 and 12 July, but my diary notes it merely as an attempt and gives no details. Two days later I was to visit the famous old pub, quite derelict for several years, called The Hoop and Grapes in Aldgate, London, a seventeenth-century timber-framed building still retaining much character inside and out. It was in a parlous state and the subject of a proposal to rehabilitate it and do various other things many considered highly controversial. However, one often has to swallow unpleasant proposals when they are part of a parcel which in the main is acceptable to everyone.

In early August one of the peacocks in the garden saw itself in a reflection in the side of the car and promptly attacked it, causing hideous scratches all along the side. That month I visited Cornwall again, and Branscombe in Devon. I also saw Tapeley Park, the home of Miss Christie, a sister of Sir George Christie of Glyndebourne, with its remarkable collection of late nineteenth-century porcelain, bronzes and furniture; and a tame parrot on her head, Smedmore and Athelhampton, Enmore Castle, Barford Park, Combe House at Gittisham, Breamore and home.

In September I went on the Historic Buildings Council's tour of churches in Lincolnshire. I remember when we were all having lunch in a pub in Bourne I remarked to the Duke of Grafton that one of the historic cases of the SPAB (of which he was chairman) had been the Old Red Hall at Bourne, an interesting and important house of about 1600 that had been stranded by the side of the railway track and had become used as the stationmaster's house. Off we went to see this formerly worrying case and Hugh Grafton went on ahead. It had been saved as a kind of community centre and he walked in and was met by an officious looking caretaker with a broom who said that the place was private and not open to the public, and as for the Duke he could say that he was the Prince of Wales because he would not know who he was and we could not go in. However, laughter ruled the day and we were allowed a very limited view. At least the house was safe and in use. We need worry no more.

At the start of 1981 I visited Pallant House in Chichester again. On the 23 February I made arrangements with the Court of Protection for the custody of my mother's affairs. On 13 March I visited Heythrop in Oxfordshire, the great Thomas Archer house built for the Shrewsburys and burnt in the 1830s. It had been restored in the 1870s for Lord Brassey. Long a Catholic college, it had become the training head-quarters of the National Westminster Bank. I spent the weekend at David and Rosemary Verey's charming house at Barnsley in Gloucestershire, and James and Alvilde Lees-Milne were there. The Vereys visited me at Bedfont with their son Charles at the end of the month.

The week before Easter was spent in Brighton, and the weather was fairly good. I met Commander Campbell Johnston at his house in Royal Crescent and was impressed by his splendid family portraits, furniture and relics (in the form of pictures) of Horace Walpole and Strawberry Hill, and a very fine bust by Mrs Damer. At the end of April I visited Shirburn Castle in Oxfordshire, the great seat of Lord Macclesfield and never before visited, I believe, by anyone. I was astonished at the variety and quality of its contents, particularly the Stubbs pictures. I visited Dorney Court the following day, a very early house much restored in Tudor style in the 1930s and now badly in need of structural repair and extensive redecoration. The medieval great hall was a big surprise and really good. A young family had inherited the house and is battling bravely with it. I do wish that something could be done about the story of King Charles II being presented with the first pineapple grown in England there. The great house in the painting depicting the incident with the king cannot ever have been Dorney Court.

In May 1981 I saw two then rarely seen houses. Elton, the seat of the Probys, and Milton Hall. This was very big and full of good things, many of them just about to leave for St Osyths Priory in Essex, as they had been left to Lady Juliet de Chair. Later they were taken to Bourne Park in Kent, bought for the purpose.

After the royal wedding at the end of July a lodger, Ken Aubrey, took me as his guest to Egypt – a place, I confess, I have never really wanted to visit – and he chose August! We flew in two jumps, changing at Rome and arrived in Cairo at midnight. We stayed in a brand-new Sheraton hotel, visited the Citadel, the Museum with the Tutankhamen treasure and the Pyramids, where we went inside the Great Pyramid. Then we boarded a Sheraton Nile steamer for the usual tourist cruise. Towards the end of the week I was so ill in my stomach that I could not have cared less about the Valley of the Kings, Luxor, Karnak, Thebes, Memphis, Philae and the rest. We were supposed to be away for two weeks – it turned out to be only one and one was enough. In spite of the series of injections that I had received before I went, I was really ill; the injections had been no good. The last day was 9 August and we rose at 5.30 in the morning to catch a plane at 8.00 for Rome with Alitalia Airlines. We arrived at Rome at noon only to have it confirmed that the airline had gone on strike. We were marooned at the airport for nine hours before we could get a flight back to England, but the wait turned out to be more dreadful than dull, for at 4 in the afternoon in the main departure lounge, where we were waiting, a bomb went off, completely destroying the El Al airline offices, showering the place with glass and overwhelming it in seconds with soldiers, police and ambulances for the injured. We eventually left Rome at 9, arriving at Heathrow at about midnight where the bloody-minded English taxi drivers just wanted long fares to London and were not interested in short runs in the neighbourhood. That seems to me to be the worst part of giving a select group a monopoly. However, we did eventually arrive home. The following day my companion had been too upset by the bombing to go to work. However, I left home the day after and went to stay in Plymouth with my friend Alvin Gamble until the following Saturday.

It was after this that the extensive thefts that had been taking place under my nose in the house were first brought to my attention, the chief loss being the William III domed-top quart-sized silver tankard that had been used on the dining table for biscuits for years and had been in the family for a century. The police were informed. I saw PC Adams on Thursday afternoon but nothing ever happened. Also discovered to be missing were many silver and all my principal gold coins, including my Henry VI gold noble and a William IV sovereign.

On 11 September, Robert McKenzie the television political commentator had invited me to celebrate his birthday at a small party he was to give at Bramerton, his cottage on Ham Haugh Island at Shepperton. I arrived there as arranged to find the house in darkness and deserted. What on earth could have happened? I searched around the outside, found nothing, and then decided to sit in the gathering darkness on the doorstep to await his arrival. I waited and waited, and waited. It grew darker and darker. More and more creepy, with just the distant sound of water rushing over the distant weir. It was not my scene at all – far too lonely at night; but there it was. Eventually the garden gate burst open and there was Bob, advancing slowly up the path carrying some tonic-water bottles in a bag. But he was bent double and clearly very, very ill. I greeted him normally as if nothing was wrong, but he immediately said that he was far from well, that a friend, John, was expected and we would have to do our own supper, and could I please take his keys because he could not open his own front door. I was most terribly shocked; I had seen him only a few days before. He was going straight to bed; would I please find myself a drink, and John would arrive any minute, which he did. Somehow or other John and I found something to eat and drink and we talked quietly for some hours about what this all meant. I felt Bob was dying of something and told John so, but neither of us actually knew. He went into hospital on the Monday.

On 17 September 1981, I went to Hawkstone Park in Shropshire for the office, to inspect the historic gardens and park there, to report on the present position about the then state of ruin and dereliction. My visit and report helped to save it all later. On the Sunday my host in Egypt moved out, to a furnished flat in Richmond, and on the Saturday, Bob having recovered, he decided to cover the Labour Party Conference in Brighton, staying at the Grand Hotel. I left for a holiday in Cornwall, but before the week was out I had a message to say that Bob was really ill and had been taken back into hospital. I returned on the Saturday, saw him the following day when he asked me to notify his cousin and various colleagues, and I visited him every day until the day of his death, Monday 12 October. He was sixty-four and had been ill for just four weeks. The funeral was at West London Crematorium on Monday 19 October. Bob was a Canadian-born political commentator and the inventor of the swingometer used on election nights. He was a professor at the London School of Economics and had first sprung to notice with his book on the British Political Parties. He had travelled the world as a lecturer.

On 1 December I myself became ill, the early signs of a nearing retirement. The strain of everything had been too much. It was Bob's death, which had brought with it my executorship, and my responsibility for his Shepperton house, and sorting out his possessions and personal treasures, plus Egypt plus Rome, plus mother, plus the silver thefts, and the responsibility load at work. On 7 December I went to Bob's memorial service at the University Church of Christ the King in Gordon Square, which was addressed by Sir Huw Wheldon, and where I sat immediately behind the Speaker of the House (later Lord Tonypandy) and was surrounded by the well-known and famous. Nothing however could conceal from me the essential misery of the year as a whole. I could not cope with it all. Christmas certainly did not exist.

The year had also seen the redecoration of part of the house inside. July had seen the extraordinary sight of a stolen lorry with waste paper being crashed through the gates in the early hours of the morning and being set alight in the drive. I never heard any more about it.

I suppose there are never years that one hopes will be repeated again, because to hope that this could be possible is to deny the nature of life. But there are, and always will be, years that can be regarded as regrettable, sad, tragic or are utterly horrible. One such year for me was 1982; one would not want that year again for all the tea in the world. Father had now been dead for ten years and heavy snow fell on 9 January; his anniversary. My mother, who had now been in hospital for some time, had a fall and broke her hip and was removed to Ealing General Hospital. On 21 January I returned to the office, feeling much better, but it was not to last. In February I had the first of several parties of visitors to see the house, this one led by the Comtesse de Chêne. On 9 February I went to Bill Drummond's gallery in Covent Garden and there met Sarah Ferguson (later the Duchess of York). On 18 February I went to Rousham on a visit for the office in connection with the gardens and historic buildings there, and on the 20th had another group of visitors to the house, this time led by Sir Ian Isham. On 4 March I lunched with Raleigh Trevelyan at 18 Hertford Street, his elegant eighteenth-century London house, and on the 15th I had what turned out to be my last day at work in the office. Exhausted from overwork and overwrought over Bob McKenzie's death, mother's failing health and other disasters, I could not carry on. Further disasters only emphasised what my doctor had told me – that if I carried on as I was, I would suffer a total collapse or stroke or drop dead before the end of the year. My old friend Gilbert Bradley arrived to stay on 23 March for a couple of nights and after twenty years he is still with me in 2002.

Mother died on 10 April at the age of eighty-eight, and on the 16th was her funeral at Bedfont, attended by just a handful of people. On 1 May my kind friends Richard Jeffree and Anthony Frater took me to see Elton Hall and Grimsthorpe Castle, a wonderful day out followed by supper with them at their Richmond home. On 4 May I had another examination at St Mark's followed by a three-day operation visit two weeks later. All the time this was going on I was looking after Bob McKenzie's house at Shepperton and helping to turn it out. On 14 June I was back at St Mark's. On 7 July there was yet another burglary at home, this time early in the morning; my diary tells me no more, but two days later a car was abandoned halfway up the drive, and within a few hours had been vandalised by local children. Thirty-two members of the Middlesex Society arrived to see the house on 24 July and on 15 August sixty people from a National Trust Centre in the Midlands came. On the 17th I went down to Cornwall to stay with friends but was far from well and suffered a minor collapse on 1 September. I returned home on 7 September. On the 20th I was back at St Mark's for further consultations, but worse was to come.

A cousin, Igraine Innes-Hamilton, called for tea on 21 August, and left at about 6.00. At 7.30 precisely, when I was expecting Timothy Mear to arrive, the doorbell went and after looking through the burglar lens, I decided that he had arrived with some friends. I opened the door to a gang of gunmen who rushed in and, with a gun stuck in my ribs, tied me up and put a carrier bag over my head so that I could see nothing. I was forced to stay like that for two hours while the house was ransacked. They had come for the best pictures they said; they knew which ones they were and were having them all. They said it was a pity that they had not brought a larger van because then they could have taken everything. After some time I was forced to go along to the drawing room, still at gunpoint, to unlock the door which they were unable to open as the key only worked upside down and backwards. Once in there I was sat down again and my ankles were tied together, and a black cushion cover slit open and placed sack-like over my head again. The feather stuffing went everywhere. At about 9.15 there was a commotion in the hall. My 7.30 visitor had just arrived only to be tied up like me, but more loosely. When the raiders left at about 9.30 he was able to set me free. The police arrived quite quickly but I broke down at one point and could not continue. The press, police, relatives and friends arrived the following day and all told me, either personally or over the phone, that I would have to sell up and move before I was killed. The following Friday I visited Brighton, a week later Plymouth. Where was I to go? On 1 November Timothy Mear moved out. I had seen comparatively little of him for some time.

Things now moved very fast indeed. My kind friends Brian and Jack in Cornwall found me a place in Plymouth, which did not suit me as it was a working hotel (and needed a great deal of attention and restoration) but it was in a spectacularly placed situation. Brian and Jack then borrowed for the three of us a flat in Hove so that we could spend a week househunting. Not many complete houses survive on Marine Parade in Brighton, but there was one, partly converted into flats, which interested me. I was to prevaricate into the following year until finally deciding upon it. Only Brian and Jack ever helped me. Practically no one else ever lifted a finger.

On 22 November there was a further visit to St Mark's Hospital, and in December I spent the last Sherborn Christmas at Bedfont, after 650 years. It was as good a Christmas as kind friends could make it in a wrecked and partly dismantled house, for packing-up had already begun. I was compulsorily retired on health grounds on 27 December.

I visited Bletchingley on 4 January 1983 with my friends Michael le Garst and Andrew McGuffog, and bought a porcelain group after Thorwaldsen, for £60. The following day I bought a fairly decent Georgian mahogany sideboard at Christies, South Kensington, for £140. I was off to Brighton again on 10 January and 13 January, meeting my old friend and colleague, the architect Edward Salter. Salter was a great friend and very supportive and he volunteered to do a complete survey of the potential new home in Marine Parade and to look after all the building works which were necessary and quite extensive. On 24 February I agreed to buy the house for £84,000. At the same time I had to move out of my bedroom at Fawns because of all the packing up that was taking place. On 8 March, not being able to stay safely in my house any longer, I agreed to sell Fawns. I sold it for the bargain price of £215,000, with nearly three acres of land, and years later it was resold for over £1 million. However, prices were depressed at that particular time. It was not quite all doom and gloom on all fronts, because I was very lucky in finding a number of pieces of furniture in an auction, which had come from various royal residences, and I bought them all for the Brighton house. I could imagine them looking very appropriate there, and they did.

I was still doing voluntary work for the Gardens Committee of the Ministry, even interrupting all my other domestic activities. I bought enough fabric to cover all the drawing-room furnishings on 22 March, and a Coalbrookdale cast-iron grate which was ideally suited for the drawing room.

On 14 April, Igraine Innes-Hamilton brought an astrologer or soothsayer or whatever to the house, and she said, not knowing the house at all, that she sensed royalty in the dining room. She singled out one picture that would return separately from all the others.

242

She was quite right on both counts, because the dining room did contain a number of things of royal origin, and the picture she picked out, a huge one, was to arrive back separately at the house, but not until many years later.

On 20 April I went to Vaccaro's at Richmond for lunch with Danny Stevens and the following day went to Kingston to collect a pair of turned wooden electric table lamps (which I now realise were made from fine Georgian stair balusters), but the taxi stopped at Hanworth on the way, burst into flames and was completely destroyed. It was another surprise for me. Was someone trying to tell me something?

On 11 May I had a shock message that I had to leave Fawns Manor by the 19th and on the following day the move actually began. I was completely alone. For some time things had been transported to local sale rooms and also to Sothebys and Bonhams, and the church chandeliers I had in store in the stables had had to be returned. By the 18th everything had gone. The most awful thing about moving is choosing the right house, and then one has to consider how to furnish it, what furniture one takes with one, and then what things will not fit in, the furniture one needs to buy, and how it is to be arranged. I had had about six months to think about the impending move, but before settling on the house in Brighton, I was given to understand that the proposed purchasers of Bedfont were not concerned about getting vacant possession and that I could stay there as long as I wished. It was something of an earthquake to be told that they would need possession in ten days and I had to be out. Their bank would not advance the money for their purchase without having complete vacant possession.

It was also something of a minor tremor to be told by Coutts that they would not allow me a bridging loan between the exchange of both contracts. Gilbert Bradley, who was in any case almost permanently travelling abroad, and had hardly been around during the packing up process at all, was actually touring America and had to be brought back for one night to look after his own possessions, but he was away again to Leicestershire the day following my lonely move to Brighton. The only way to move the contents of a large house in a few days is to go to a very large firm who can draw furniture vans from a number of different places. A total of thirteen furniture vans was eventually organised from all over the place – London, Reading, Brighton etc.

All my early furniture, particularly the walnut and beech caned chairs of late seventeenth-century date, my pair of painted dummy board figures of a similar period and my pair of Charles II silver framed wing easy chairs, upholstered in needlework, tapestry and velvet, were all sent to Sothebys in Bond Street. My kitchen fittings, including spits, spit jacks, the kitchen range and dresser, the ladder-back and Windsor chairs, plus knife machine, candlesticks, candle moulds, irons, goffering irons, sugar cutters, brass dog collar, yokes, meat dishes, plates, mugs, copper and brass saucepans and measures, mangle, travelling bath, brass fire blowers, paraffin lamps and domestic odds and ends were all sent to Bonhams. It was a shame because the old kitchen at Bedfont was attractive but there was not going to be any old kitchen again.

I set off by myself to Brighton the following day as arranged, having more or less carefully packed what things I wanted for use in the house immediately. The removal firm attacked the problem with zest, not always wisely and in fact I took a film of them at work which reveals a very funny incident in which the men carrying a Victorian glazed bookcase from the house walked into a tree and broke off the cornice top, it being shot like an arrow towards the front door, and the men having to duck their heads to avoid it! I had done a great deal of packing myself – 160 tea chests – and there were loud complaints from the removers because I had filled the chests too full with books and they were quite unable to lift them! Oh dear, what a disastrous thing the move turned out to be, what with all the breakages, losses and thefts from the removers. Most of the furnishings had to be stored while the house in Brighton was made ready because of the work that had to be done. Large items of furniture, like Georgian tallboys and secretaires, arrived in Brighton with their bracket feet broken off. My great pair of Canton vases was broken and my equestrian statue of the Duke of Wellington by Count D'Orsay was never to arrive at all. Regency plaster lamp statues had their arms or heads knocked off, or were broken in half at the waist. Also lost completely was a plaster death mask of the composer Tchaikovsky, an eighteenth-century plaster library bust of Shakespeare and a set of nine Chinese Fitzhugh pattern armorial plates were broken. Even worse was the total loss of items including: an extremely fine

Victorian carved and inlaid rosewood trumpet-shaped work table on elaborate carved legs which had belonged to my great-great grandmother Sherborn; a Continental mahogany work table with cross-framed legs and satinwood interior (also hers); a very fine William and Mary walnut candlestand with a laburnum oyster veneer top; a fine and important small bronze relief portrait of the mid-eighteenth-century Frederick Prince of Wales; a Cromwellian basket-hilted mortuary sword; a late eighteenth-century miniature of a Miss Sherborn of Bedfont; a pair of circular plaster reliefs of Night and Day in gilt frames after Thorwaldsen; a Regency decorated work box with a coloured print of Brighton Pavilion on the top; a blue/green leather folding travelling barometer, thermometer and clock; a small oval watercolour of an old lady in a bonnet of about 1840; a small round silver ashtray of 1899, engraved with the coronet and initials of the then Earl of Chesterfield; a table magnifying glass of good quality, with a carved marine ivory handle from a parasol inscribed on a silver band 'S.A. Jennings, Victoria Place, St Ives'; a Victorian plated sugar basin on four legs; a long stemmed Meerschaum pipe; and a set of mounted deer antlers. Worst of all was the loss of the completely irreplaceable samplers by my two grandmothers as children, both in maple frames. Fifteen items of good antique furniture, badly damaged, had to be sent away for restoration.

A year later, in May 1984 I was still corresponding with the removers about broken and missing items and had to write to the Chief Constable in Brighton about the possibility of theft. None of the important lost items were ever found or delivered to me. The compensation ran into many thousands of pounds, and greatly exceeded the cost of moving and storage. My claim took the best part of five years to settle.

On 6 June I called in a firm to report on installing central heating and a hot water system. Builders had now taken over the house completely and the central heating engineers were pulling up floors. There was hardly a room where one could sit or anywhere that wasn't covered in confusion. It was a situation that was to last for a very long time indeed. Obviously with so much going on, I do not remember it all nor have I noted everything down. What I really wanted at that time was a certain amount of activity to try and trace my pictures and other things that had been stolen in Bedfont. I desperately wanted the people concerned to be arrested and charged for their offences. But it was to go on and on for years. I have noted in my diary the names of many police officers who visited over a period, but exactly what they did or said, I no longer remember. In August I had news about ten of my pictures, and an enquiry about what reward was on offer.

September started off with three days of violent storms, but like all storms they only lasted for a comparatively short while, and then the weather became calm again. On 16 September I attended the funeral in Tunbridge Wells of my old friend Terence Davis, the distinguished architectural historian and biographer of John Nash.

Fortunately it had been a very fine summer and the complete re-roofing of my new house in slate and lead, replacing of rotten sash windows and the restoration of glazing bars to the windows had gone off without a hitch. The new external shutters for the drawing room and the reproduction iron balcony railings were also in hand. The central heating and hot water system had been installed and was turned on on 3 October. A few days later there was a leak in the airing cupboard and hot water was found running in a lavatory.

On 6 December I attended the memorial service at the University Church of Christ the King in London for Sir Nicholas Pevsner who I had known for a great many years, he having been on the Minister's Advisory Committee for Listing and having published an article by me on the Georgian theatre I had discovered on holiday in Penzance in Cornwall, in the *Architectural Review*. Pevsner was one of the great architectural historians of England, perhaps the greatest, and I remember him so clearly visiting Committee meetings, half dozing through endless rather boring discussions, at times almost falling asleep and then suddenly waking up, taking notice and contributing something in his remarks which made everybody else stop and think.

I had an excellent first Christmas in Brighton with endless invitations to other people's houses. I suppose they felt rather sorry for me, and all the things that I had been through recently. But there it was, I was crashing into the pool of entertainment and fun which is so typical of Brighton. I was splashing around and swimming around and eventually I was to settle down very happily there. Very happily indeed, and I ceased to regret Bedfont completely. There was no place for me there any more.

*   *   *

On 4 January 1984, the brass picture rails which I had ordered for the house were completed and hung in the dining room. The ceiling rose went up and the balcony railings arrived to be put up the following day. Four van loads of furniture arrived and on the 10th the drawing-room decorations were started. On the 16th my friends Brian and Jack unpacked about a hundred tea chests of books which they left piled high on the floor of the library, as most of the bookcases had been sent away for repair. Next day they returned home to the West Country, and on the 14th the carpet was put down and the chandelier was put up in the drawing room.

I mentioned earlier that I had had a new central heating system installed at the house. There had been some teething problems with it, but it was on the night of 21 February that all hell was let loose. I had a huge flood during the night from the top floor right through to the basement, which caused the most enormous amount of damage. The central heating engineers had been at the house that day doing some work and the piping had come apart in the night. All the rooms at the back of the house from the top right through the five floors to the basement were soaked, all the decorations wrecked, the furnishings wrecked and everything had to be started all over again. Over 300 volumes of books were completely destroyed and others were so badly damaged that they had to be sent away for rebinding. Fortunately there is a firm at Crowborough which specialises in restoring furnishings from houses that have had floods, fires and other disasters, and they were able to take away with them all of the furniture, carpets, mattresses, bedding, curtains and other things that had been affected by the flood, for drying out and, where necessary, repolishing and restoring.

During the Brighton Festival in May, numerous visits to the opera are mentioned, plus a visit to Portsmouth to see the tudor warship the *Mary Rose*, of which Sir Henry Shernborne had been captain in 1514.

On 22 May a firm of bookbinders came to the house to take away those books that needed to be restored, rebound, cleaned, washed or otherwise attended to. We had of course, in the meantime, made sure that everything was dried out properly, by spreading things out on the floor with the books upright and their pages opened outwards.

247

On 12 June scaffolding was put up outside. On the 15th the external shutters arrived from the builders and a week later they were put up. On the same day the builders finished their work. They had of course had to redo all the rooms at the back of the house, restoring all the ceilings, repapering the walls and painting them as necessary. The repairs and other work had cost £40,000.

The very severe flooding of my home had a sequel in that on 1 August the central heating engineers sued me for the remainder of my agreement, which naturally I had not paid, and because my then solicitors were not paying proper attention, judgement was delivered against me. However, they were able to appeal and have the judgement set aside, and that left us just where we were. In March 1985 a leaking radiator had to be replaced in the drawing room; in September 1985 a two-way valve in the top floor cupboard in the back kitchen was leaking and had to be replaced by someone else; in May 1986 the joint between two pipes in the top cupboard simply came apart and water gushed from the open end of the pipe, causing damage to the bedroom ceiling and the library below. If I had not been in at the time this could quite easily have been a flood of the same proportions as the original one which had caused all the previous damage. I was able to catch it early and arrange for emergency repairs to be done by another firm. This necessitated further redecoration to rooms and restoration of damaged furniture. In February 1987, in order to make good progress on the claim for damage and all the other problems relating to the central heating system, it was agreed to approach the National Heating Advisory Council, which is an independent body of experts on heating and plumbing matters. Correspondence with them and with the opposing solicitors went on and on, for an unnecessarily long time. I have a note that on 28 May 1990 approximately seven years after the central heating was installed, we were still waiting for a visit from Mr De Lury of the National Heating Advisory Council. Eventually he did come, and he inspected the installation and said the whole thing was an absolute disgrace and I shouldn't pay a penny for any of it. He thought it was the most appalling installation he had seen in his entire practice.

On 13 September the furniture that had been taken to Crowborough for restoration was returned, and I went on holiday to Cornwall to stay with my kind friends, visiting on 17 September John Betjeman's grave in the churchyard of St Enodoc in Cornwall. At the end of my holiday I went to stay with my friends Douglas and Catherine Chome-Wilson in Dorset, leaving them to have lunch at Athelhampton with my friends Robin and Jenny Cooke. On 14 October a great friend who lived in London telephoned very anxiously to find out if I was all right. Yes, of course I was but what I did not know, and had not heard, was that there had been a great terrorist outrage in the night and activists had blown up the Grand Hotel in Brighton in the early hours of the morning. As is common in such incidents the principal targets escaped and comparatively unimportant and innocent people suffered most. On 21 November I went to the funeral of Commander Colin Campbell-Johnson, and three days later went on the beach and in the sea (September and October had been very poor weather). Then before one could say very much more, Christmas had come round yet again with its usual round of parties here, there and everywhere. Brighton is marvellous like that.

On 21 February removal people came to take things away from the house which I had decided I no longer needed, the furnishings all having been sorted out. It was a quantity of furniture destined for Sothebys, who then had a place in Pulborough. On 20 March I attended a banquet in the Drapers Hall in Throgmorton Street to honour Dame Jennifer Jenkins on her retirement from the Chairmanship of the National Trust. She had made an enormous contribution to conservation, firstly as secretary of the Ancient Monuments Society and then as Chairman of the Historic Buildings Council. I was very sad about it as I think she made a wonderful contribution to everything she ever did.

April was not a bad month weather-wise, and in May was the Brighton Festival. Between 16 and 22 May I went off to the Loire to see the castles there. They are so completely unlike English houses, so much greater in their fortification and with such a small amount of furniture.

On 3 July Roedean School celebrated its centenary and opened its doors to the public. I thought that it might be the only chance of seeing the inside of the school, and so I satisfied my curiosity by going.

On 13 August I was off on my travels again: I went to Honiton, Truro, St Austell and Polperro, and on the 23rd I left St Veep to stay at the Royal Glen at Sidmouth, a charming hotel which was the house where the Duke and Duchess of Kent were staying in 1817. The Duke caught a cold from wearing damp socks and died as a result of his condition, thus leaving it clear for his daughter Princess Victoria to ascend the throne.

On 26 September I had to visit Hounslow police station in connection with the burglary at the house in Bedfont. On the 30th, Brian Leach and Jack Anderson arrived from St Veep to stay with me. We had some very hot weather and on Wednesday 2 October we went to Chichester and to see the *Mary Rose* in Portsmouth. On Sunday 6 October we went to Goodwood House and to Boxgrove Priory; both looked extremely good. Goodwood, although not the most beautiful house one has ever seen, has really pulled its socks up over the years and shows itself very well indeed.

Around this time I had inserted a full-page advertisement in the *Antiques Trade Gazette* in connection with the armed robbery at Bedfont. It had an almost immediate effect, and on 20 October I had news from the police telling me that four people had been arrested. In addition, four of the stolen pictures had been recovered in a swoop by armed police on a layby on the M4, where armed villains had been arrested.

I began 1986 with an interesting trip to Holme Lacy in Herefordshire, a vast country house of late seventeenth century date which had been the home of the Craven family. It was known to have some marvellous plaster ceilings and woodcarvings ascribed to Grinling Gibbons, although it was also known that it had been used as a hospital for many years and had just been chucked on to the property market by the local authority. I was asked to go and see it by an American friend called Dewey Curtis, who had spent much of his life taking Americans round England on cultural tours. He had long nursed the idea that he would like to have a country house in England where he could spend his declining years. I set off for Holme Lacy and stayed in Hereford; I was taken to the house and looked round. It is an enormous building with vast rooms and vast kitchen quarters, but the thing that I thought went very much against it was the fact that there was no land in front of it, merely a very tall hedge. A great deal of the interior of the house was also twentieth-century reproduction. The Gibbons carvings had been removed and altogether I found it a colossal project and had to advise Dewey that I didn't think it was a sensible thing to pursue. He was very upset, but never mind, I think it was the best thing in the end.

On 17 February, there was a remarkable exhibition in Brighton about the 'China Trade', a wonderful event showing all the things that are made in China – porcelain, pewter, silver, paintings, furniture and woodwork – for export to the European market. It was quite an eye-opener and something I shall never forget.

On 8 April my two cousins, Leonard Terry and his wife Jean Sherborn (known to me as Biddy all my life), came to see me and I took them to the Taverna Sorrento just by Hanningtons in North Street. There was nothing exceptional about it at the time, but I was astonished the following morning to find that the restaurant had had a fire in the night, and had been completely destroyed. On 18 April I had to go to the funeral of a friend, Godfrey Parker, who stayed nearby, whom I met soon after coming to live in Brighton. Godfrey had an Egyptian friend called Wagdi Morsi, who stayed with him from time to time. Wagdi was a nice chap and I felt for him very much when Godfrey died. Godfrey had actually gone off to Australia househunting as he was thinking of moving there to live, but sadly was to die on the way back. I felt sorry for Wagdi so several weeks later, after the funeral, I telephoned him to see if he might like to come to a supper party at the house. Much to my amusement I got a recorded message saying, in Godfrey Parker's own voice, 'I'm sorry that I'm not available to take your call at the moment but I'll return your call as soon as I am able'! Some chance!

On 30 April I collected my friend Peter Rose in order to go to Arundel to see James Cartland's house with its (as we discovered) very remarkable contents. James was such a nice man, it was a shame that he moved to Derbyshire but he did rescue a very important house which I'd actually listed myself many years before, when it was standing empty and virtually derelict. He had it restored and opened it to the public.

On Monday 26 May I set off for Burghley House near Stamford

(which is actually in Northamptonshire), and also went to Island Hall at Godmanchester, which I had seen in dire straits years before; to Tallington which is near Stamford and where members of the Gilbert family are buried; and to Otley Hall in Suffolk, which is a lovely old house. The following day I visited Gainsborough's House at Sudbury, Belchamp Hall in Suffolk and Haughley Park in Suffolk, which looked marvellous outside. On the Wednesday I explored Lavenham Priory, which is a collection of timber-framed houses right in the middle of Lavenham, and went to Ickworth, the extraordinary round house built by the Marquesses of Bristol.

Next was Anglesey Abbey in Cambridgeshire, which started life as a medieval priory, was then dissolved with the Dissolution of the Monasteries in 1535, and then suffered various vicissitudes, getting smaller and smaller and eventually becoming a farm house. It was bought by an American called Huttleston Broughton, who loved England. He was born in 1896, the son of Urban Broughton, who made a fortune in the United States in mining and railways between 1887 and 1912, later returning to England and sitting as MP for Preston from 1915 to 1918. Huttleston Broughton's mother was Cara Rogers, a New York heiress. Mother and son were deeply attached until her death in 1939, and distant cruises on her sumptuous yacht, *Sapphire*, which carried a crew of sixty, were almost an annual event. Huttleston Broughton succeeded in being granted a barony on his father's death in 1929. Lord Fairhaven, as he then became, was a gay bachelor and in 1961 a second barony was conferred on him with the remainder to his brother Henry Broughton, who succeeded in 1966. It is really wonderful what money can buy. Lord Fairhaven restored the house very sympathetically, added to it very sympathetically and it still incorporates the thirteenth-century undercroft of the priory. What makes the house so remarkable now is the incredible collection of pictures, bronzes, statuary, tapestries and furniture as well as smaller items, plus an enormous library. Also as part of the project was the creation of a magical garden round the house in which was incorporated statuary, vases, urns, gate piers, gates and other features which were then available having been taken from their original settings and put on the market. It's a beautiful garden, it's a beautiful house with beautiful contents; I love it.

The following day I went on to Gunby Hall in Lincolnshire, a Queen Anne house, described by Tennyson as a 'haunt of ancient peace'. From there I drove into Skegness just to remind myself of my time in the RAF during the War.

From the 16 to 24 June I went with the National Trust to Belgium, staying for a part of the time in Bruges and visiting Brussels, Ghent, Antwerp and various other places. It was a marvellous tour; Bruges is so wonderful.

On 8 January 1987 I visited Croydon with Ronnie Power to see a production of *Black Eyed Susan*, an old play I had heard about for many years. On the 10th I went to *The Phantom of the Opera* at Her Majesty's and on the 25th to the Beethoven Gala at the Dome in Brighton. On 22 February my cousin and godson, John Wilsdon, and his wife and children came to see me. On 1 March it was *Turandot* at The Dome and on the 3rd *King Lear*. I then went off by through train from Brighton to Glasgow with Gilbert Bradley, and of course as soon as we arrived it started to snow, but it did not last. We managed to go to the Cathedral, St Andrew's Church, Pollock House with its wonderful collection of pictures, and the Burrell collection, which is more famous but quite different. We also went to the Hunterian Gallery, the Willow Tea Rooms, which were associated with Charles Rennie Mackintosh; we went to the lovely Theatre Royal in Hope Street, and the College of Art, which is a marvellous building by Charles Rennie Mackintosh. We also went to Edinburgh to see the National Gallery, the National Portrait Gallery and other things. It was a wonderful trip. From Glasgow we took a train to York where we visited the marvellously restored Fairfax House with its beautiful collection of furniture and works of art.

On the 15th I had a distant cousin of mine, Michael Dodson, to stay from Solihull in Warwickshire. The Dodsons were descended from the Sherborns of Odiham and it was nice to exchange notes about family matters.

On the 29th I had further meetings with the police. On 2 May I went to Brickwall at Northiam, a lovely old timber-framed house with some very remarkable late seventeenth- and early eighteenth-century plaster ceilings inside and an interesting garden; a lovely house.

On the 13th I went to Hinton Ampner, and to Uppark again for the umpteenth time. On the 15 June I went to Rye in Sussex to see that lovely old town again and on the 17th I was up at five and went up to Northamptonshire to see Canons Ashby. This is a remarkable old house, home of the Dryden family. I also went to a house which I had never seen before called Baddesley Clinton, which is near Solihull in Warwickshire. I stayed with the Dodsons, my cousins. The following day I went to the National Trust-owned Fleece Inn at Bretforton; Hanbury Hall; Stanway House; Aldsworth to see my cousins the Terrys; and to Clifton near Bristol. I then went on to Wales to see Llansannan House, Hensol Castle, Gileston Manor and Fonmon Castle, the latter having a marvellous roccoco drawing room constructed inside a medieval castle keep. On the 21st I went to see Penhow Castle, where Steven Weeks (who when a very young boy had achieved fame in Gosport by taking on the local council as vandals) was living and had restored the building, and then went straight on to Trevelyan at St Veep in Cornwall.

On 10 July an American, Tom Standish, from Hartford, Connecticut, came to stay, bringing back for me one of the pictures that had been stolen from Bedfont in the great armed raid. It was very generous and kind of him because he had bought the picture in good faith in an auction in America. It was rather an unfortunate occasion when he arrived because we had a flood in the basement (as if we hadn't had enough of floods) and the lights had fused. I was not surprised that Tom left the following morning. On the 17th the lights on the landing outside the drawing room fused as well. On the 31st I journeyed to Lydd in Kent where one of my ancestors had lived, went to see Port Lympne, a remarkable house built by Philip Sassoon with its great garden and painted and decorated rooms, and also to Folkington Manor in Sussex, a lovely timber-framed house now largely known for its collection of old motor cars. The following day I went to Ashdown Forest, to Groom-bridge Place and had lunch at the Dorset Arms at Harting. My friends Roger and Ray having come from Christchurch in New Zealand to stay, we did a few things including going to the Open Air Museum at Singleton and to Boxgrove Priory, but they were only here for a few days.

On 5th September I had the good fortune to meet Peter Wiley, the artist, on the beach and we have been friends ever since.

On 16 October there was the celebrated so called hurricane which did so much damage. The noise was horrendous. It started about 2 am in the morning. All the lights went out just after 4. Chimney pots and slates came off the roof, the chimney stacks were rendered unstable, a rear window of the car was smashed, wing mirrors were torn off and the car body itself was peppered with holes. However, we didn't realise just how bad it was until we set off the following morning to view an auction in Lewes, only to find that Dawsons Auction Rooms near the station had been half destroyed. It was a big corrugated iron-faced building and half of it had come down, doing serious damage to the contents in the sale room stores. Trees were down over the road from Brighton to Lewes in great numbers. We actually saw seven vans which had been blown off the road into fields and on The Level in Brighton we saw a great many trees down. People had chimney-stacks through their roofs and all hell was let loose. A most awful experience.

On 10 November I went to a performance of *La Cage Aux Folles*, and also at about that time. I went to the Rodin Exhibition at the Hayward Gallery and the exhibition of pictures from Fyvie Castle at Agnews, which I thought was quite wonderful. The pictures from Fyvie had been bought by the nation for retention and return to the Castle from which they had been removed.

On 17 November the trial began at Isleworth Court of the people arrested and charged with handling my property as a result of the armed raid on the Fawns. I was there for just two days but the trial lasted for six weeks. The people arrested were sent to prison for three years each. On 22 December I had a meeting with Detective Sergeant Morrison of Hounslow police prior to going away the following day with Gilbert Bradley to stay at the St Vincents Rocks Hotel at Clifton overlooking the Clifton Suspension Bridge. It was a nice hotel to stay in, having visited it several times before. The next day was Christmas Eve and we went to stay with Gilbert's sister and her husband at Naunton in Gloucestershire for a couple of nights. When we got to Naunton, we were told we had been invited to drinks at a neighbour's house, and the neighbour turned out to be Nicholas Ridley, later the first Lord Ridley. It was a sticky evening; Ridley's house was all right but he was there with his new wife and there was a rather frosty atmosphere. There were only four of us as guests and the conversation didn't flow at all. I tried to make my contribution by saying how I spent my working life on listing historic buildings in the Ministry of Town and Country Planning; how I was a friend of Robin Cooke, who was then MP for Bristol West. I made all these remarks because Nicholas Ridley, in the days after the War, was one of the few MPs who ever asked questions about conservation, preservation, or listed buildings, and I felt that my remarks would be well received. But somehow or other the conversation became more sticky and eventually I saw on the stool in front of the great fire a copy of the catalogue of the exhibition of pictures from Fyvie Castle, and I said helpfully how wonderful it was that these pictures had been saved and that they'd been returned to the house. I was astonished to get the rejoinder that Ridley didn't approve of this at all – pictures should be on the walls of people's homes and if people couldn't afford them then they should be sold to someone else! He didn't approve of galleries of pictures open to the public at all to which I replied with some astonishment, 'but what about the National Gallery?' 'I don't approve of the National Gallery,' he said, 'the pictures should be on people's walls!' Then I began to realise what an absolute fraud he was. A completely maverick politician. How could he have deserved his reputation?

The Christmas ended rather badly. We were leaving Naunton on the 29th but the gearbox and transmission went and we had to be returned to Brighton by AA Relay, a marvellous service which the AA provides for motorists in difficulty.

On 15 February 1988, there was the official opening of the exhibition of photography by Gordon Antony at the museum, which we all enjoyed very much indeed. On 6 April I went up to London to see the Robert Mapplethorpe Exhibition and also called in at Somerset House and St Catherine's House for research of several kinds of family history. In May it was the Brighton Festival, and every day seemed to produce something of importance or interest, or both. On 9 May I went to see *The Deep Blue Sea* with Penelope Keith playing the lead which was awfully well done; she was outstanding. On the 12th, in a most inadequate setting, I saw a production of *The Flying Dutchman* at the Dome; somehow or other they managed to get two ships and quays on the very tiny stage. On the 14th Timothy Bond was giving a recital on the organ at the Chapel at Lancing College and that was excellent. On the 17th I saw the Ballet du Nord at the Theatre Royal but I'd hurt my back going to see the Flying Fruit Fly Circus in a tent on the Sunday and the result was that I had to cancel my trip to Glasgow on the Thursday because my back hurt so much.

On 12 June I had a strange experience when I saw a ghost in the house. It was in the middle of the day and suddenly when I came out of the drawing room there was this little girl in a cut-off crinoline of the 1860s, running up the stairs from the drawing room to the floor above. I called to my friend Gilbert Bradley to look but he didn't quite hear or understand what I was saying and didn't see anything. It is the only time I have ever seen a ghost in that form, although people staying in the basement flat have reported seeing an old lady down there and I did once see part of a trousered man's leg disappearing up the stairs. All I actually saw was the leg, not the body nor head.

On 13 July I set off at 6 am from Brighton with Ronnie Power. We stopped at Saltram for tea and to look around the house and arrived at Trevelyan at 6 pm. The following day, Thursday, we had lunch in the Rashleigh Arms and visited Fowey; on Friday we went to Lanhydrock to look at the house and gardens again, and on Sunday we went to Mevagissey, Trerice, Newquay, Trevose Head and various other places. On Sunday we went to Polperro, and on the Monday we went to Carlyon Bay. The following day we went to Padstow and Prideaux Place. On the 20th Ronnie's visit had to come to an end so I took him to Bodmin Road Station to return to Brighton.

On 22 August I visited Hastings, Lydd, Romney and Hythe and various other places and it was quite a good day out. On 26 August I went to see Standen near East Grinstead, a house by Phillip Webb, the former home of the Beale family of solicitors. On the 29th I took my friends Ray Penney and Roger Balson to Kidbrooke Park, Brickwall at Northiam and Great Dixter also at Northiam. Great Dixter is a marvellous medieval timber-framed house restored by Edwin Lutyens and Nathaniel Lloyd. It has a most gorgeous garden laid out by Gertrude Jekyll.

On the 7th my friends Peter Rose and Albert Gallichan and I went off to see Highclere Castle which we all much enjoyed. It's a house by Sir Charles Barry belonging to Lord Caernavon, with interesting contents. We went to Sandham Memorial Chapel and also visited churches at East and West Woodhay. The following day I set off for Derbyshire to have tea at Carnfield Hall, the home of my friend James Cartland and his wife. The house was one I had listed years before when it was derelict, and they had restored it and it was absolutely marvellous. The following day I dashed off to Ruthin in Wales where I was staying at 'The Castle'. This sounds straightforward enough, but in Ruthin there is a Ruthin Castle Hotel and a Castle Hotel. Of course I arrived at the wrong one only to be redirected. Anyway it all makes for jolly fun in a way. I went on from there to see Erthig again, Chirk Castle again, Brynkinalt, Brynbella, Nerquis, Leeswood and then from there went to Barlaston Hall in Staffordshire, an empty shell of a house designed by Sir Robert Taylor which had been derelict for years. I also went to see the remains of Knypersley Hall and Park, and to Hanch Hall in Staffordshire which many people believed had been demolished years before. It is a house of 1730s, very Gibbsish in its way, but by a local chap called Trubshaw. It had enormous later additions which rather spoilt it, but never mind. I was staying with Brenda and Sid Bailey at Tunstall in Stoke-on-Trent, wonderful friends of mine and distant cousins.

Back home in Brighton I went up to Petersham near Richmond where Richard Jeffree was conducting a group of people around Petersham House, Petersham Church and Douglas House for the Georgian Group. If anyone knows Petersham they will know that it is stuffed full of marvellous late seventeenth and early eighteenth-century mansions in their own grounds, most of them still extremely well preserved, although one of the best ones, Rutland Lodge, was unfortunately largely burnt out a few years back completely destroying the magnificent early eighteenth-century main staircase.

Back in Brighton I went up to London to the ceremony naming a room in Falmouth House in Bayswater Road in honour of Bob Mackenzie. There I met Barbara Kelly and her husband Bernard Braden, who had been great friends of Bob. Barbara ran an organisation providing distinguished speakers for functions of various kinds and Bob had been one of her main speakers.

On 7 October I went off to stay in the West Country. I had a private view of the sale at Avishays in Somerset, I went to Dartmouth, and arrived at the Cliffe House Hotel in Torquay in the evening, in an absolute cloudburst of torrential rain which didn't do either the place or me much good. The following day I went to an astonishing house in

Paignton called Oldway; a late nineteenth- early twentieth-century house built by the Singer Sewing Machine family, with American money. It had most lavishly decorated interiors and stunning gardens. I also went to Tor Abbey which belonged to Torquay Council and is an ancient house operated as a museum. I visited Knightshay once again and Castle Drogo by Lutyens. On the 9th I went to the Maritime Museum at Exeter and visited Paignton church. On the 10th I arrived in St Veep and viewed a sale at Par, which was all very interesting. I left some bids and a couple of days later I went there again to collect the things I'd bought. On the 14th, having arrived at Trevelyan to stay with my friends, we were invited by Raleigh Trevelyan to go and have drinks at his house St Caddix which is nearby, on a little inlet of the river. It was a lovely moment in my holidays. On the 16th I went to Northill Church, to Place at Fowey and then on to Moretonhampstead in Devon. I had a terrible job getting across Dartmoor in thick fog and arrived hours and hours late. On the Monday I left Moretonhampstead to see Okehampton church and to view the auction of the contents of Southwick House in Hampshire and then go back to Brighton.

The year ended with a pleasant Christmas in friends' houses, and in the New Year I was given the name of a photograph retoucher called Len Day in New Church Road Hove, to whom I went for help with two old photographs I had discovered from Aunt Ada's, which had been popped inside a book and had been lost for many years. One photograph showed the great aviator Charles Lindbergh and Ann Morrow on the day of their wedding, and together with that was a letter of thanks to my Aunt Ada from Ann Lindbergh for the wedding gift they had been sent. The other photograph was one of the Morrow-Lindbergh family with the baby that was to be kidnapped for a ransom demand and then murdered. The Morrows had been friends of the Sherborns for many years and it was through a family called Reeve that there was a distant family connection. The Lindberghs always used to see Aunt Ada when they came to England, which explained why I had the photographs. But both the photographs had been slightly damaged and I needed them to be touched up. The retoucher was so proud of the fact that he had been given the job of retouching them for me, he refused to accept any payment, which was marvellous of him. Thank you very much, Mr Day.

On 7 February I went to an amateur production of *Oklahoma* in Brighton, and on the 9th I went to another organ recital by Timothy Bond, this time at Lancing College, My friends Brian and Jack arrived again in April and we went to Charleston, the former Bloomsbury Group house with fascinating decorations, to the Priests House at Alfriston, to East Dean Church, to Alfriston Church and the Star at Alfriston for tea. On the 12th we went to Nymans Gardens near Haywards Heath and to West Hoathly and its Church. On the 14th we visited Pashley at Ticehurst, and the following day we went to Brickwall, a timber-framed and gabled house with lovely late seventeenth-century plasterwork. We also went to Tenterden Church. On the 19th we were off again to Parham near Pulborough, and to Billingshurst. A couple of days later we were off to the Isle of Wight, visiting the Roman villa at Brading, and Brading Church. We had tea at Shanklin in pouring rain, and arrived at the Royal Hotel in Ventnor. It was Brian Leach's birthday on the 25th and we celebrated it by going to Appuldurcombe, Carisbrooke Castle, and Osborne House. We stayed in the Fountain Hotel in Cowes. On the 26th we visited Whippingham Church near Osborne where all the royals are buried; Shalfleet Church; Yarmouth Church; and Alum Bay, which has an interesting glassworks and amazing coloured deposits of sand. We then returned to the mainland to stay in Southsea and visit the sights in Portsmouth. We visited the Tudor battle ship the *Mary Rose*, the Victorian iron clad ship, the *Warrior* leaving behind the *Victory* which we had all visited before.

On 30 May I was elected vice-chairman of the Conservation Areas Advisory Group at Brighton Council. I had been a member of the group for some time, representing the Regency Society, so to be elected Vice-Chairman was really rather nice.

At the end of the month I left for Wales on holiday. I stayed at the Bear Hotel in Crickhowell, which was very nice, and the following day I visited Abercamlais, Tretower Court and other places. I also went to see St Fagan's Castle, near Cardiff – a Jacobean house in a medieval Castle setting. I then left Wales for North Devon to stay for the first time with my friend John Stevens Guille, and was expected to arrive at Yatton Court at six in the evening. Most embarrassingly the car broke down on the very top of Countisbury Hill and the AA had to take me all the way to Exeter, wrecking our arrangements. John very kindly rescued me from Exeter, and the following day arranged for me to visit the little-known but architecturally exciting house, Kings Nympton Park for tea. This is a Georgian house, virtually a copy of Marble Hill at Twickenham, which had been designed for Henrietta Howard, Countess of Suffolk, by Roger Morris and the Earl of Pembroke in 1724. Designed by Francis Cartwright of Blandford for James Buller in 1746, it is astonishing that the house has never been completed by being rendered externally, in all that time, 250 years.

After leaving John's, I spent a couple of nights in Penzance and then crossed over by boat to the Scillies. I had a splendid time and actually saw some sharks close to for the very first time. I left two weeks later, driving up to St Mawes where some newly discovered cousins of the Bances lived. I went there to lunch, and then up to Martock for the night. In the village is an eighteenth-century column called the 'Pinnacle'. It had been hit by a truck years before when I was in the office and pressure had been put upon me to let it go as only the base survived. However, I dug my toes in and said that it should not be demolished or removed but restored as it was – and lo and behold it had been!

From Martock I drove to Hungerford, to East and West Challow in Berkshire, to Childrey and Newbury in search of the Bance graves and then back to Brighton.

On the 16th I had a very nasty experience which I have never recovered from. I was driving out of Brighton up the A23 at Bolney and had to stop in the middle of the road to allow for a car turning right into one of the roadway restaurants. There was no room to overtake on the inside. I was just over the brow of the hill and I could only wait for someone to crash into me. A chap with a van came and to avoid me he threw his truck into the ditch. Behind him came a fast car driven by a man who crashed headlong into me, knocking my car forward into the car in front. It was a four-car pile up and a mess. I was going to have tea with my cousins, Commander and Mrs Innes-Hamilton in Virginia Water and then to supper at Cobham with my friends Michael Le Garst and Andrew McGuffog. Obviously I couldn't go; the car was far too badly damaged and I was badly shaken, though there were no signs of blood or broken bones. I thought at the time that I had not been hurt at all, but before long muscle tightness and aches and pains announced that I had started on a lifetime sentence of osteoarthritis and what became permanent disability. The breakup of the body physical had begun.

November 11th was the occasion of a visit to Bramber and to Worplesdon to see the church there where the deaths of two Selous cousins of mine during the First World War are recorded.

On 18 December I took my dear friend Gary Holt to lunch at the Grand Hotel in Eastbourne. We did not know then that he had only a short while to live.

16

The Brighton Bolthole

January 1990 was rotten. On the 25th there was a great gale with widespread damage and more five days later. I had tea with the famous actress Dora Bryan at her flat in Marine Parade on the last day of the month. Gilbert Bradley was off to Zimbabwe on 2 February, having suffered a nasty fall just a couple of days before. Nothing would ever stop him from travelling!

More storm damage occurred on 7 February but then the weather settled down and became very warm; a nude sunbather was visible on the beach on the 16th! There were various site visits with the Conservation Areas Advisory Group, including one to Barry's classical St Andrew's Church in Waterloo Street. On 2 March I attended a performance of *Turandot* at the Gardner Arts Centre with Pauline Tinsley, which was marvellous. Later on in March I was elected President of the Kingscliffe Society, an amenity group concerned with the half of Brighton to the east of the Steine. This was immediately followed by a major crisis in the Committee, with the then chairman handing in his resignation!

On 30 March, Charlotte Bonham Carter having died a couple of months before, there was to be a memorial service for her at the crypt of St Paul's Cathedral. All the other Bonham Carters assembled with a considerable number of other personalities – Charlotte had been a great character.

In April Gilbert, having returned from Zimbabwe, set off for a tour of Peru. I had Peter Reid, the great country house historian, to stay – his one and only visit to me in Brighton! We visited all the Bloomsbury Group places like Monks House at Rodmell, Charleston and Berwick church, plus Shelley's Hotel in Lewes which occupies a wonderful old house in the High Street. I also managed to arrange a privileged visit to a very little-known house called Clayton Priory, formerly the seat of the Podmores near Burgess Hill, which had an absolutely stunning staircase hall with a flying Imperial-style stair.

Peter having left, and Brian and Jack having come to stay again, we set off to stay in Ely to see the cathedral, to explore Cambridge with its college buildings and then to stay at The Bell in Thetford. As part of our stay, we visited Burghley, the Cecil's great Elizabethan house near Stamford with all its treasures. We also went to the great Georgian house, Wimpole Hall, and explored Godmanchester in the car. We then set off for King's Lynn as a base for seeing the town and for visiting Felbrigg Hall, a Jacobean and Wren period house altered by James Paine with very lovely interiors. We went to Fakenham for lunch and then to the great Jacobean house of Blickling Hall, where an eighteenth-century Norwich architect, Thomas Ivory, had had the strangely brilliant idea of refixing the main staircase in what had been the great hall by adding extra parts to match. He had also painted the whole thing with white paint (now long removed), and the later parts are all made in softwood rather than in oak – the original wood for the rest of it. The following day was occupied by a visit to Houghton Hall. This surely has to be one of the greatest houses in Europe, designed by Colin Campbell, William Kent and James Gibbs (who added the domes on the roof) with interiors and contents almost beyond compare. In Norwich we saw Strangers Hall, a medieval courtyard house and now an excellent furnished house museum, and the Cathedral. We then went to stay in Lavenham, exploring the place itself, plus The Grange at Ditchingham and many churches. The following day was the last but we managed to visit Audley End, another great Stuart palace, Flatford Mill and the extraordinary and very early recently ruined, but now restored, Grange Barn at Coggeshall which, the experts now believe, dates from the twelfth century and was part of Coggeshall Abbey.

Now into May, the Festival was on again and I went to many different things, including a concert by the Moscow Radio Symphony Orchestra at the Dome which included as an unbroadcast encore, Elgar's *Pomp and Circumstance* No. 5, Land of Hope and Glory which brought loud cheers from the audience for this generous compliment.

However, it seems that I had been overdoing things greatly, and during the night of 29/30 May I suffered a heart attack in the early hours of the morning. Too much culture I suppose, and for the first half of June I laid low going nowhere at all.

On 18 July Brian Leach came to stay and we set off by train the following morning to Paris. We stayed there for a few days principally to see the Musée d'Orsay in a revitalised railway station, with a splendid collection of nineteenth-century art. We did a chunk of the Louvre with its great pyramid entrance and various churches, then spent two nights in Rouen to explore it. Then it was Dieppe and the museum in the Castle. It was highly successful but the heat at midnight in the Champs Elysées in Paris made me wonder if I was about to collapse and die.

I was still not very well when I returned and congestion of the heart was diagnosed on 22 August. All my medication was stopped immediately by the hospital, and on Sunday 25 August I collapsed and was close to death. My friends and relations were sent for to see me. I kept going into a coma at the hospital, and it eventually transpired that I was suffering withdrawal symptoms as a result of being cut off from my medicines. As soon as these had been restored and a cardiac tracer had been installed to monitor my progress, I began to recover swiftly. I left hospital at the end of the month.

In the middle of September I was a great deal better. On 23 September I heard one of Nigel Kennedy's amazing violin recitals at The Dome.

Brenda and Sid Bailey, my cousins from Stoke-on-Trent, came to stay in October and we went to an antiques fair, the marvellous exhibition on the Crace family of decorators in the Museum, Preston Manor, Ditchling Beacon and Church, Berwick Church, Alfriston Church and the fifteenth-century Star Inn with its fascinating timber-framed front and carved oriel windows. On 6 November I bet Ronnie Power that Margaret Thatcher would lose the general election because of the Poll Tax disgrace and discovered that the electorate had forgotten about it, so I lost my money. How can people be so silly?

Christmas soon arrived and John Wilsdon, my cousin and godson, came to see me in Brighton.

On Tuesday the 15th I saw *Volpone*, on the 17th *The Merchant of Venice*, on the 21st January *Reversal of Fortunes* with Jeremy Irons, and on the 23rd I went to the watercolour exhibition and fair at the Park Lane Hotel and found myself within a security cordon with the Prince of Wales!

The weather had improved enormously enabling a visit to the beach at the beginning of March, but on 19 March a flood was discovered in my entrance hall following a visit the previous day by a gas engineer who called to balance the radiators. The emergency handyman, who called promptly found three radiators leaking. The water had affected the hall table which had belonged to George IV at Windsor Castle, the desk box, made originally for Henry Duke of Cumberland, and the Duke of Cambridge's hall chairs, plus the ceiling, of course.

On Sunday 8 April 1991 Brian and Jack having come to stay again, we set off for Oxfordshire to stay the night at Swalcliffe Manor near Banbury, a marvellous medieval house with a vaulted undercroft. We visited Charlecote Park and Coughton Court, and the following day went to Calke Abbey and stayed at Monsal Head. Next day we did Bolsover Castle, Sutton Scarsdale, Edensor Church and Chatsworth, popping in for quick looks at Tissington Hall, Okeover Hall and Hassop Hall. On Wednesday we had been invited by the James Cartlands to visit their restored house Carnfield Hall, which I had listed years before, and we did Hardwick Hall and Rode Hall and lunched at the Bells of Peover. On Thursday we went to Tatton Park, that magnificent house owned by the National Trust and Tatton Old Hall which I had played a significant role in preventing the National Trust from demolishing. From there we went to Blackpool, which made quite a change for us. I was able to see the Grand Theatre which again I had played a significant part in saving from destruction. There was also the famous Tower designed by Maxwell and Tuke in 1894 and the magnificent Tower Ballroom designed by the eminent theatre architect Frank Matcham in 1899, which I had campaigned for years at the office to get listed, and it is now graded 1. We then went to stay in Lancaster from where we visited Lancaster Priory Church, the Castle, the Music Room in Sun Street and, the Harris Art Gallery in Preston. Then we saw Gawthorpe Hall, and York. On the 18th/19th the car broke down with a flat battery in York, but we had plenty to do while it was fixed and went to Fairfax House now fully restored internally, the Castle Museum, and then left to see Allerton Park and Low Hall at Dacre to

266

stay with Mrs Holliday. The following day we did Harewood House very thoroughly and greatly admired the new sculpture of a male nude by Astrid Zydower which had been installed in one of the fountain basins in 1984 on Charles Barry's terrace. I was enormously impressed by the redecoration and rearrangement inside the house, which had been designed by Alec Cobbe of Hatchlands and Lord Harewood. The rearranged picture gallery I considered a triumph. After Harewood we decided to make for home, and did the 250 miles in five hours, ending up at the Elizabethan Tandoori at Patcham for supper, 1,276 miles later!

On Saturday 18 May 1991 there was a splendid day out with the Royal Archaeological Institute visiting places in Kent: the mediaeval Old Soar at Plaxtol, Dukes Place at East Peckham and Mereworth Castle, that marvellous Colin Campbell evocation of a large Palladian villa with porticoes on each front and a domed roof, with magnificent interiors – though I thought the rooms on the bedroom floor had been altered rather a lot.

On Wednesday 5 June my friend Michael Norman, the archaeologist, had arranged for me to see over Castle Goring – an eccentric Georgian house by John Rebecca with one front like a Gothic castle and the other an impeccable Palladian villa. At the same time I discovered that a very old friend, Alvin Gamble the antique dealer, been found dead on the moors near Plymouth, having committed suicide over money worries. Two more friends were to die that week on the same day, 12 June, both involved with the theatre: Lewis Aronson and Sunny Russell Hay: Sunny was a great character who had been taught dance by her aunt, Lilian Baylis.

On Sunday 7 July I was delighted to take the opportunity never before available of seeing Rotherfield Park in Hampshire with Peter Rose and Albert Gallichan. It is an interesting house, largely of nineteenth-century date, with an impressive central staircase hall and exciting contents, and we tacked on Stanstead Park and a few churches. On 6 August there was a very good amateur production of *Privates on Parade* at the Little Theatre. There was to be yet another death with a funeral on 18 August, that of the brilliantly talented and young John Dinkel, Director Emeritus of the Royal Pavilion and museums and galleries in Brighton.

267

In September 1991, fed up with things generally, I went off by myself for a restorative stay at Broadstairs, visiting Faversham to see what had been achieved in the way of restoration following all my professional visits years before to Court Street and Abbey Street, and this was a joy and a delight. I also visited Dunkirk to find the graves of Mr and Mrs Henry Sherborn, who when in the late 1840s at Mornington Place, London had had Alfred Lord Tennyson as a lodger, and it was while staying with her that the manuscript of *In Memoriam* was lost until found in Mrs Sherborn's kitchen cupboard; Surrenden Dering to see how much remained of that seriously fire damaged seat, now a redecorated and restored house; Fordwich, and Margate, one of my favourite old seaside towns; and then to the Royal Albion Hotel on the seafront in Broadstairs. The following day was not quite as hectic and I just visited Ramsgate to have a look round there and to St Nicholas at Wade where I had a record of an ancestor visiting it centuries ago.

On the Friday I visited Canterbury, Herne Bay, Ramsgate, Dunkirk to search all over again, and Kingsgate, but while still in Broadstairs I searched out a house called Little Chart in Castle Avenue, which had been owned before the war by the Farrows. I had been privileged to stay there as a child. Returning home the following day I found time to visit Leeds church, Charing Church and Goudhurst Church, where the tower had been rebuilt by the mason John Young and others in 1638–40. He also built the remarkable classical church at Berwick-upon-Tweed in 1649–50 and, sticking my neck right out, it would not surprise me if it was discovered that a whole group of seventeenth-century country houses in Kent with pilastered fronts might be attributable to him (Lees Court, Syndale Park and Bayhall at Faversham for example); but there is absolutely no evidence yet. He must have done other work somewhere.

On the 15th October I travelled by train to Stoke-on-Trent to stay with my cousins the Baileys, and they took me to the Moat Hotel which incorporates Josiah Wedgwood's Etruria Hall, to the Theatre Royal at Hanley for a musical version of Arnold Bennett's *The Card*, to the gardens of Biddulph Grange and to Knypersley Hall, where the remaining fragment of the house has an extremely sumptuous eighteenth-century plaster ceiling.

On Monday 4 November, I went with Brian and Jack to Seaford, Newhaven, Bishopstone church and Alfriston.

On 29 December my great friend Richard Jeffree died. We had both helped each other enormously, I by driving Richard around searching for things often in Eton High Street and elsewhere, he doing a great deal of research. He was a unique authority on Mary and Charles Beale and had a great knowledge of the works of Kneller, Lely, Borsselaer, Wissing and their contemporaries. He left his Beale collection to Bury St Edmunds Museum, near to where the Beales had originated in Suffolk.

On 2 January 1992 I had the most unusual experience of having to sue the police for the return of a picture of mine and appeal to the Court in Horseferry Road, Westminster. The picture had been seized by the police following a tip-off from the National Portrait Gallery who had spotted it in a sale catalogue at Christies at South Kensington and the procedure that had to be followed was that there had to be a hearing in Court. The picture had evidently been in a sale before at Christies and had been bought in, but it was one of the pictures that had been stolen in the big armed raid at the house at Bedfont ten years before. My solicitor had advised me that the cheapest thing to do was to pay the alleged cost of the picture (£150) and had offered to do so. However, there was a difference of opinion about the alleged value of the picture, and the owner responded by saying that he wanted £700. I was not prepared to pay this much and in any case I felt it was legally mine. At the hearing the man turned up and both he and I had to appear and give evidence. I was armed with photographs of the picture, including one of it hanging on my staircase. When asked where he had bought it, he said, to the Court's amazement, that he had 'bought it off the back of a lorry' – no defence being offered at all. The magistrates retired and returned with their judgement that it was undoubtedly my legal property, and it was returned to me for nothing! The picture, I should have said, was a very large one, a portrait of Jane Gore, Mrs Travell, mother of Sir Thomas Travell, MP for Milborne Port, and was by John Vandervaart and had originally cost me, years ago, just £1. The fine contemporary carved giltwood frame has never been recovered.

*   *   *

On 4 March I took my great friend Mukesh Pattni to see the new production of *Me and My Girl* which had been put on in London. Mukesh is from Tanzania and this was to be his first visit to an English theatre and we both enjoyed it very much. I had seen the original production of the show at the Victoria Palace Theatre in 1938 with Lupino Lane. I thought the revival better because it had been completely rewritten and now incorporated some extra songs from other works by Noel Gay.

On Tuesday 9 April we had a general election which was won by the Tories. On the 29th I set off for the Moat House at Longnor in Shropshire in order to see Pitchford Hall and from there travelled to Bettisfield Park to see that lovely Georgian house, rescued by Mrs Bailey of Plas Teg in Mold. I also visited Market Drayton and Erthig. I stayed at Golden Grove at Llanasa. From there I went to Bodelwyddan Castle, Levens Hall and on to the Pheasant at Bassenthwaite Lake, and then drove up to Edinburgh for the Festival, joining Ronnie Power, calling at Mellerstain and Traquair on the way. I was staying at the University and we were entertained by John and Rita Seton-Hill at the New Club in Princes Street to see the fireworks. After seeing the sights of Edinburgh (the Castle, the Royal Mile, Holyrood Palace and the Georgian House in Charlotte Square) there were houses to be seen with Ronnie Power: Dalmeny, Hopetoun and Glamis Castle. For one night we went to stay with our friends John Jarvis Smith and Roger Cave at Wallbut near Lockerbie, from where we visited Maxwellton House famously associated with the song 'Annie Laurie'.

On 6 September I visited Thirlestaine and Floors Castle, followed in the next few days by Paxton House, a very fine William Adam building with original Chippendale furniture and a great display of pictures from Scottish National Collections. I also saw Belford Hall, Lindisfarne Castle, Cragside and Axwell Park. I stayed at Bradley Hall near Gateshead, and from there went to stay the night with John Martin Robinson at his house at Barbon, taking in Sizergh Castle and Naworth Castle on the way. John's house is a lovely Georgian building. Leaving the following day I went to Eyam Hall in Derbyshire, stayed at Monsal Head for the night and then returned home. Well over 2,000 miles were covered.

On 29 September there was a memorial concert for Richard Jeffree at

Leighton House in Kensington, attended by close friends. In October I went to stay with my friend Danny Stevens at Whitton and did research at the Bank of England Record Office at Roehampton into the accounts of John Bance of Challow in Berkshire. He was presumably one of 'my' Bances and he was a director of the Bank in the first half of the eighteenth century. On the 12th I saw *Swan Lake* performed by the London City Ballet and on the Friday I went to see the National Theatre production of *Billy Liar*. Brenda and Sid Bailey came for the weekend. On the 27th Brian, Jack and I arrived in Bath to stay at the Kennard Hotel in Henrietta Street where the only place to sit was on a sofa on a landing (apart from our bedrooms), but during our stay we visited The Red Lodge in Bristol, the Georgian Houses at Bath and Bristol and Dyrham Park. When we left Bath we called in at Lydiard Tregoze and were given a royal welcome because of my gift years ago of the Highmore state portraits of Lord and Lady St John. On Sunday 22 November 1992 Gilbert Bradley had a party for about thirty people for his birthday.

On Friday 8 January 1993 I had a lunch party for the Rev. Prebendary Irvine, his sister Rosemary and Mark and Valerie Chinnery. On 21 January I went to the Connaught Theatre, Worthing and saw the very best non-West End performance of *La Cage Aux Folles* that I have ever seen, and I must have seen the show about twenty times now. This time I took my friend Roger Miller. On the Sunday was a Brighton Cares show at the Dome. On the 29th was the opening of the Country House Lighting Exhibition to which I was lending several items. John Brushe came to stay and we visited that marvellous old house, now Shelley's Hotel at Lewes. Folkington Church next, a charming unspoilt church with interesting features. There is a monument in the church to the distinguished harpsichordist Violet Gordon Woodhouse, and another to Viscount Monckton of Brenchley, a close confidant of Edward VIII during the abdication crisis. In the churchyard lies Elizabeth David, the celebrated cookery writer. Also Berwick Church with its remarkable Bloomsbury Group painted decorations. We went to Eastbourne the following day. We enjoyed the splendours of the Kings Arms Pub in Seaside Road, saw Beachy Head, talked our way into Compton Place, the Duke of Devonshire's seaside house, and visited the Towner Art Gallery.

On the 4th I went to the funeral of Antony Dale, my former colleague and boss. I was delighted to meet Carole Ryan there after so many years. Antony had enjoyed a peaceful retirement for 17 years in his beloved Brighton. On the 9th I took Mukesh to see *Anna Karenina* and heard that Gary Lee-Holt had been taken to hospital and that he was very ill. On the 15th the Conservation Areas Advisory Group of Brighton had a site visit to Patcham Place, that enchanting-looking Georgian house faced with black mathematical tiles, seen as soon as one enters Brighton from London and presently a youth hostel. There was a proposal that it might be sold on as a hotel and the Youth Hostels Association chucked out. We felt the house was better left in their hands. There was another site visit on the 19th to Moulscombe Place in Brighton – another, slightly later, Georgian house which Brighton Council was proposing to sell to the University. It contains, interestingly enough, a series of doors given by George IV which had been displaced from Brighton Pavilion by the alterations under John Nash. On the 23rd Gary Lee-Holt was collected from Hove Hospital so that he could return home.

Gervase Jackson Stops from the National Trust came to stay on Sunday 14 March bringing his friend Ian Kirby to see me here.

On 30 March we went on a site visit to the Art Deco Butlins Ocean Hotel at Saltdean.

On 16 April Brian and Jack and I set off to explore Kent in depth for five days.

The first stop was at Ightam Mote, a medieval moated house of great interest which was undergoing a massive restoration programme. I was interested to discover that the upstairs chapel is now thought to have originally been the long gallery and that there is a suggestion that the painted roof timbers could possibly have come from some temporary structure built for the Crown, possibly for a pavilion for the Field of the Cloth of Gold. One obviously reserves judgement on this interesting speculation. As the National Trust was seeking sponsorship for the restoration of the leaded windows and their diamond-shaped quarries of glass, we felt that we should support this and did.

For lunch we searched out the Kentish Rifleman at Dunk's Green, a country pub which I had visited as a small boy, as the people there then were cousins of cousins of mine, the Boreham family. From a modest country establishment, it was now a restored timber-framed building with the internal timbering and substantial fireplaces opened up. And good food.

, After lunch we visited Chiddingstone Church where we looked for the grave of my old friend Rupert Gunnis, whose funeral I had attended in 1965. After Chiddingstone we visited Hever Castle, the first time for me for about twenty years or so, when the Astors still had it. I was very pleased to find that most of the contents had been bought by the new owners, and the rooms looked as splendid as ever. The gardens are quite magnificent and the flowers and trees were all in full bloom. There was formerly much more ancient classical sculpture here, but the essential atmosphere has survived.

We stayed at an old farmhouse called Saywell Farm, at Bedmonton, Wormshill, near Sittingbourne. The house was, and is, an ancient one. It is timber framed, and difficult to date, but has an inserted brick central chimneystack dated twice, clearly, 1611. The outer walling had been heightened, to give the upper floor headroom space. Originally, no doubt, it had just been a single-storey building. We were to spend a very happy four nights there.

On Saturday 17 April we set off for the south of the county to see Walmer Castle, which none of us had ever visited. One of Henry VIII's geometrical castles, it had been in use also as the official residence of the oddly titled Lord Warden of the Cinque Ports, an obsolete function performed by many leading dignitaries over the years. Parts of the interior are quite pleasant, but the furnishings favoured by the famous Duke of Wellington, who died here in 1852, lacked all comfort and aesthetic sense. One was amused that these famous people had tolerated ordinary painted weatherboarding *inside* their living rooms. there was some quite good mahogany furniture of the Georgian period, and a collection of Wellington souvenirs. One was surprised, if not warned in advance, that some of the alterations this century were to the designs of George Devey.

From there we drove to Broome Park, a gorgeous Charles I brick house, now in use as a golf club and quite happy to admit strangers for food and drinks. It is a perfectly preserved house, but with a great deal of totally imitative alteration and restoration. The interior is wholly reproduction, done for the first Earl Kitchener. The same goes for many external changes too, confirmed by a Victorian photograph in my collection. The front had sash windows of later date. It is very nice, and important, for all that!

After Broome we set off for Belmont. This had only been recently opened and was new to all of us. It is a very fine house designed by Samuel Wyatt and, although not built by them, still in the Harris family after 200 years. There is a very extensive collection of clocks, but the house was more interesting to us for its architecture and furnishings. Belmont is quite close to Faversham, so we explored Abbey Street and its neighbourhood, and were much impressed by the restoration of the old buildings, the pedestrianisation of much of it, and the treatment of the new, old-style pavement surfaces.

Sunday 18 April was the busiest for us. Firstly, Chartwell, Winston Churchill's country house, which I had not seen for a great many years and which now had a new entrance drive, a vast restaurant and other facilities. A house largely of the 1920s, by Philip Tilden, it is extremely liveable with a particularly delightful study and an ingenious dining room surrounded by windows in the daytime, and halved in size in the evenings by a wall of curtains. It has a lovely situation and views. From there it is just a few yards to Quebec House, General Wolfe's birthplace; an attractive, gabled brick house, with a massive staircase, panelling and Wolfe relics. From there, and still in Westerham, is Squerryes, the seat of the Warde family, a perfect Queen Anne red brick house with astonishingly important pictures, a suite of furniture with embroidered armorial seats, and much else of interest. Like Firle Place in Sussex, it has never quite recovered from wartime use and has modern brick splays to all its fireplaces and dull, colourwashed or painted walls everywhere, which detract terribly from the quality of the rooms and their contents. The colours are now too cold and featureless.

As if we had not done enough, we then went on to Finchcocks at Goudhurst, a very fine Queen Anne baroque house which I had not visited since the house had been the home of the Lycett Green family years before. It was now a museum of antique keyboard instruments owned and played by Richard Burnett, and we were delighted by recitals that took place at intervals about twenty minutes apart. A great surprise for me was to discover that my Broadwood grand piano of 1801, which I had sold in 1982 at Sothebys from Fawns when I had installed central heating was now here and in regular use. Indeed I heard it played and was also able to buy a tape of some Haydn pieces being played on it. I discovered it at the end of the war for sale in a draper's shop in The Brittox at Devizes in Wiltshire, for just £10! I had it restored by Morley's then at South Kensington and it was regularly tuned at Fawns by Broadwoods. At Streatham it had actually been housed in my bedroom!

It was upsetting to see that the great family group picture of the Bathursts, by James Maubart, which had been fixed over the hall chimneypiece when the house was built, had gone. One wondered whether any proper consent had been given for its removal as it was an original feature of the house.

It was not a good day for seeing houses on a Monday, so we visited shops in Faversham, went to the Sir John Falstaff at Gads Hill for lunch, looked at the outside of Gads Hill Place, and then drove into Rochester having seen the exterior of Cobham Hall. Rochester had greatly improved since my last visit, with the High Street freed of traffic and full of antique and arty shops – and tourists. It has a modest-sized cathedral, with very fine Norman parts, and there is much to see.

On the last day, Tuesday 20 April, we set off for Port Lympne, a house by Herbert Baker and Phillip Tilden for Philip Sassoon, which originally had magnificent gardens with a great cascade and pool. Unfortunately, that had a very short life due to structural failure. However the gardens are still quite fine, as long as one avoids the lions, tigers, wolves and other wild animals! Inside the house there is a clever staircase and entrance hall, and a lovely painted room by Rex Whistler.

From Port Lympne we visited Lympne Castle, a substantial medieval building, restored and enlarged by the 'Scots Lutyens' Sir Robert Lorimer. It is vast, rather unloved and unfurnished house, which looks as though a great injection of affection and money is needed.

Tuesday the 27th was to be remembered because my never-before-seen first cousin Arthur Allman and his wife Anna from Vancouver came to see me. But they stayed only a couple of hours, preferring to head off to the shops rather than tour the Royal Pavilion.

On 6 May, as a birthday event, Gilbert Bradley and I set off for Frogmore House, so beautifully restored and furnished by English Heritage. What genius some of these people have! We then saw the mausoleum and the fire ravaged Windsor Castle, so fascinating to see in its damaged state. May was the start of the Brighton Festival again but I felt that much of it was dreadful. Things greatly improved with James Galway's solo concert at the Dome. Sunday was The Siobhan Davies Dance Company at the Gardner Centre. On 13 May there was a Festival event involving a trip on the Bluebell Railway with theatrical incidents on various railway platforms.

I despatched all of my most valuable books for sale at Sothebys, to be followed by all my estate papers and archives which I sent to the Greater London Record Office in August.

But I was spending money too fast and I was burning up my energy quota. Things had to slow down as neither my money nor my strength was inexhaustible. But things stayed the same! The books were sold at Sothebys for £25,000 – mainly the most precious and rarely used ones (I still have several thousand I suppose). In a lifetime I had built up a fine collection of books illustrating country houses inspired entirely by the manuscript reference notes compiled by James Lees-Milne and given to the Ministry of Town and Planning way back in 1947 when listing really began. I had bought them all purely for use at the office and I was no longer there.

On 13 August Matthew Saunders from the Ancient Monuments Society came to stay and we toured various houses and churches.

On 10 October there was a show at the Dome with Hinge and Brackett called the *Last Night of the Brighton Proms*, which was absolutely excellent.

Friday 19 November started off with me viewing auction sales in Lewes and Heathfield, and then I struck up northwards into Kent via Maidstone and made for the village of Lynsted, because I had a photograph of the 1860s showing the church which I wished to visit because of the splendid monuments inside, including the masterpiece of the Elizabethan sculptor Epiphanius Evesham. However, as so often these days, the church was locked up and no access was possible, but a helpful notice announced that the key was to be had from Glebe Cottage, which would have been fine if anyone had been there. Another time, perhaps on the journey home! But there was one reward, and that was to discover that one of my photographs was actually of the Vicarage and had been taken in the 1860s or 70s.

276

So another unidentified subject in an old photograph had been solved. The house was still there, of medieval origin altered in the Regency period, but the attractive trellis verandah and the slatted shutters had all gone.

Onwards from there I made for Lenham, the nearest sizeable village to Chilston, and explored this pretty little place and patiently waited for a popular funeral to end, so that I could see the Church. It then took what seemed like two hours to find my way to Chilston, which was only about three miles away, but cut off from much of Europe by newly-constructed motorway-type roads not shown on my inadequate old maps! Surprisingly I did not have a one-inch map that covered Chilston. Beginning to get desperate and the day dark, I eventually arrived at a very handsome early eighteenth-century red brick house with a pedimented front and slightly projecting wings. The house is grand but simple externally; internally it appears, probably incorrectly, to be entirely a seventeenth- and eighteenth-century pastiche of Edwardian date, the Georgian style stuff being very lavish and rather over the top, and the central courtyard filled with a staircase hall with a sort of Stuart staircase on an imperial plan, all in dark brown oak. A room was allocated to me called the Boswell Room and this turned out to be in the attic storey, with sloping ceilings and dormer windows, and I had a comfortable double bed. But otherwise there was much to be desired, for there was absolutely no wardrobe and nowhere to hang anything: a small chest of drawers stood furtively behind a baggage rack, there were two Italianate gilt chairs designed for children, and the toilet glass stood on a ledge just fifteen inches from the floor. The bathroom adjacent was fine except that there was only one round shaving mirror attached to the cheek of the dormer window and one could only comb one's hair by scraping the comb along the ceiling. There was ample space where adequate mirrors could have been placed but had not been.

The hotel is run as a 'country house' and is only lit downstairs by candles and log fires. The rooms seemed spooky and dark, even in the dining room, where one was left wondering if there were several servants standing ready or whether the room was totally empty. It was impossible to read, there was no bar and no ballroom, and the supernatural effect was enhanced by a grand piano which played electrically by itself. The food and service was however very good, the food elaborate and plentiful.

The following morning I complained about my inadequate room, and was told that I would be moved, and was given one on the principal floor called 'Byron'. This had everything one wished, except only that the bathroom mirror and its attached lighting were still substandard; one fifteen-watt candle bulb and a pull cord hanging down the centre of the mirror were disappointments to say the least.

I headed for Canterbury in the morning, the chief objective being the Cathedral. Canterbury was swarming with visitors from overseas, in spite of the time of year, and in spite of flakes of occasional snow. However the day was pleasant and sunny, with no sign of a recession or closed up shops, and the whole place was immaculately kept. A simple lunch at Slatter's and a further walk round the town threatened by dark black clouds told me that it was time to leave before a snowfall. Stopping only to look at the church at Boughton Malherbe, where the owners of Chilston are buried, I hurried back to the candlelit gloom.

During supper the clouds opened and by the morning the park was deep in snow and all the trees covered in it. After breakfast and parting duties Danny and I decided to head for home after retrieving my white facecloth which the management had removed for washing, the hotel providing its own. The main roads were perfectly easy for the journey home, particularly as they were mainly motorways, and I arrived back in Brighton to find no snow whatever.

Unpacking the luggage, there, to my shame, I had two white face cloths not one. I suppose I shall have to drive back to Chilston to return it to them some time!

It was sad to miss Linton Church with the splendid monument to Lord Broome by E.H. Baily, but really this will have to wait for another visit . . . If only I had not come away with one of their facecloths! But then maybe their bills allow for accidents of this kind to happen.

Did I enjoy it all! Who does not enjoy a summer holiday even if it only amounts to two days in a snow covered county. It will at least be remembered.

On 17 February the Conservation Areas Advisory Group visited Ovingdean Grange, a highly complex and greatly altered medieval house where works had revealed some remarkably fine early carved panelling and other interesting features.

I had been suffering considerable problems with my arms and shoulder for some time and in spite of every kind of treatment had virtually lost the use of both arms. My doctor, always very good, had been laid low by a broken hip and a series of temporary doctors had only prescribed a varying series of coloured pills. I decided that I would have to go to the casualty department at the hospital, where they pronounced me as bad as I could possibly be and made me turn up for examination in detail by a Mr Turnbull the following day. This was later followed by an appointment with another consultant when arthroscopic sub-cronial decomposition and rotator cuff syndrome were diagnosed, chronic osteoarthritis.

In the meantime I had taken Gary, who was temporarily feeling much better to *Tosca* but I collapsed twice on the Tuesday after having had lunch with Danny Stevens and Michael Caldon. Mukesh Pattni took me to the curiously titled Adventures in Motion Pictures production of *Highland Fling* at Sadlers Wells but I was slowing down considerably. On 1 June I was taken into hospital for an operation on both shoulders and my left knee, and I was put on a morphine drip for several days. On 9 June I was discharged from hospital but was still paralysed and in pain. Nonetheless I was on the mend, and I spent four hours on the beach on Saturday.

In September I set off for Dorset to visit Kingston Lacy but I found the journey very tiring and had to sit down in each room at the house as I went round. It was fascinating that the persecuted gay owner William Bankes had built the house when in enforced exile abroad, not able to return to England without arrest and imprisonment. I stayed, most comfortably, with the High Sherriff of Dorset and his wife at Abbey House, Cerne Abbas.

Back in Brighton, Matthew Saunders invited me to supper at Glyndebourne as part of the Royal Archaeological Society trip round Sussex. I had a little holiday on 17 October at Bury St Edmunds, staying at The Angel which was very nice indeed, and visited the Athenaeum and the Manor House Museum where I was to see Richard Jeffree's picture collection in its new home. All those old friends!

On 25 October I had to travel to Dengie in Essex for the funeral of my cousin Joan, John Wilsdon's mother. It was a wretched wet day

On 2 December the funeral took place of the oldest surviving Sherborn, Joan Moore, at East Grinstead where she had spent her declining years. The mother of three daughters, she had reached a very ripe old age.

17

The Century Ends

'What's life all about Derek?' said my jolly friend Danny Stevens. So what's it all about? Danny was fond of making remarks like that even in crowded public rooms when he could be heard by anyone. But in this case he was standing on the balcony of my house in Brighton staring out to sea. It was an intellectual reflection on life. Has it all been worthwhile? What has been achieved either for myself or for the better good of the world in general? Well, of course it has all been worthwhile!

For the moment one reflects on what has gone on. One has spent a lifetime pursuing historic trails, artistic trends, political campaigns, collecting and discovery. Collecting is largely a selfish pastime since one acquires objects for oneself. Things in fact that others would not want to own. I view auctions and antique fairs all the time and others do occasionally. They usually complain that they never see anything to buy ever. All auctions and fairs should be explored for the odd discovery. To collect seriously one must devote a great deal of time and care to it.

Conservation and the study of buildings of architectural and historical interest is likewise a whole time occupation which should embrace intensive sightseeing but also the careful absorption of everything that is written and published on the subject. My own library was to include several thousand volumes although pressure of space and usage has forced me to sell my most valuable 18th and early 19th century books. Very few of these are available anywhere outside the British Library but they were important for my researches into houses when in the office.

I have compiled many lists in my lifetime. Not just as a result of my field surveys of local authority districts but also of the finest towns and villages. They include the list of outstanding country houses submitted to the Gowers Committee [for which the Ministry of Works was thanked!]; the original lists of historic parks and gardens in England, irreplaceable monuments in time of war, houses with or possibly without outstanding contents, theatres throughout England and cinemas too. What's it all about then? I am proud of what I have achieved in my chosen life. I regret having been passed over for promotion to the head of my professional branch in favour of a comparatively inexperienced outsider. I regret not having been remembered by my friend Rupert Gunnis in his will and I regret and am angry that certain recommendations I have made for listing in Brighton have been rejected and that the Imperial Theatre in North Street was eventually demolished. This splendid building dated from 1940 and was one of the finest theatres in the south of England. I was glad that I was able to help save Calke Abbey in Derbyshire, Witley Court in Worcestershire, the Shaftesbury Theatre in London, Cowick Hall in Yorkshire and hundreds of other lesser but important buildings.

My collecting has been an unqualified success and I have derived much pleasure from having given those two great portraits to Lydiard Tregoze in Wiltshire and thus started the refurnishing of this magnificent empty house by Swindon Corporation.

I esteem the fact of my endeavours for the change of the laws about homosexuality and I am pleased that my own gifts for Aids charities and the fact that I was able to channel many thousands of pounds to their cause has made a real difference. Life has not been all achievement as I have already explained but it has had a rich enthralling pattern. One has done one's best.

Brighton was an enchanting place to live in but its charm was rudely shattered in the night of 30 July 1999 when burglars struck by smashing the panel of my front door and carting off a great quantity of treasures. No doubt pleased with their haul they came back for more by smashing a ground floor window in the porch of the house next door during the nights of 2 September and 5 September 1999.

Even worse was the occasion on 23 March 2001 when the Brighton *Argus* carried a front page banner headline declaring that I was being sued for thirty two million pounds and the action had to be defended in the High Court in London.

Brighton is a popular and historic town with lovely terraces of Georgian and Victorian houses. At the end of the War it was practically unscathed, but unbridled development in the last half century has wrought havoc to several of its lovely squares and streets, so that now the majority of them have lost some at least of their fine old houses, or if not complete houses then some of their decorative features such as pilasters, cornices or, more importantly, their delicate balconies and verandahs. A highly successful start has been made in recreating the decorative iron railings to the squares and crescents of Kemp Town and nearby, which were all scrapped during the War, but some of the post war lamp posts are completely out of scale with their surrounding architecture and resemble a juggler's variety turn twiddling plates on the end of sticks. It is pointless lighting the sky; good taste should be a consideration when installing street furniture.

Brighton is a kind of Bingo City by the sea. Its major theatre, the Hippodrome, a fine example of work of Frank Matcham in 1901, has been used for bingo for years in spite of being badly wanted for its original purposes.

The Imperial, designed by Samuel Beverley, opened at that most unfortunate of times, April 1940, was designed on a lavish scale with seating for 1,846 people and a stage 37 feet deep, complete with flytower, and was said to be one of the largest in the south of England. Its splendid Art Deco style interior with a marine theme was largely intact, and the theatre would have been absolutely wonderful because it could have staged the largest opera, ballet and musical performances in the country. I blame obduracy, lack of imagination and pedantic stubbornness on the part of English Heritage for not listing the building as one of special interest; an opinion of criminal stupidity. Apparently the matter hinged on whether or not John Alexander did or did not execute the interior decoration, as if it matters two pins what names can be associated with what when assessing a building for architectural merit. Listing is not the same as a university thesis. The Dome itself can never be a full 'Lyric Theatre' in the current meaning of the term because of the lack of stage depth and the absolute impossibility of building a fly tower for the scenery and it can never be a building as suitable for this purpose as was the Imperial in North Street.

English Heritage's obduracy in not listing the Imperial Theatre has resulted this year (2002) in the loss of this priceless theatre building, one of the very finest in the whole of the South of England. Its comparatively modern date meant that it was ideally suited for all types of theatre usage today. The provision of extra shops and a handful of flats is no justification for this appalling vandalism. English Heritage has similarly been bloody minded over not listing the surviving parts of the Prince Regent's Barracks in Old Barrack Yard and a similar nonsense scenario for several years dogged the future of the magnificent Astoria Cinema in Marlborough Place designed by EA Stone and partners in 1934. Messrs Stone and Partners were the architects for the well known Whitehall Theatre in London.

Jubilee Street is not the only 'bomb' site in the centre of Brighton unused for twenty years; there is another huge one up near Brighton Station which now perhaps stands some chance of being built on with a greater provision for housing also.

There are other wasted assets in the town like the gorgeous early Georgian country house, Stanmer Park, where a preservation trust has done noble work in re-roofing and making watertight this long disused house, but where they have as yet no firm proposals for its future management later.

East Street, Duke Street and Pavilion Buildings have been pedestrianised and there is a much improved shopfront initiative in St James's Street which should do good, but so much more needs doing.

It seems almost impossible to believe that the West Pier has been closed since 1970 because of its dangerous condition. It was first built in 1863 to the designs of Eugenius Birch as a promenade pier so that people could walk above the sea without getting their feet wet. In 1890 a central windshield was added. In 1893 a large pavilion was added to the sea end and was converted to a theatre 10 years later. The large concert hall at its centre was erected at the height of the First World War in 1916. From then on the Pier slumbered without much change for the rest of its commercial life. Since its closure, it has been the focus of endless controversy and argument with those in favour of its preservation as a Grade I building asking for greater financial support and those others belligerently stubborn to the proposals in the opposite direction. It is now in such bad condition that it is almost impossible to believe that any scheme of restoration without complete rebuilding can possibly succeed. Surely the whole structure will end up being an almost complete replacement or a copy of the Pier people have come to love? A tour of the structure today is both an exciting and an awful experience, whilst the stench of bird droppings is almost beyond endurance.

Brighton is changing, but it comes over as a town failing to care for its thousands of townsfolk – acres of unwanted and empty offices have been built here – and it comes across as inadequately caring for its architectural heritage and cultural heritage. A town with tunnel vision without an overall compelling strategy. Brighton needs a good kick up the backside. And English Heritage too. And they surely have to have been expecting one for a long time.

INDEX

Abel Collins Almshouses, Nottingham 158
Aberffraw, Anglesey 57, 77, 100
Abergavenny, Lord 131
Aberglasney, Wales 223
Abermarlais, Wales 223
Abernethy House, London 54
Acrise Place, Kent 137
Acton Park, Denbighshire 177
Acworth, Angus 112, 136
Adam, Robert 111, 136, 137, 138, 156, 172,
    184, 189, 191, 196
Aikman, William 134
Aislabie, John 107
Albany Trust 121
Albert, Prince 17
Albyns, Essex 182
Aldenham, Lord 104
Alderley Hall, Shropshire 183
Alfreton Hall, Derbyshire 193, 202
Algarkirk Hall, Lincolnshire 174
Alkincoats Hall, Lancashire 156, 187
Allman family 62
    house 67–9
    shop 66–7
Allman, Ann (née Clews) 61
Allman, Arthur 275
Allman, Arthur William 63–5
Allman, Charles 61
Allman, Edie (b.1890) 62, 70–1
Allman, Hannah (née Heton) 61
Allman, Mary Ann (née Savage) (d.1947) 62,
    69–70, 108
Allman, Maud (b.1876) 62, 70, 83
Allman, Percy 64
Allman, William 63–5
Allman, William (b.1772) 61–2
Althorp, Northamptonshire 139
Alton Towers, Staffordshire 175
Ampthill Park, Bedfordshire 145

Ancient Monuments Act 144
Ancient Monuments Society 276
Anderson, Jack 241, 247, 250, 260, 266, 269,
    271
Angle, Wales 223
Anglesey Abbey, Cambridgeshire 252
Annesley Hall, Nottinghamshire 191
Anthony, Brian 166
Antony, Gordon 256
Apley Castle, Shropshire 182
Aramstone, Herefordshire 186
Arber, Agnes 39–44
Archer, Thomas 236
Architectural Publication Society, *Dictionary
    of Architecture* 152
Arley Castle, Worcestershire 207
Army and Navy Club, London 207
Asgill House, Richmond 183
Ashburnham House, King's Road 37
Ashburnham Place, Sussex 137, 193
Aspenden Hall, Hertfordshire 202
Assington Hall, Suffolk 163, 189
Athelhampton, Dorset 119
Atherstone Hall, Warwickshire 208
Attingham Park, Shropshire 5
Aubrey, Ken 237
Audley End, Essex 264

Baddesley Clinton, Warwickshire 254
Badger Hall, Shropshire 177
Bailey, Brenda and Sid 258, 265, 271
Baker, Herbert 275
Baker, William 184
Baldwin, Thomas 192
Balson, Roger 257
Bance family 27–8, 261
Bance, Franklin Arnold 26–7
Bance, Harriet (née Bailey) 26
Bance, John 28, 271

287

290